Social Costs
in Modern Society

Social Costs
in Modern Society

A QUALITATIVE AND QUANTITATIVE ASSESSMENT

Edited by John E. Ullmann

Q
QUORUM BOOKS
Westport, Connecticut • London, England

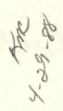

Library of Congress Cataloging in Publication Data

Main entry under title:

Social costs in modern society.

  Bibliography: p.
  Includes index.
  1. United States—Economic policy—1981-
2. United States—Social policy—1980-   . 3. Economic
policy. 4. Social policy. 5. Externalities (Economics)
I. Ullmann, John E.
HC106.8.S636 1983   361.6'1'0973   82-18590
ISBN 0-89930-019-7 (lib. bdg.)

Library of Congress Catalog Card Number: 82-18590
ISBN: 0-89930-019-7

First published in 1983 by Quorum Books

Greenwood Press
A division of Congressional Information Service, Inc.
88 Post Road West
Westport, Connecticut 06881

Printed in the United States of America

10 9 8 7 6 5 4 3 2 1

TO THE MEMORY OF
K. WILLIAM AND LORE L. KAPP

Contents

Tables and Figures

Figures

Preface

Most economic activities generate social costs and externalities that affect third parties or society at large. Their scope and extent and the way they are allocated or alleviated form the substance of much political action in modern societies and are at the center of perennial debates on the nature and function of organized life. The most immediate issue is the politically determined process of change of social costs into business costs and vice versa. This book examines the methodological problems involved and analyzes social costs and their treatment in the most significant sectors.

This volume resulted from the continuing series of MBA research and thesis seminars of the School of Business at Hofstra University. For each of these seminars, a director (subsequently, editor) chooses a topic. The work is shared among the participating students, each of whom drafts a chapter. The chapters are then edited and prepared for publication by the director. In this volume, the original submissions had to be shortened to keep the total length of the book within bounds while at the same time substantial new material had to be added due to rapidly changing developments in the field. The responsibility of each participant is thus limited to the final drafts submitted by each of them and subsequent changes are the editor's sole responsibility. Past or present employers of the participants were in no way involved in the study, nor did it receive or seek any additional outside support.

We are very much indebted to Mrs. Marion Anderson of Employment Research Associates, East Lansing, Michigan, for contributing valuable research materials for chapter 15; to Professor Marvin Berkowitz of Fairfield University for permission to reprint a concluding table from his pioneering work on the social costs of poverty in chapter 9; and to Mrs. Ruth Leger Sivard for permission to reprint Chart 13 of her book *World Military and*

Social Expenditures 1982. Our particular thanks likewise go to Mrs. Dorothy Trombecky for her indispensable help in getting the manuscript into final form.

JOHN E. ULLMANN
Hempstead, New York

Social Costs
in Modern Society

1
The Structure of Social Costs

JOHN E. ULLMANN

It is for the public
good that no one use his
property badly.

The Roman Codex

Introduction

During the last generation, the problem of social costs has attracted increasing
public attention, especially insofar as it involves the transformation of social
costs into business costs and vice versa. Social costs are costs of an economic
activity that are borne in some way by society at large, rather than by those
involved in it as producers or users. The concept is therefore implicit in such
major contemporary endeavors as legislation for environmental protection
and safety of products and processes.

This book attempts to summarize what can be readily determined about the
scope and extent of social costs in a wide variety of areas. The assessment is to
a large extent qualitative. Social costs are often very difficult to measure
because there are problems both of what to measure and how to do it. On
occasions social costs reflect a net effect of costs and benefits; the latter typically present even more difficult problems of definition and measurement.
The definition of social costs and an investigation of their origins is a prerequisite of all such analyses.

It is not meaningful to combine the social costs of various activities into a
grand total with which our society is afflicted. Rather, the chapters of this
book ought to be considered individually with full awareness of the great volume of work that still remains to be done. The organization of this book

reflects the fact that social costs can be generated by business practices that have an impact on society beyond the activity involved. The book thus starts with an examination of the extensive recent attempts to have reports on business activities take these externalities into account in some way. The chapters following discuss various ways in which business has avoided—or has been permitted to avoid—what could be defined as the full costs of the various parts of its operations. Pollution, unemployment, energy production, job-related accidents, and sickness are among such problem areas. Since these raise questions on how human life and health are to be valued, they are preceded by an analysis of court cases in which these matters were the focus.

The costs of various social dysfunctions are, however, also turned into externalities by government. Old age and poverty, for example, to the extent that they are cared for, are a cost to all of society and to the extent that this care is inadequate, produce further deleterious effects. Government subsidies and some of the cost of government itself further add to this burden. Finally, certain products have social costs of their own: food, because of the way it is subsidized, the automobile, and drugs. All of these are considered in their appropriate chapters. A final chapter deals with the enormous and, as is shown, all-pervasive costs of the military sector.

In a real sense, the process by which social costs are created or redirected to those directly involved in the activity is a political one. Resolving the issue of who ultimately pays for the troubles of a society is certainly a significant bottom line of politics, if not the principal one. The dynamics of this political process are currently characterized by the emergence of a powerful lobby against government regulation. A large part of this body of law and administrative decision making has resulted in the transformation of social costs into business costs; a concerted effort at reversing this trend is now underway.

In the next section of this chapter the structure of social costs is examined. This is followed by a historical survey of the study of social costs. Finally, the problems are examined in the current context, which is essentially in terms of the deregulation process referred to above.

The Structure of Social Costs

The definition of social costs of K. W. Kapp is still appropriate as "all direct and indirect losses sustained by third persons or the general public as a result of unrestrained economic activities." These social costs may take the form of damage to human health, destruction or deterioration of property values, the premature depletion of natural wealth, or impairment of less tangible values such as quality of life.[1]

Social costs come in three broad categories. The first is that of the direct social cost in which it becomes possible for an economic activity to slough off on the general public or third persons the cost of carrying out an economic activity when those costs should really be borne by those engaged in it or benefitting from it. If, as a result of bad environmental practices, for example, a company reduces its costs, the difference between its actual costs and those that would be incurred if the trouble were avoided are borne in one way or another by the general public, be it workers, customers, communities, or anyone else. The cost to third parties is that part of the damage that was *not* abated; it is not what a company spends to clean up its water pollution, but the cost of what it still dumps into the river.

A second type is the outright subsidy. If a government subsidizes an economic activity, the costs of carrying it out are shared among all taxpayers, but the beneficiaries are still the managements, workers, and customers of the subsidized sector.

The third variety is that of the social opportunity cost. Any action that society takes that is less than optimal, meaning the best that is available, exacts a cost as well. A product manufactured more expensively than it has to be obviously must, if price reflects cost, exact a penalty from society at large. However, there are considerable problems with this category. First, the "one best way," which was espoused by the school of scientific management early in the twentieth century, has long been dismissed as a bit of wishful thinking. Given the fact that most business decisions of any substance have multiple objectives, it is not possible to single out one best way. Best with respect to what? Unless a usually arbitrary set of valuations is put upon the objectives, there is no way of answering the question. A second problem lies simply in the fact that opportunity costs under many conditions are practically open-ended and limited only by the imagination of the person who proposes to assign them. How much better can something be? What are the limits of improvement?

The above limitations and strictures must not, however, be taken to mean that opportunity losses are a useless concept in the analysis of social costs. Quite the contrary, they are an indication of social efficiency or inefficiency and as such are an extremely important aspect of determining the course of economic development of a society. Indeed, opportunity cost is a very important concept in the analysis of industrial investments of all sorts, whether related to social costs or not. Any firm buying a new machine considers the opportunity cost of not using it. Indeed, a major problem in the current decline of productivity in manufacturing (chapter 15), is precisely that the decline of nonmilitary technology has limited progress in equipment for many industries to such an extent that new machinery costs too much in relation to the benefits it can bring.

Furthermore, as will be seen throughout this volume, it is often possible to define quite clearly what else could be done, and, regardless of whether the amount can actually be quantified, make a judgment at least as to the *existence* of a social cost. If resources such as labor hours are wasted as a result of heavy unemployment, for example, a definition of what might have been is not difficult. Opportunity costs and social efficiency or inefficiency are therefore important ingredients of a proper analysis of social costs.

In general, the definition and estimation of social costs presents at least six major areas of concern:

1. The *nature* of social costs is often not nearly as clear as may at first appear. Whether a given pollutant is in fact harmful often requires medical judgments based on substantial uncertainty. The causation of many diseases is fraught with sufficient uncertainty to produce long arguments as to whether a social cost has actually been incurred.

2. The assignment of *responsibility* is likewise often a matter of controversy. Do pollutants come from a specific process, or from somebody or something else? Is acid rain the result of burning sulfurous coal in the Middle West or do automobile emissions cause it, or is it "natural"? The responsibility for social costs in such contexts is a grave matter, implying as it does legal responsibility, litigation, regulatory activity, and the like.

3. *Who is affected* is yet another issue. How far does a given effect extend physically? If by virtue of a tax-financed subsidy the costs of a certain economic activity are borne by the public at large, who exactly pays for it, and how does it percolate throughout society, both directly and indirectly? What are its multiplier effects with respect to the rest of the economy? A determination of who is affected is important for another reason. In many cases the effects are so widely dispersed that each individual suffers only minimal, if not negligible damage. Yet there is a question of equity involved in essentially absolving anyone from responsibility for social costs if only they can be shared out among a sufficiently large number of people.

4. The *time factor* is an important element. From a clinical standpoint, for example, it is well known that diseases, including cancer, have very long periods of latency. The problem is further complicated when it was not known at the beginning of that period that the substance involved was in any way dangerous. These are questions that bear heavily upon legally assignable responsibility on *ex post facto* grounds.

5. *Scientific uncertainty* is pervasive in many social cost problems. Some of the uncertainties were described above. There are now many specialties in the sciences that relate to the physical analysis of processes and conditions leading to social costs and comparable work is done in the social science field. One would be foolhardy to claim that this enterprise has been crowned with success. One could indeed argue that uncertainty increases all the time, were it not for the fact that some of it is due to deliberate obfuscation on the part of those seeking to escape responsibility.

6. Finally, there is the matter of *social values*. This is no doubt the most difficult of all issues because it is possible for someone to justify a great many things as proper that would be considered barbaric and totally unacceptable by other individuals. "You can't make an omelet without breaking eggs" is perhaps the extreme position on the subject of economic development in which social costs are brushed aside as an essential feature of industrial progress. It is an ideology that constantly makes itself felt in all public controversies relating to any significant technical development. In this volume, nuclear power is probably the one in which this kind of argument is most often encountered, but it relates to one's basic views of what government can do, and indeed of what human beings can do in joining together in reasonable freedom to solve common problems. In fine, it relates to the very foundations of reasonably cohesive human societies and whether they can be sustained. For a time, it had been the fashion to espouse "value-free" social sciences in which everything would be cozily quantified and decisions could be made "objectively" on narrow margins of the superiority of one choice over another. However, this ideology ran into several obstacles, not the least of which was that substantial portions of the social science professions and the general public would not buy it. The inability to measure things "objectively" was an obvious problem, and so was the discovery that, echoing the old Jewish proverb that "no choice is also a choice," no values are also values.

All of this suggests the likelihood of an ideological cast to the debate. This is unavoidable because the treatment of social costs has long been at the top of the agenda of the political process. In one way or another, decisions on how to cope with social costs are made politically, and there is no such thing as an "objective" analysis remote from the political process.

In this connection, it is important to note that a comprehensive analysis of social costs should not cast itself as related entirely to private enterprise. If there ever was a substantial view that social costs are only the result of the depredations of private business and that governments are innocent of them, it must surely now be consigned to the waste baskets of history. Government-owned industries throughout the world behave in much the same way as private ones with respect to the treatment of those production problems that cause social costs. Government ownership does not of itself produce greater or lesser safety in the workplace, or better or worse quality. Rather, the issue as between public and private enterprise relates to the *activity* involved. A public steel mill is much like a private one, a public railroad the same, even though it may originally have been planned with a better eye to a coordinated transport system, as discussed in chapter 10.

A second element of distinction between private and public activities is the fact that if a profit is to be expected, then revenues must be maximized and costs minimized. It is precisely in the minimization of costs that, as noted above, social costs can be created. It is simply convenient to have someone else pick up part of the bill. Some public enterprises the world over make a profit; it is simply untrue that none ever do. The only difference is that deficits are often picked up explicitly by the public exchequer but then so in increasing measure are the deficits of private corporations. Corporate welfare clients, such as Chrysler and Lockheed in the United States, are well known as are comparable enterprises elsewhere in the world. In the United States, moreover, companies have been able to place into the public sector the most unprofitable parts of their activities. Amtrak, Conrail, and, possibly before long, the local telephone operating companies, are in that category. All of these situations have caused a convergence between the characteristics of management in the private and public sectors, a point which the present writer has treated at greater length elsewhere.[2]

The Historical Development

The earliest awareness of social costs related very closely to environmental conservation. The care of forests particularly goes back a long time. Sumerian law prescribed a fine for cutting down a tree. A wildlife preserve was established by Ikhnaton, king of Egypt, more than 3,000 years ago, and others were created throughout the ancient world.[3]

Nevertheless, early times also have their share of environmental disasters, even though some of them may be the result of long-range climatic changes rather than human error. Ancient Greece and North Africa were successively deforested, as was China throughout much of its history. The Romans were strongly aware of the need for conservation, but they overused the forests of

Dalmatia in present-day Yugoslavia and the ruin was completed by the Venetian Republic, all for the construction of ships. The major result today is seen in long stretches of the Dalmatian coast which resemble nothing so much as the badlands of the American Dakotas, where the remnants of dunes were left over from prehistoric seas and not the results of human depredations. The examples cited, however, have left a legacy of misery for the afflicted areas that is unlikely to be alleviated in the foreseeable future.

The classical economists from Adam Smith on sought support for their views in moral laws. But even for Smith, *laissez-faire* had its limits. In his *Theory of Moral Sentiments,* he asserted that a "prudent man" should improve himself only in fair ways, that is, without doing injustice to others. Historicists like August Comte took the view that the principle of self-interest is in fact not able to promote social welfare and that there was therefore a need for government planning and regulation of the economic process more pervasive than the classicists had advocated.[4]

The early socialists placed social control at the center of much of their advocacy. Sismondi said in 1827 that an entrepreneur may realize "returns in far excess of the costs of production . . . because he does not pay the total cost of his enterprise; he fails to give an adequate compensation to the worker. Such an industry is a social evil."[5] Engels, Fourier, and Liebig likewise considered the problem along those lines. A particularly trenchant rejoinder to those who maintain that social costs are "transitional" phenomena associated with the building up of business is offered by Karl Marx who said that "these temporary evils have implied for the majority the transition from life to death and for the rest a transition from a better to a worse condition."[6] In the early twentieth century the Fabian socialists of Great Britain, notably J. A. Hobson and Beatrice and Sidney Webb, did major work in identifying social costs in the industrial structure as it then existed. Their approach was succeeded by that of welfare economics of which the most important exponent was A. C. Pigou. He formulated the issue in a variety of ways one of which was identifying the difference between the marginal net social product of a given unit of investment and the marginal private net product resulting from it, which may in fact be considerably smaller. This is because the value that society realizes has been diminished by social cost.

In 1917, Thorstein Veblen called for an investigation of the social costs of business enterprise in these terms. "It will be necessary to investigate . . . in a convincing way what are the various kinds and lines of waste that are necessarily involved in the present businesslike control of industry."[7] Veblen concluded from this that engineers and economists, given the task of reorganizing the job on the basis of unified "social" control, would do better, but this has become a somewhat questionable notion in our time. What is important in the present context, however, is that Veblen thereby clearly identifies opportunity cost as one of the elements to be considered in the analysis of social costs.

Deregulation

Discussing the pervasive effects of social costs in modern political processes, Kapp has said:

> It is no exaggeration to say that . . . a large part of governmental activities in modern society is devoted to the repair and prevention of a number of social losses caused by modern industrial activities. . . . No doubt this increasing recognition reflects to a considerable extent a shift in the balance of power in favor of those classes and groups in society which have borne the brunt of social losses in the past and who now are using their political and economic power in an effort to protect themselves against the negative consequences of progress. The political history of the last 150 years can be interpreted as a revolt of large masses of people, including small business, against social costs.[8]

As a comment on American domestic politics of the last generation, Kapp's statement, which itself dates back some twenty years, certainly provides an accurate summary. There is no doubt that in many different areas, notably those relating to product and process safety, to honesty in the marketplace, and to environmental protection, a substantial degree of government intervention has been strongly favored and considered essential to the functioning of modern government. As is noted at many points in this volume, this process has gone on against sustained challenges and resistance from wide areas of the business community and has therefore become increasingly involved in the major political shifts that have beset American society. Essentially what the argument boiled down to was that the regulations designed to alleviate the problems of social costs have fallen unfairly upon business and that the effects should be ignored forthwith, and that the political efforts at alleviation should be abandoned or reversed. The grounds for this were, of course, in large measure ideological, but they also rested upon the concept of cost-benefit analysis, again involving the kinds of measurements discussed earlier in this chapter.

It would consume far too much space to recount the general argument in detail. Again, throughout this volume examples are presented as they relate to particular industries or other conditions. There is, however, an excellent reference which, though dating back to October 1979, still sums up the argument. It is a record of the joint hearings before the Subcommittee of Oversight and Investigation and the Subcommittee on Consumer Protection and Finance of the Committee on Interstate and Foreign Commerce of the House of Representatives and deals with the use of cost-benefit analysis by regulatory agencies.[9] It is interesting in that within one volume it presents an exhaustive debate between those who sought to dismantle regulations for consumer and workplace safety and the marketplace generally, and those who sought to preserve what had been attained with so much difficulty. The former group included Murray L. Weidenbaum and James C. Miller III, both then affiliated with the American Enterprise Institute. Among the latter was Ralph Nader of the Center for Responsive Law and Allen Ferguson of the Public Interest Economics Center. It is instructive in view of what was to follow later that Dr. Weidenbaum served until August 1982 as Mr. Reagan's chairman of the Council of Economic Advisers and that Dr. Miller was appointed by Mr. Reagan as chairman of the Federal Trade Commission. Events since the time of the hearings have demonstrated rather clearly who "won" that particular debate at least temporarily.

The volume includes the monograph *Business' War on the Law* by M. Green and N. Waitzman, who were associated with Mr. Nader. On the other side of the scale appears an elaborate response to them by Weidenbaum, "The Continuing Need for Regulatory Reform," and a further one by Miller. Weidenbaum's critique and that of Miller strongly espouse cost-benefit analysis and apparently accept regulation only if the evidence of benefit is quite overwhelming. There is a sustained debate between Dr. Weidenbaum and Representative Albert Gore, Jr. (D. Tenn.) on page 445 and following. A particularly interesting point, however, is raised by Dr. Ferguson who points out (page 435):

> Even if it were possible to measure all the benefits of regulation in dollar terms and to compare them with dollar costs (both properly measured and so on), and even if that analysis showed that costs exceeded benefits, that, even that, would not show that there was an excess of regulation. . . . The conclusion could mean either that there was too much regulation, or that regulation was inefficient. Regulation could be inefficient in that the emphasis in regulatory programs was inappropriate—relatively minor hazards, say, were being guarded against while major ones were ignored—or that, within individual areas of regulation, regulations were so designed or so enforced as to be ineffective.

In effect, what is being said here is that a mere comparison of costs says very little about possible efficiencies and effectiveness of regulation.

There is throughout this debate a profound reluctance to come to grips with ethical issues or, rather, the desire seems overwhelming on the part of the deregulators to cover their own sociopolitical judgments with a quantitative fig leaf. A previous article by Dr. Weidenbaum[10] discusses benefit-cost analysis of government regulation but appears rather shy on comprehensive data. On page 3 he shows a graph which purports to plot the extent of regulation against economic impact, eventually showing the cost outweighing the benefit. The graph, however, is without benefit of scale, even of units, and beyond that we are only favored with a quantitative example which assumes that certain numbers can be measured; at the minimum such analysis violates the old Talmudic precept that "for instance is not proof."

The results of all this have been well covered in the news media. The changes are extensively referred to throughout this volume in which a number of chapters start by giving a report on progress in public protection and must necessarily end on a note of discouragement and reversal. As early as March 1981, *Business Week*[11] published a "Regulatory Hit List" which not only included the environmental and safety problems but also such matters as an easing of meat labeling requirements, making it possible to sell tubercular pork and mechanically deboned sausage meat. It is instructive to set such a reversal against one of the earliest exposés of conditions in the meat industry. Upton Sinclair's *The Jungle*, in which among many other horrors of the industry at the time, sausages were described in terms of a variety of unwelcome mysteries. Thus, in an almost literal sense, we were in places back to square one; Sinclair, whose own work was intended to bring sympathy to the oppressed workers in the meat packing industry, only got better meat inspection laws instead. "I aimed for the public's heart," he said, "and I hit it in the stomach."[12]

A further significant development in the antiregulation battle took place in March 1982 when the Senate voted to give Congress veto power over virtually all regulations. It was pointed out by the very few legislators in opposition that this was more or less an open invitation for lobbyists to use their strength in order to win privileges. It was expected that only those interest groups able to come up with suitable political contributions would be able to make their voices heard and get inconvenient regulations canceled. One is most uncomfortably reminded of Tacitus' comment on the last years of the Roman Republic: "And now laws were made not for the public only but for particular men and in the most corrupt period of the commonwealth, the greatest numbers of laws were made."[13]

Conclusion

It is clear from the foregoing that this study of social costs is being undertaken at a very difficult period. It is, however, important to keep an eye on what is involved, especially with respect to the gains achieved so far. It is also well to bear in mind the objectives. It is *not* merely to shift monetary responsibility from one sector of society to another. Rather, it is the alleviation of a particular condition. Even if in supreme wisdom we could compensate precisely for pain, suffering, and injury, or impairment of property values, by far the best strategy and practice would be to avoid the damage altogether. This is the essentially constructive aspect of the whole analysis. The problem is clearly shown to be one with an ancient history and in a real sense determines the nature of the world to the extent that humanity can influence it. The following detailed studies of areas of concern elaborate on the foregoing general formulations.

Notes

1. K. W. Kapp, *Social Costs of Business Enterprise* (Nottingham, England: Spokesman-B. Russell Foundation, 1978).

2. J. E. Ullmann, "Nearer My God to Thee," *The Management of Nonprofit Organizations*, R. M. Cyert et al. (Lexington, Mass.: Lexington Books, 1975), p. 141ff.; J. E. Ullmann, "Tides and Shallows," in *Management for the Future*, ed. L. Benton (New York: McGraw-Hill, 1978), ch. 27.

3. R. M. Alison, "The Earliest Traces of a Conservation Conscience," *Natural History*, May 1981, p. 73.

4. Kapp, *Social Costs*, p. 32.

5. Ibid., p. 32.

6. Ibid., p. 34.

7. T. Veblen, *The Portable Veblen* (New York: Viking, 1948), p. 543.

8. Kapp, *Social Costs*, p. 7.

9. House Committee on Interstate and Foreign Commerce, Use of Cost-Benefit Analysis by Regulatory Agencies, Ser. no. 96, 157, 96th Cong., July 30, October 10 and 24, 1979. Vol. 2 is cited here; for an earlier congressional study, see U.S. Senate, Committee on Governmental Affairs, *Study on Federal Regulations*, 95th Cong. (Washington, D.C.: U.S. Government Printing Office, 1977-1978), 6 vols.

10. M. Weidenbaum, "Benefit-Cost Analysis of Government Regulation," *Toxic Substances Journal*, Autumn 1980, pp. 91-102.

11. "Deregulation: A Fast Start for the Reagan Strategy," *Business Week*, March 9, 1981, p. 57.

12. The history of regulation in this context is discussed in detail in J. E. Ullmann, "Science and the 'Regulation' Bogey," *Annals of the New York Academy of Sciences*, vol. 403, 1983.

13. Tacitus, *Works of Tacitus* (London: Henry Bohn, 1854), Annales, 3: 27.

2
Social Costs and Social Accounting

BERNARD BELITSKY

Little Jack Horner
Sat in a corner,
Eating a Christmas pie.
He put in his thumb
And pulled out a plum
And said "What a good boy am I!"

Anon.

Introduction

In chapter 1, it was noted that awareness of social consequences of business activities led to demands for more comprehensive cost-benefit analysis of operations. Social accounting (sometimes called "social audit") is one of the principal attempts at developing a methodology for responding to this need. A number of serious proposals on the subject were made and these are the subject of this chapter. None has so far been commonly adopted and, indeed, comprehensive rather than selective analyses are seldom found in practice. Nevertheless, the issues raised are important concerns of executives and educators in the continuing debate over corporate purpose.[1]

The principal reason for the difficulties is that the job of measuring individual items is largely beyond the current state of the art and may well be irremediably subjective, rather than quantifiable. Thus, as applied, claims of social benefits from business operations are often self-serving while social costs tend to be downplayed. The line between an attempt at serious measurement and a public relations exercise then becomes rather blurred.

Social Accounting: Aims and Problems

Numerous theories and techniques have been advanced on how to measure the social consequences of business activities in such areas as:

1. Pollution of the environment
2. Depletion of nonrenewable natural resources
3. Community and regional impact of plant closings
4. Improvement in product safety and quality
5. Affirmative action programs
6. Other aspects of ultilization of human resources
7. Community activities
8. Urban renewal and development

Recent efforts at quantification of corporate social costs have revealed both the extreme of questionable activities and the broad scope of societal activities that are affected.

In response to the public criticisms concerning the social purpose of their business activities, many corporate policymakers have undertaken some form of review or "social audit" of their operations which attempted to deal with these issues, as shown, for instance, in the Corson-Steiner survey, "Social Audit: Actions and Opinions,"[2] made for the Committee for Economic Development in 1974. It was based on 284 usable replies to a questionnaire sent to 750 companies. Some of the findings were:

1. Of all responding companies, 76 percent reported that they had attempted an assessment or social audit. The larger the company, the more likely it was to have undertaken one.

2. The ten most frequent social activities out of fifty-eight listed for which corporations had committed significant amounts of money and personnel are (in rank order): employment of minorities, financial aid to schools, recruitment of the disadvantaged, improvement of work opportunities, installation of pollution abatement equipment, increasing productivity, financial support to art institutions, employee training programs, improving management's performance, and engineering new facilities for minimum environmental effects. It is noteworthy that the authors of the survey made no attempt to separate activities that corporations undertake voluntarily and those required by law, nor did they single out those undertaken in the

normal course of business, for example, employee training or increasing productivity. The final ranking of these activities raises questions as to the objectivity used by corporate managements in responding to the questionnaire.

3. Despite the public pressure for corporate disclosures, U.S. corporations do not have an established obligation to render an accounting to anyone on their overall social performance. Most corporate social reports continue to be used for internal purposes.

4. There is continuing need for government standards where corporate activities affect health, standards of living, and related areas. Hence, the two greatest obstacles to effective corporate action are the inability to develop measures of performance against a standard that everyone will accept and thus to make credible cost-benefit analyses.

A *Business Week* study[3] based on a random sampling of annual reports from 100 large U.S. industrial companies revealed that "companies went out of their way to display their concern for social responsibility." In 1971 and 1972, 60 percent and 64 percent respectively made prominent mention of social issues in their annual report. However, in 1973 the upward trend of disclosures fell to 22 percent as the energy crisis issue moved to front page importance, displacing much of the discussion on social activities. Moreover, the avowed concern for corporate responsibility to the public included the many monetary settlements made with the government for noncompliance with regulatory provisions, such as the more than $100 million of settlements with the Equal Employment Opportunity Commission by AT&T and nine steel producers.[4]

The accounting firm of Ernst & Ernst[5] analyzed social measurement (SM) disclosures in annual reports of Fortune 500 companies for the years 1971-1973. The authors defined SM as any disclosure stated in monetary or nonmonetary terms related to a specific social project. It was not required that companies measure project benefits to society. (This writer suggests the term *"cost* measurement" as a more appropriate one for this study.) While an increasing number of firms reported such disclosures, most of them were not monetary and some were merely a few sentences in the president's letter in the annual report.[6]

In 1974 David Linowes saw a "snowballing movement" toward social responsiveness by U.S. corporations.[7] He cited examples of corporate reporting programs at Scovill Manufacturing Co., First Pennsylvania Corp., First National Bank of Minneapolis, Consolidated Edison of New York, Cummins Engine Co., Dayton Hudson Corp., CNA Financial Corp., Quaker

Oats Co., Chrysler Corp., Whirlpool Co., Polaroid Corp., Owens-Illinois
Co., Levi Strauss and Co., Fairchild Camera Corp., American Metal Climax
Corp., Rouse Co., Campbell Soup Co., Atlantic Richfield Co., AT&T Corp.,
and Bristol Myers.

More recently, a study by M. Lovdal, R. Bauer, and N. Treverton[8]
uncovered thirty-five corporations that have formed public responsibility
committees on their boards of directors. However, the study noted that 2,000
corporations were queried and only 35 answered in the affirmative.

Such low participation is one reason why there are critics of these corporate
efforts. They further tend to view them as lacking substance and undertaken
primarily to improve the company's image and reduce political pressures for
legislation.[9]

A sampling of opinion among 200 certified public accountants (CPAs),
chartered financial analysts (CFAs), and controllers of the Fortune 500 companies[10] reveals that they acknowledge the need for social accounting but take
a dimmer view of its prospects and implementations.

European firms may be making better progress toward meaningful social
accounting reports than their U.S. counterparts.[11] The French Parliament
enacted legislation in 1977 requiring corporate reports in 1979 for their 1978
operations. In Germany and the United Kingdom there are pressures for
mandatory reports. The giant Swiss supermarket chain Migros-Genossen-
schaftsbund has made the boldest attempt thus far. Its reports, along with
the more conventional subjects, discuss such activities as pricing, competition, labeling practices, work environment, and cultural activities. In West
Germany alone some 20 companies publish a "Sozialbilanz" and 100 to 150
companies were reported to be considering it.

However, the reports were criticized as lacking objectivity and having been
motivated by pressures from the left and movements toward restrictive legislation. Still, James E. Heard of the U.S. Department of Commerce said, "the
state of the art is more advanced in Germany than the U.S., and we have a
good deal to learn from them."

The status of social accounting today is still unclear. Although a substantial
body of authoritative literature exists on the subject, effective debate remains
inhibited. Corporate managements themselves often seem of two minds. In a
candid moment, one businessman observed, "when a business statesman
makes a public speech, he has to talk in terms of social responsibility and long-
term profit maximization, but the deep truth—the deep secret he can never
admit to anyone except the lady that shares his pillow—is that he is a short-
term profit maximizer."[12]

Still one can point to numerous corporate social programs that seem to be rooted in an altruistic social concern of corporate management and recognize the interdependence between social progress and long-term corporate survival.

Measuring Socially Relevant Corporate Activities

In general, the inability of business, the public, and the government to develop a consensus on measures of performance has been the major roadblock to progress.[13] However, a precise measure of how much a particular corporate activity has enhanced the quality of life need not be a prerequisite to efforts to adapt social accounting practices to business reports.

Neil Churchill[14] has suggested that a corporation can measure its social performance on four levels. The first consists of ascertaining the set of activities with social relevance. This level of study addresses the question, "What are we doing?" and identifies the universe of activities for possible future measurement. In a sense, this is taking an inventory.

The second, or input, level involves determining the extent of the efforts being expended in each of the identified, socially relevant activities. This level of study addresses the question, "How much are we doing?" in terms of resources used and actions taken. Examples are dollars of contribution, number of man hours of released time, amount spent on minority hiring or training, and so forth. At a more sophisticated level, these inputs can be calculated in terms of common measure—cost to the organization—but this involves a number of accounting questions as will be shown later.

The third level of measurement counts the immediate outputs of an action or process, number of employees trained, tons of water filtered, tons of particular residue captured in precipitators, and so forth. Costs may be calculated for this process and be subsequently allocated to products—costs per loan, cents per bottle reclaimed, and so on. What is *not* done at this level of measurement is to make an evaluation of the worth of the output.

The fourth level measures the worth of the output, that is, the results. This involves both an identification of what is being accomplished and an evaluation of its worth to society. This is more than an enumeration of the immediate results and often requires consideration of second- and third-order effects, foregone alternatives, and displaced activities. Most of the demands for social measurement call for level four, that is, for the value of the results of socially relevant actions. There is no question that these measures would be of great value, but there are serious questions as to where and how rapidly they can be developed.

For instance, in promoting members of minorities to executive positions, not only are there immediate benefits to the minority community of having their members in higher decision-making positions, but there is the role model effect on the young which may not be measurable until some years have passed and even then could only be measured by some form of statistical association rather than directly observed causes and effects. In spite of the difficulties, this is an important area for serious study. Even if general measures are not available, what can be measured may be useful in specific business decisions.

In the next section we review several detailed sets of guidelines for social accounting which have been set forth recently.

Recent Efforts in Social Accounting

David F. Linowes' Socioeconomic Operating Statement

Perhaps the most significant work toward adapting social accounting theories to business accounting practice was Linowes' proposal for a socioeconomic operating statement (SEOS).[15] Structured like a formal operating statement, the SEOS includes as positive items ("improvements") any expenditure that enhances the welfare of either employees or the public or improves the safety or quality of the product or of environmental conditions. The decision to expend funds would have to be voluntary. Actions required by law or union contract are excluded. Examples of such improvements are:

1. Installing safety devices on the premises or in products
2. Setting up facilities for the general good of employees or the public
3. Contributing cash or products to social institutions
4. Building playgrounds or nursery facilities for employees or the community
5. Landscaping of strip-mine sites or other environmental eyesores.
6. Upgrading of health, beauty, or safety standards of a business facility
7. Prorating salaries of personnel who spend time with civic organizations

Several of these, of course, have large elements that are legally required.

A negative item ("detriment") is charged against the company when a responsible authority brought the need for action to management's attention, but management did not voluntarily take action. Examples are:

1. Any action required by law or union contract but ignored or postponed through delaying actions by the company

2. Neglecting to install safety devices to protect employees or the public where available at reasonable cost

Linowes also proposed that Congress enact legislation allowing companies a deduction against taxable income for net social expenditures which are shown on the socioeconomic operating statement for the year and exceed a certain percentage (he suggests 1 percent) of the taxpayer's net worth. This would be in addition to all other expenses and depreciation allowances already made for these same items. Such a tax allowance would consciously assert the collective responsibility for environmental and social problems by having government and the citizen-consumer indirectly share in the costs.

While Linowes' proposals have been widely discussed, research indicates that not a single corporation of any size has issued such a financial statement for external uses. In addition, neither the Financial Accounting Standards Board (FASB) nor the Securities and Exchange Commission (SEC) has sanctioned, encouraged, or promulgated any accounting practices that would endorse Linowes' concepts.[16]

There appear to be four practical drawbacks:

1. The omission of expenditures means that SEOS does not show fully what a company is doing in this area. Legal compliance is often costly. On the other hand, however, this rule is understandable if Linowes' SEOS is to serve as a basis for a tax deduction; individuals should not expect to get tax deductions for not having broken the law. Furthermore, voluntary material expenditures are unlikely when long-term financial profits might be adversely affected by the furtherance of a social objective.

2. Because of the highly subjective nature of the data, the statements do not appear to lend themselves to audit by an independent third party. Without this attest, it is unlikely that a net bottom line called "social improvement" would really be credible.

3. Some specific items in Linowes' suggested schedule of possible social accounts are questionable. For instance, he lists one as "executive time—hospital trusteeship." Was the time spent productive? Were funds raised? Was the presence of the executive useful or a barrier to progress? Such questions cannot be avoided any more than the need to assess the *quality* of the executive's regular work as a condition for keeping him as an employee.

4. Under "detriments," a company would surely feel compelled not to list

items that border on the illegal or could serve plaintiffs in civil suits against the company. Self-interest or possibly self-incrimination would dictate a very limited response here.

The Social Financial Statements of Abt Associates Inc.

The 1975 social financial statements of Abt Associates Inc.[17] was the first comprehensive and quantitative social audit completed by a private corporation and presented to the public along with other conventional certified financial statements. Abt is a consulting organization which proposed its system as a service to be introduced to its clients. It demonstrated its application by subjecting itself to a social audit. The statements consist of two parts, a "social balance sheet" and a "social income statement." It is an elaborate scheme, with dozens of different accounts. Here, no distinction is made between voluntary and legally required activities.

As with conventional financial statements, all corporate assets and liabilities are accounted for on the balance sheet. For example, proposed "social assets," valued at their present economic worth, include: staff available for three years, training investment, creation of the organization, and public services paid for by taxes, that is, the difference between value of services consumed and taxes paid (an interesting exercise in itself, as further discussed in chapters 14 and 16).

"Social liabilities" include future wages payable to staff, future financing requirements, and accumulated pollution to the environment caused by company operations.

The "social equity" (net worth) of the company is the difference between the assets and liabilities—thereby simulating the tradition balance sheet.

The social income statement reflects all of the activities of the company as either a social benefit (positive impact on society's resources) or as a social cost (resources consumed). The activities are further classified as to the constituencies they affect: stockholders, staff, clients or general public, and the community. Illustrative of social benefits and their recipients are:

Benefit	Recipient
Contract revenues	Stockholders
Health, dental, and life insurance	Staff
Value of research	General public
Federal taxes paid	General public
Local taxes paid	Community
Environmental improvements	Community

Benefit	Recipient
Pollution abatement	Community
Career advancement	Staff
Tuition reimbursement	Staff
Child care facility	Staff

The total list is extensive and seems overly complicated and some items are called by unnecessarily unfamiliar terms. For instance, career advancement means salary increases for the year. Moreover, for many of the above items, there appears an equal and opposite entry in social costs. Since costs are subtracted from benefits, a net social income of zero results. How is one to interpret this? Are these wasted corporate resources? Do tuition reimbursement expenditures, for instance, result in a social benefit of zero? Surely it is avoiding the central issue when, in a cost-benefit analysis of this sort, a social benefit like pollution abatement is carried only at the value of related equipment. Abt says that since resultant benefits may not be quantifiable in dollars, this is the way to do it. But what is the purpose then?

In 1977 Abt decided to drop its annual social audit at a saving of $10,000 per year.[18] Again, it does not appear to have been a success.

Social Auditing as Proposed by
Raymond A. Bauer and Dan H. Fenn, Jr.

In contrast to the relatively complex financial statement approaches of Linowes and Abt, Bauer and Fenn propose that the initial thrust of social accounting have a more limited but attainable objective.[19] They would have management commit itself to a more systematic nonfinancial assessment of those business activities that have social impact on the firm's more immediate geographic area. The reporting would be on an activity-by-activity basis which would not require an accounting for the totality of corporate resources. In addition, reporting initially would be used for internal purposes only—that is, for helping officers assess the company's social performance with a view to its vulnerabilities and to changes that management may want to make.

The focus on the more easily measurable items thus results in a kind of "creaming" approach. Within each activity, performance is measured by cost and it is suggested that overhead, executive time, and other indirect items be omitted, since they offer extensive opportunities for padding. Benefits are given internal measures such as number of people served by lenient bank loans to a housing rehabilitation scheme. However, many such efforts are far more difficult to evaluate than this and the results, when obtained, may not be very meaningful. For instance, if a company ascertains the number of high school students who use the computer it has donated, what has it really learned? Probably not very much. In summary then, Bauer and Fenn appear to suggest that one should use rough estimates for whatever can be measured rather than attempt an equally rigorous approach to all possible items.

Other Social Accounting Concepts

Dierkes and Bauer[20] refer to some other approaches to the problem. Thus Sater[21] suggests that firms be rated by outsiders and compared to local, national, or industrial norms. His intention of reducing all this to a single index, however, proved too difficult. Shulman and Gale[22] define the constituencies that a firm must serve, for example, employees, community, consumers, and so forth, as well as its owners, but they do not go much further. Gardner[23] proposed another rating scheme and Marlin[24] discusses the evaluation of pollution abatement in detail. Finally, in 1978, the Department of Commerce started a project to develop a social performance index for business,[25] but nothing appears to have been published as of 1981.

The Social Audit—An Illustration

Social audits are particularly useful when they focus on a specific corporate decision. Industrial plant relocations are particularly good examples. They have had a major impact on city life—especially on its labor force. The exodus of labor-intensive operations to Puerto Rico (Operation Bootstrap), the sunbelt states, and more recently to Taiwan and other Far Eastern countries has left stranded human resources and production facilities, most notably in the northeastern states.

The present writer has prepared numerous studies for the senior managements of two major corporations on moves away from northeastern locations. Although social impacts were discussed at the highest policy levels, they were only minor factors in the final decision to move.

It would appear feasible for the Securities and Exchange Commission to require that public companies have an outside independent social audit conducted one year prior to a contemplated move. This audit, similar to the one illustrated below, would be available to interested parties such as government agencies and unions. With this kind of information, steps could be taken to ameliorate the hardships to the affected communities—or, indeed, to propose tax incentives or alternative actions to the moving corporations.

An illustration of how a social audit and social operating statement might be constructed to reflect a plant closing was prepared in 1975 by the Committee on Social Costs of the American Accounting Association.[26] An actual plant closing was audited in order to obtain realistic data and to expose the auditors to social-measurement problems that otherwise might not surface. Most of the analysis is based on actual data—some estimates and assumptions had to be made. The text, partly edited for reasons of space, follows.

The plant (Plant X) was owned by a major U.S. corporation and operated in a company town (Atown in Kentucky) for over half a century. Most of the homes and community buildings were built by the company and generations of Atown residents worked at Plant X. The general area of Atown had a total population of 19,500 of whom 1,500 worked for the five other major employers.

In 1965 Plant X employed 1,300 people. By the time the plant closing was announced in 1971, Plant X had decreased its labor force to about 825 employees. Although the published reason for the closing of the plant was the inability of Plant X to conform to new and stringent water pollution and control standards, many of those involved felt that a lack of employee productivity and company profitability were also important factors in the decision to terminate operations.

When a company locates in a community, it provides employment, increases the tax base, and provides other benefits, thereby creating a social asset. Although precise measurement is difficult and perhaps impossible, the existence of the social asset is evidenced by numerous examples of communities donating land and other property to companies willing to locate within their jurisdiction. A reverse situation arises when operations in a community are terminated. That is, a decrease in social assets associated with industrial operations is a social cost of closing or scaling down an industrial facility. This is the rationale behind the major social cost measurements suggested below for the closing of Plant X.

The four principal items in the social operating statements are disposal of the plant itself, loss of the tax base, unemployment benefits, and subsequent underemployment. When Plant X closed down, it did not attempt to sell its plant and equipment but rather donated it to Atown. Several measurement problems arise from this donation. Disposal plants used in Plant X's operations continue to emit mercury into a nearby river. As a result of accepting the property, it would seem that Atown has assumed a social (or legal) liability for pollution which should be offset against the social asset acquired, but this was not considered.

The social benefit of the plant and equipment to Atown is particularly difficult to measure. Current value would seem to be the appropriate measure; however, because no alternative use of the plant has been found and no bids have been received, current value of the plant is indeterminable. The assessed valuation at 100 percent of value was $37 million. Rather than use this obviously excessive valuation, the plant and equipment are included in social benefits at an estimated $6 million based on sales of similar equipment by the company.

The loss of tax base resulted from the acceptance of the plant and equipment by Atown, thus removing the property from private owner-ship and completely eliminating it from the tax base. Had Plant X sold the property or given it to another enterprise, at least a portion of the tax base would have been retained. Atown may be able to sell the plant and reestablish taxable property, but the loss of tax base from closing Plant X remains a social cost of a plant closing.

Unemployment benefits actually paid are among the certain and most accurately measurable of all social costs. Actually, the net social cost is the amount paid out in unemployment benefits, related supplements, and welfare minus the previous contributions in the account of the firm in the state unemployment insurance system, but this refinement was not used here. All employees at Plant X qualified for the $59 per week maximum unemployment benefit then applicable and this was used in the analysis.

The largest single item appearing on the social operating statement is called underemployment costs. These result from many well-trained and highly skilled employees being displaced from relatively high-paid positions. Rather than relocating, most of these people accepted low-paying jobs as unskilled workers in nearby towns. Some were unable to find jobs or unwilling to accept underemployment. It is assumed that such employees would receive the average welfare benefits for families in the area.

No attempt was made to quantify the social costs of such items as bus-iness contractions, loss of charitable contributions, foreclosures on home and auto mortgages, loss of employee health and retirement benefits, continuing water pollution, and other factors which would be included in a complete social audit.

Accountability, Responsibility, and Actions to Be Taken

The major obstacle to the integration of social accounting data into corporate reporting, both external and internal, is not the lack of criteria of social value of operations and other actions, but the question of accountability. Who decides social priorities? Who determines operating standards for socially relevant outputs? Who decides the content, format, and data of corporate reporting? Who shall attest to the fairness of published data? In effect, who protects the public interest?

The task of determining the proper balance between corporate profit-seeking and social goals is the responsibility of the elected representatives of the public. It follows that the accounting records of the corporation should reflect the dollar cost and the liabilities of any social projects that this political process has deemed desirable. In other words, *compliance with existing laws* and timely reporting as required by them are the primary responsibilities of business. It is the concern of government to *measure the benefits of the outputs* and to procure these benefits at the lowest economic cost—through laws, regulations, persuasion, tax incentives, and so on.

The past decade of federal regulatory history gives convincing evidence that the major social improvements in pollution control, product safety, employee safety and welfare, affirmative action, and other areas were not a result of corporate self-critical accounting exercises, but rather of fairly precise performance standards developed by government agencies empowered with litigation authority.[27] Accordingly, such activities might serve as initial focus of analysis.

Currently, corporations are required by the FASB and the SEC to disclose the results of their operations through the issuance of four audited financial statements: (1) balance sheet, (2) statement of income, (3) statement of changes in financial position, and (4) statement of retained earnings.

A fifth statement should be added. Its primary purpose is to quantify the contingent liabilities of the business entity to comply with government-mandated programs. Its form might be as shown in table 2.1 which, in practice, would have to be supported by appropriate budgeting analyses.

The annual audited report would accomplish the following objectives:

1. It would provide government bodies and other users with financial and performance data regarding corporate expenditures, liabilities, tax credits (if any), and progress of each program. The report would also measure the degree of compliance and indicate projected expenditures (contingent liabilities) necessary to meet government specifications. Also embodied in the report is a cost distribution of who shall bear these costs, that is, government, corporations, and the public.

2. It would provide the corporations with a method of separating those activities which it currently would not voluntarily undertake in the course of its regular business activities. Thus, adverse affects on profitability, if any, could be evaluated.

Table 2.1
XYZ Corporation: Statement of Expenditures, Liabilities, and Income from Government-Mandated Programs as of December 31, 19XX

	Current Year	Estimated Next 5 Years	Prior 5 Years
		(amounts in thousands)	
Estimated Cost to Comply with Government-Mandated Programs			
Direct Continuing Cost	$10,000	$ 50,000	$20,000
Allocated Continuing Cost	2,000	10,000	4,000
Capital Expenditures	32,000	50,000	10,000
Finance Costs	4,000	9,000	2,000
TOTAL	$48,000 (A)	$119,000[1] (B)	$36,000 (C)
	100%		100%
Actual Expenditures for Government Programs			
Direct Continuing Expenditures	$ 8,000	—	$18,000
Allocated Continuing Expenditures	2,000	—	4,000
Capital Expenditures	21,000	—	15,000
Fines, Assessments	2,000	—	—
Finance	3,000	—	3,000
TOTAL	$36,000 (D)	—	$40,000 (E)
	75%		111%

Unrestricted Net Current Assets Available for Operations and Government Programs[2]

				5-Year Average
Current Assets	$340,000			
Less: Current Liabilities	180,000	$160,000 (F)	---	$263,000 (G)

Actual Current Year Expenditures for Government Programs as a Percentage of Year-End Net Assets

$36,000/160,000 = 22.5%

	22.5% (H)	---	3.0% (I)

$$\frac{\$40,000}{(\$263,000)\ (5\ \text{years})} = 3.0\%$$

Income from Government Sources for Government Programs

Tax Credits, Subsidies, Contracts, and so on[3]	(J)	$16,000	42,000	-0-
Costs Applicable to Above Income[4]	(K)	13,000	32,000	$40,000
Net Income Before Tax		$3,000	$10,000	($40,000)
Applicable Federal Tax[5]		-0-	-0-	($20,000)

---

[1] Will now appear in the liability section of the balance sheet.

[2] Assume these figures come from the balance sheet.

[3] Arbitrary figure.

[4] Arbitrary figure.

[5] Assume net income is derived through a 100 percent tax credit. Also assume that there were no tax credits given in the prior five years, and the tax rate was 50 percent.

Table 2.1 (continued)

	Current Year	(amounts in thousands) Deferred Next 5 Years	Prior 5 Years
Income from Business for Government Programs			
Unrecovered Government Program Costs			
Applied to Product Costs[6] (L)	$7,000	$17,000	$40,000
Average Trade Markup[7] (M)	3,500	8,500	60,000
Billings to the Trade (N)	$10,500	$25,500	$100,000
Total After-Tax Income from Trade (Item M × 50%)[8]	$1,750	4,250	$30,000
Total After-Tax Income from Government (Item K)	3,000	10,000	—
Total Combined Income	$4,750	$14,250	$30,000

Consolidated Corporate Income

Total Combined After-Tax Income, Government Programs	(O)	$ 4,750	23%
		$ 30,000	15%
Total After-Tax Income, Non-Government Programs[9]	(P)	16,250	77%
		170,000	85%
Total Corporate Income		$21,000	100%
		$200,000	100%

[6] Current cost equals actual expenditures, Item D Less: Noncurrent capital expenditures, assume $16,000. Less: Cost recovered from government, Item K. ($36,000 − 16,000 − 13,000 = $7,000) For the five-year deferred ratio, the same ratio as the current one was used:

$$\frac{7,000}{13,000} = \frac{x}{32,000} \; ; x = 17,000$$

[7] Assume 50 percent; this is quite normal in many industries. However, the actual average markup would be used for the current year and prior five years.

[8] In the example it is assumed that all costs can be passed along to customers, as in the case of a public utility. However, in the case where competition is a factor, earnings would be adversely effected.

[9] Arbitrary figure based on 77.5 percent of assets used for nongovernment programs because 22.5 percent used for government programs. Prior five years used 85 percent for nongovernment.

3. While its focus on mandated activities is the opposite of that proposed by Linowes, it has the advantage that its various accounts are much more readily defined and evaluated.

Proposed Corporate Reporting Requirements

Which companies should be required to issue financial data regarding compliance with government-mandated programs?

Many reporting criteria could be used: assets, employees, property, plant and equipment, type of industry, regulated or unregulated, public or private companies, and so on. One recommendation might be that all U.S. corporations whose compliance with government-mandated social programs would require a commitment of at least $10 million over the next five-year period would issue these annual, audited reports.

Only a small percentage of the 1.5 million U.S. corporations would be reporting; possibly not even as many as the 2,641 corporations listed on the New York and American stock exchanges. However, these 2,641 corporations accounted for approximately 60 percent of the $2,552 billion in sales for the nation's manufacturing, trade, and retail sectors, and about 90 percent of the $75.4 billion of corporate profits after tax, using average annual data for the years 1974 and 1975.[28]

The reporting requirements would be enforced by the Securities and Exchange Commission and the Federal Accounting Standards Board.

Conclusion

The past decade has seen an unmistakable shift in priorities regarding what society expects from the business community. The *quantity* produced is no longer the prime consideration. Today, because of its many social watchdogs, a company's method of production and final output must also be related to the *quality* of our social environment. As a result, the need for a method of corporate social accounting should not be mistaken for a fad; rather it is based on society's long-term requirement that there be an accounting of corporate actions or inactions so as to determine whether increased social costs are being generated and passed on to others.

Obviously, the attestation of the fairness of such social reports must be made by independent third parties, such as public accountants, engineers, and government regulatory agencies. Experience has shown that corporations cannot both formulate operating policies, which are profit motivated, and objectively assess the value of these policies to society. One can only expect that, with a few exceptions, such corporate reports would reflect the self-serving interests of management.

Social accounting practices can be implemented by structuring corporate reports so that they disclose the dollar costs and contingent liabilities required to comply with government-mandated operating standards. Presently, corporations do disclose to governmental bodies data regarding individual products and services, pollution abatement, operational practices, employment practices, financial operations, and so forth. However, they do it on a piecemeal basis and the result is of little help to anyone who desires to form an overall judgment of the social performance of a particular company. It is recommended that this fragmented data be integrated into comprehensive social accounting reports which should be embodied in a company's certified annual report. The FASB and the SEC have the authority to make such social accounting reports a reality. As this chapter has shown, a variety of approaches may be used. The time is appropriate to make a serious attempt to establish standards for the task.

Notes

1. For a comment by the American Assembly of Collegiate Schools of Business, see R. A. Buchholz, "Business Environment/Public Policy," Working Paper No. 55, CSAB, St. Louis, Mo., May 1980; for a general and comprehensive treatment, see L. J. Seidler and L. L. Seidler, *Social Accounting: Theory, Issues and Cases* (Los Angeles: Melville Publishing Co., 1975). See also, *Whistle Blowing: The Report of the Conference on Professional Responsibility*, ed. R. Nader, P. Petkas, and K. Blackwell (New York: Grossman Publishers, 1972), ch. 3.

2. J. J. Corson and G. A. Steiner, Measuring Business's Social Performance: The Corporate Social Audit (New York: Committee for Economic Development, 1974).

3. "A New Diet of Data Fattens Annual Reports," *Business Week*, April 27, 1975, pp. 63-64.

4. American Accounting Association, "Annual Report Committee on Social Cost," *The Accounting Review*, 1975, p. 74.

5. J. Backman, *Social Responsibility and Accountability* (New York: New York University Press, 1975), p. 97.

6. American Accounting Association, "Annual Report Committee on Social Cost," p. 58.

7. D. F. Linowes, *The Corporate Conscience* (New York: Hawthorn Books, Inc., 1974), pp. 157-79.

8. M. Lovdal, R. Bauer, and N. Treverton, "Public Responsibility Committees of the Board," *Harvard Business Review*, May-June, 1977, pp. 40-60.

9. J. Ryan, "Costly Counsel: Regulations and Fees Boost Legal Expenses; Firms Try to Cut Them," *Wall Street Journal*, April 13, 1978, p. 1.

10. R. H. Strawser, K. G. Stanga, and J. J. Benjamin, "Social Reporting: Financial Community View," *The CPA Journal*, February 1976, p. 7.

11. "When Businessmen Confess Their Social Sins," *Business Week*, November 6, 1978, p. 175.

12. Quoted in L. Silk, "Multinational Morals," *New York Times*, March 5, 1974, p. 33; see also "Hilfe fuer den Fiskus," *Der Spiegel*, August 21, 1978, p. 80.

13. Corson and Steiner, *Measuring Business's Social Performance*, p. 36 and table 4; also see Seidler and Seidler, *Social Accounting*, pp. 1-42.

14. N. C. Churchill, "The Accountant's Role in Social Responsibility," paper presented in the *Distinguished Accountant Lecture Series*, University of Florida, February 17, 1972.

15. Linowes, *Corporate Conscience*, pp. 103-37.

16. Financial Accounting Standards Board, *Original Pronouncements* (New York: Commerce Clearing House, 1976). Also see note 23.

17. C. C. Abt, *The Social Audit for Management* (New York: Amacom, 1977), pp. 254-64.

18. "When Businessmen Confess Their Social Sins," *Business Week*.

19. R. A. Bauer and D. H. Fenn, Jr., "What *Is* a Corporate Social Audit?" *Harvard Business Review*, January-February 1973, pp. 37-47.

20. M. Dierkes and R. A. Bauer, *Corporate Social Accounting* (New York: Praeger Publishers, 1973), pp. 3-40.

21. C. Sater, "A Supplement to the Bottom Line: Rating Corporations on Social Responsibility," Stanford University Graduate School of Business *Bulletin*, Summer 1971, pp. 18-21.

22. J. S. Shulman and J. Gale, "Laying the Groundwork for Social Auditing," *Financial Executive*, March 1972, p. 38.

23. B. B. Gardner, *An Audit of Corporate Social Responsibility* (New York: Social Research, Inc., 1972).

24. J. T. Marlin, "Accounting for Pollution," *The Journal of Accountancy*, February 1973, p. 41.

25. "When Businessmen Confess Their Social Sins," *Business Week*.

26. American Accounting Association, "Annual Report Committee on Social Cost," pp. 78-84.

27. For a discussion and debate on corporate responsibilities, see M. Friedman, "The Social Responsibility of Business Is to Increase Its Profits," *New York Times Magazine*, September 13, 1970, and R. L. Heilbroner, et al., *In the Name of Profit* (Garden City, N.Y.: Doubleday & Co., 1972), pp. 223-64.

28. Committee on Government Operations, U.S. Senate, 94th Cong. 2d Sess., "The Accounting Establishment: A Staff Study," *The Journal of Accountancy*, March 1977, pp. 104-20. For the AICPA's position on this matter, see "AICPA Testifies Before SEC on Social Reporting," *The Journal of Accountancy*, June 1975, p. 14.

3
Valuation of Human Life and Health

ROBERT M. PEREZ

> The person who injures another must
> make good five kinds of damages:
> Loss of bodily substance and
> function, pain, cost of healing,
> loss of income and mental anguish.
>
> The Talmud, *Baba Kamma*

Introduction

In chapter 1, we noted the importance of assigning some sort of value to the impairment of human life and health as the result of an economic activity. As further noted, this raises most important issues of ethical values and social policy. However, society now endeavors to assign such values whenever cases involving damages, liability, and negligence are before the courts. This, in turn, means that accidents are the main topic of investigation. Sicknesses caused by products or processes are much more rarely encountered in litigation, probably because many of them have only recently attracted public attention but, even more, because causation is so much harder to prove than in accidents. Moreover, industrial sickness is usually a matter for workers' compensation (see chapter 6), as are several broad classes of accidents. In the present chapter, the focus is principally on the legal treatment of accidents resulting from the use of products.

To start with, there is the question of which of the costs described here are true social costs. First, any costs to the court system itself that are not borne by the litigants are obviously social costs although they are probably small relative to the awards and other costs. Second, if a firm pays for accidents it causes, it will eventually pass the cost on to its customers and the users of the product will have to pay; thus it is not a true social cost in that it is not spread amongst the population, users and nonusers alike. On the other hand, one can argue that liability insurance of one kind or another covers nearly all products and the risks are spread among industries by the insurers, thus raising the general price level even for nonusers of the product. Thus a major part of the awards won by plaintiffs mentioned below is indeed a social cost. Certainly the reverse holds true: making a product safe surely confers a social benefit, although it may be offset in part or entirely by the additional costs of making changes in the products.

If damage awards of one kind or another are considered as indicators of the valuation of life and health, the difficulties in the way of a comprehensive approach immediately present themselves. First, much damage to health and, no doubt, many deaths, are suffered without any attempt to hold anyone legally responsible. Data on claims in casualty insurance are scanty and, in any event, encompass other kinds of damage, for example, to property. Finally, even if a suit is filed, a settlement out of court occurs frequently and its details are often secret, or if not, seldom find their way into the legal literature.

In this chapter, therefore, it is necessary to rely on a sample of cases that came to trial. The chapter concludes with a statistical analysis of the sample and the factors that appear to influence the monetary outcome. The number of potential cases is very large. As table 3.1 indicates, more than nine million people required emergency-room treatment for accidents relating to home equipment alone. Automobile and work-related accidents add enormously to this number, as shown in chapters 6 and 12. In this chapter, a discussion of the legal approaches to various aspects of the problem draws upon and is illustrated by a random selection of ninety cases which are described briefly in the appendix beginning on page 255. These also serve as the basis for a statistical correlation analysis in which monetary awards are related to various factors within them.

Damages

Estimating the amount of damages in any one particular case involves consideration of the pain, suffering, financial and personal inconvenience, and all other ill effects on the injured party's life. The objective is to return the plaintiff to a position as close as possible to the one occupied before. The variety of such effects leads to wide discrepancies in awards. Compensation for physical pain and suffering, for example, requires the jury to consider the amount of pain that could reasonably be expected from the injury, given the damage and the area of the body affected and the age, health, and physical condition of the plaintiff at the time of the accident. The duration of suffering is yet another factor. The injury may cause great pain for a short period immediately after

Table 3.1

Estimates of Injuries Requiring Emergency-Room Treatment Received from Consumer Products during Fiscal Year 1977

Type of Consumer Product	Thousands of Cases
Home structures and fixtures, construction materials	2,098
Home alarm, escape, and protection devices	4
Space heating, cooling, and ventilating appliances	100
Home furnishings	681
Home communications and hobby equipment	54
General household appliances	58
Kitchen appliances and unpowered housewares	604
Packaging and containers for household products	223
Home and family maintenance products	131
Home workshop apparatus	334
Yard and garden equipment	211
Child nursery equipment	46
Toys (excluding riding or ride-on toys)	94
Riding or ride-on recreational equipment	770
Ball sports and related equipment	1,373
Winter sports and related equipment	221
Other sports and recreational equipment	697
Miscellaneous	1,578
Total Estimate for 1977	9,277

Source: Consumer Products Safety Commission, *Annual Report 1978*, pp. 117–21.

the accident, or pain may be experienced intermittently or constantly for years to come. Eventually, it is up to the court to review these considerations and agree on an award. Alabama law on the subject states, "compensatory damages for pain and suffering must be left to the sound discretion of the jury to the correction of clear abuse and passionate exercise."[1] Discretion as exercised by the jury, has not, however, produced consistent awards as exemplified in cases 1-11, where awards range from $1,373 to $81,000. We will next examine some of the principal factors in the assessment of damages.

Physical Pain and Suffering

In evaluating the pain and suffering experienced by the plaintiff, the jury is at a disadvantage in assessing the intensity of pain associated with a particular injury. Generally an attending or consulting physician is required to testify to the amount of physical suffering associated with the injury as well as the expected duration. Physicans are usually asked to give a prognosis as well, that is, what operations or other therapies are needed, what the effects will be on the future life of the injured party, and so forth. In cases 12-16, a variety of medical judgments served as the basis for awards; again, the range is substantial.

Mental Pain and Suffering

With a portion of the award encompassing mental pain and suffering, the court considers the emotional strain that can fairly be expected from the injury (for example, shock, trauma, disorientation in society as the result of a handicap, psychosomatic conditions, and so on). Mental anguish is harder to assess than physical pain since it is hard to verify objectively; a plaintiff's over-reaction may be the result of acting, a poor sense of security, or just plain fright. The law, however, has tended to lean toward accepting the plaintiff's inner turmoil as a basis for compensation as stated in the *Corpus Juris Secundum*, ". . . imaginary suffering due to legitimate 'neurotic' suffering is recoverable. Recovery allowed for mental anguish i.e., disappointment, frustration, etc. and child based suffering."[2] This is illustrated in cases 17 and 18; both, to be sure, were minor cases and the low awards reflect this.

Physical and mental pain and suffering usually occur together. When the accident occurs, depending on the severity, it is an abrupt interruption of the manner of living and occupation that has provided both spiritual and financial sustenance and happiness to the plaintiff. The concert pianist whose hands are mangled and rendered unfit for playing, the pilot who loses partial vision in an auto accident, and the newlywed who loses his virility due to the wrong prescription of a drug are all examples of torment lingering long after the initial pain of the injury. People who have lost limbs or sensory acuity due to an accident suffer from disorientation in society since they feel at a disadvantage in not being "fully equipped." Emotional stress, in the same vein, is experienced when disfiguring scars, especially facial ones, are grim reminders of the injury itself. In the cases reviewed for this analysis, injuries resulting in the forfeit of love, affection, and feeling, either physical or emotional, for one's mate (consortium) are highly prominent and serve to escalate awards.

In the manufacturing of products or provision of services, contemporary business is thus financially responsible for the emotional welfare of its public as exemplified in cases 19-27, again showing a wide range of mishaps and awards.

Loss of Future Income and Wages

Yet another factor that is evaluated by the court is the plaintiff's surrendering of all future wages and income attributable to the injury. A company can be financially liable to this person long after the initial accident when continued partial or total disability makes it difficult if not impossible to work. Calculations of income loss awards involve immediate hospital expenses, future therapy, the particular occupation of the injured party, and the nature and extent of physical damage in view of the line of work familiar to this person.[3] These are the ingredients that determine the lump sum to be settled on at one payment, or payments made intermittently during the period of occupational disability. Case 28 relates to serious injuries suffered in an auto accident and is noteworthy in that it itemizes the damages awarded:

Past Pain and Suffering	$ 6,250.00
Future Pain and Suffering	6,250.00
Past Loss of Wages	4,200.00
Future Loss of Wages	19,750.00
Injuries	10,000.00
Auto Damage	1,252.50
Medical Bill	3,208.15
Total Award	$50,910.65

Other cases listed under this category are numbers 29-33.

When, according to the consulting physician's prognosis, continued disability is indicated, the loss of future income and wages is determined by the remaining life of the individual multiplied by his average yearly income. Projections of future damages may figure in the computation as further discussed in the next section. Life expectancy is ascertained by the courts through a variety of methods considering the human factors of age, health, physical conditions and habits, hereditary factors (longevity of ancestors, hereditary diseases, and so on), illnesses, occupation, and so on. Tables are then derived determining the expected remaining life period the business must be responsible for. The awards in cases 34-37 were based on such tables. When determining the average yearly income for future years, it becomes necessary to adjust these figures by projected cost of living indexes, inflation, and other indicators of income determination.

Each state court varies as to the degree of application of future income-adjusting factors. Alabama law states, "present value of dollar as compared with its value in former years must be considered in determining whether the amount of damages awarded is excessive. . . . In passing on the question of excessiveness of damages, Supreme Court will look to the amount of decreased purchasing power of money, present inflationary trends, enormous increase in cost of living, and give approval to a larger verdict than under normal circumstances."[4] California law on the subject also agrees with this philosophy that "trier of the fact may take into account future estimates of money arriving at damage award under California law."[5] Maryland also holds the same position: "In personal injury action in which lost future earnings are claimed, inflationary factors and present value should be considered together and simultaneously."[6] However, Florida legislation clearly puts a ceiling on income assessments when some settlements have stated, "effect of future inflation is not to be considered in calculating future damages, and court erred in including 2% cost of living increase in award for loss of future earnings, where inclusion was based on inflation . . . in determining damages for loss of ability to earn money in the future, an interest rate of 5½ percent would be inadmissible."[7] The rationale for the above differences among jurisdictions is beyond our present scope.

Death

Death clearly presents the most complex aspects of cost. It is the gravest consequence of the kinds of accidents and negligence described here. The United States Supreme Court states that in deaths the damages "recoverable are such as flow from the derivation of the pecuniary benefits which 'the beneficiaries might have reasonably received if the deceased had not died from his injuries.' Foremost among these 'pecuniary benefits' are the financial contributions which the decedent would have made to the survivors had he lived, from his earnings, salary or wages as well as any other financial aid that the beneficiaries might reasonably have secured from the decedent during his lifetime had he survived, including such sums as decedent might have expended for the maintenance and support of the survivors. Recovery for loss of support has been universally accepted, and includes all the financial contributions that decedent would have made to his dependents had he lived."[8]

Calculating the amount of lost contributions and attendant loss of support and maintenance involves the source of these variables—potential earnings (earning capacity), profits or income from solely owned enterprises, partnership drawings in adequate proof situations, retirement funds and other fringe benefits, and the duration of the contributions, which involves the life or work life, life expectancy of the decedent and also the life expectancy of the beneficiaries concerned, and the character and habits of the decedents and of the survivors. As a first approximation, attorneys for plaintiffs may use a formula for total lost earnings A, such as

$$A = \frac{a(e^{rn} - 1)}{r}$$

where a is present annual earnings, n the expected remaining working years, e = 2.718, and r the *real* annual rate of increase in earnings, that is, current rate minus inflation rate. If r should be found to be negative,

$$A = \frac{a(1 - e^{-rn})}{r}$$

with r entered as its absolute value. These amounts may have to be discounted to their present value.[9] Clearly, the data required for such computations involve a number of uncertainties.

The relationship between the decedent and the survivors as well as other matters relating to dependency affect the awards. For a parent, compensation is rendered for loss of love, affection, support (to which child is accustomed according to age), future school tuition, donations, emotional support, contribution to society, and so forth (case 38). For a child, compensation is granted for loss of affection, love, future contributions or gifts or awards (if child has occupation, determination of future income and rent), dependency if parents were dependent on child's earnings, and so forth (cases 39-41). For a spouse, compensation is awarded for loss of love, affection, support to which accustomed, consortium, spousely duties, future contributions, and so forth.

Punitive Damages

Portions of the awards cited above, and further illustrated below, included punitive damages. The form of compensation may be recovered "in any case where the death resulted from the gross negligence or willful act or omission, from recklessness, wilfulness or malice, from oppression, fraud or malice, or from fraud, malice, insult, or a wanton and reckless disregard of the injured party's rights and feelings."[10]

Courts and juries have often held that enterprises owe a substantial degree of responsibility to the public by reason of their financial strength, business expertise, and impact on society. Punitive damages, when introduced into a consumer lawsuit, not only serve to place higher values on human life, but are a deterrent to future business practices that endanger the welfare of the consumer. A recent Alabama decision stated, "in action for wrongful death . . . in arriving at the amount of damages which should be assessed, jury should give due regard to the enormity of the wrong and to the necessity of preventing similar wrongs, since the punishment by way of damages is intended to be a deterrent to others similarly minded."[11]

In cases 42-49, punitive damages were a substantial portion of the sums awarded. The very high judgment ($3.3 million) in case 49 was subject to the reserved decision of the judge as of the time it was reported. Actually, in many cases in which large sums are awarded, a punitive element is implicit, even if not explicitly stated.

Punitive damages appear to be levied more frequently and in greater amounts than in the past. In *Gryc* v. *Riegel Textile Corporation*, a judgment of $1.8 million was levied against Riegel of which $1 million was for punitive damages, in a case in which a child was burned as a result of wearing a highly flammable fabric. The award was sustained in the Minnesota Supreme Court, and in October 1980 the U.S. Supreme Court declined to review the case. The verdict was upheld, even though Riegel showed that it had compiled with federal standards. However, the evidence also showed that Riegel was aware that the standards in the Flammable Fabrics Act were highly questionable. Previous cases involving fabric burns should have served as a warning to Riegel, the trial court ruled.[12]

The high levels of punitive damages now being awarded in many states greatly increase corporate risks when trading off safety of products against cost. Actually, few awards of this size have been paid, because they are taxable to the plaintiff and not recoverable from a defendant's insurer; thus the cases often end in compromise and settlement before appeal. But the possibility of class actions in mass-marketed products is a substantial risk, even if jury awards are later reduced.

Negligence and Liability

Consumer Responsibility

A business defendant may not have to bear sole responsibility for the incident at issue. Apportioning the blame between the injured party and the business comes under the legal definition of comparative negligence. This now includes contributory negligence, a slightly different legal concept that was treated separately until about ten years ago. Comparative negligence refers to how a reasonably perceptive person should have behaved in relation to the handling and use of a product which resulted in injury or death. This conduct may decrease the award in part or in whole, as Dooley states: "The term 'Comparative Negligence' might be used to describe any system that by some method, in some situations, apportions costs of an accident, at least in part, on the basis of relative fault of the respective parties."[13] This aspect of the matter is called "damage apportionment" or "comparative damages." Under pure comparative negligence, where the individual has acted in such a way as to be totally incompatible with the intended use of the product, the negligent plaintiff may *still* recover even though his negligence was greater than that of the defendant's, but will have his damages reduced in proportion to the amount of negligence attributable to him.

Moving in varying degrees, the courts attempt to observe three different methods, depending on the situation, in considering comparative negligence. The equal division or admiralty rule applies when the damages are almost divided equally between the negligent parties, regardless of the actual relative contributions. Second is the "slight gross" system which is applied in all negligence actions in Nebraska, South Dakota, and in a limited number of actions in other states. Under this system, if a plaintiff's negligence is slight and the defendant's gross in comparison, the plaintiff can recover, but his damages will be diminished by the percentage of fault attributed to him. The third method is the 50 percent or Wisconsin System. In this case, if the plaintiff's contributory negligence is equal to or greater than that of the defendant, the common law contributory negligence rule applies and the plaintiff recovers nothing. In 1969, New Hampshire adopted a variant of this approach which allows the plaintiff to recover 50 percent of his damages when his negligence is equal to that of the defendant. The apportionment of blame has, incidentally, been shown to take substantial extra litigation time.

Comparative negligence does not only consider misuse of the product after the fact, but also considers whether the user should have had advance knowledge of the imminent danger. The courts, in assessing the liability of the business involved, have given weight to the plaintiff's accepting the assumed danger whereby the plaintiff "expressly assumes a risk and specifically agrees prior to the time of the injury-causing event to hold the defendant blameless with regard to his negligence."[14] In effect, when an individual knowingly and voluntarily encounters a risk, he is treated as if he has agreed to take charge of himself and relieve the defendant of any responsibility toward him. This serves to mitigate in part the damages charged to the corporation.

In cases 50 and 51 blame in that sense was apportioned, although in case 51 it consisted of preexisting disability, that is, not actual negligence. In cases 52-61, limitations of responsibility were successfully asserted by defendants and won by them as a result. Accident prevention measures by business have placed increased responsibility on the user in the use of a product. This decreases public liability for the corporation and reduces the compensation due to the injured party. It also indicates, at least in part, that compliance with federal standards may serve as successful defense provided these are shown to be technically appropriate. The current deregulation trends, if implemented, may therefore well serve to impair that kind of defense in future cases, with resultant greater judgments for the plaintiff, increased punitive damages, and more frequent and protracted litigation.

Finally, there are instances when, due to the severity of the injury, or the surrounding circumstances and resulting disabilities, awards are granted that ignore comparative negligence even though a case might be made for it. In such cases, for example, numbers 62-64, the jury believed that although full compensation theoretically was not in order, it would have been inhuman not to give full compensation. For instance, in case 63, a pickup truck owner recovered $1,760,000 from the manufacturer for the paralysis that resulted when the lockout system in the truck's quadra-jet carburetor failed to operate properly, causing the truck to accelerate and overturn. Misuse of product (readjustment and other work on the carburetor by the plaintiff) was held contributory but not grounds for denial of award. In case 64, the plaintiff's daughter fell through an open window in the common passageway of the defendant's apartment building. She received an award of $5,000 even though no unnecessary danger was presented by the actual structure of the building.

Strict Liability in Tort

Technical progress and complexity in products have changed legal definitions of corporate responsibility to their public and increased the scope of business liability. In cases where the defendant was felt to have a large impact on the public with its products and its dangers, negligence in use by the consumer (plaintiff) became an extraneous factor. These changes in attitude toward the business entity presaged a new doctrine, the doctrine of strict liability in tort, which would eliminate common rules insulating manufacturer and seller from the injured user of their products. Consumers' interests would be given priority in public policy. The maker is considered the expert and has, or should have, knowledge of dangers of its products and their components. This attitude has been growing steadily and at a pace where critics now speculate that America is approaching a "no-fault" economy where both manufacturers and sellers will bear full responsibility for all product-related injuries. Juries have been accused of being overly sympathetic to this sentiment and of having given the plaintiff "the benefit of every doubt."[15] Changes in liability law after 1976 prompted some insurance companies to raise their premiums 1,000 percent for some manufacturers.

However, the concept is rooted in long precedent. In 1944, Justice Traynor of the California Supreme Court, concurring in a food products case, reasoned that a manufacturer should incur absolute liability for placing on the market a product with a defect-causing injury. The manufacturer was far more capable of absorbing the risk than the public at large. The marketing of harmful products was declared adverse to public policy. The ability of business to profit from its products carries with it an increase in social responsibility as reflected by legislation and increased awards. As Dooley puts it, ". . . the general inability of consumers to bargain for protection against defective products, intense modern advertising, and the prevalent custom of doing business through the sale of goods in sealed packages are compelling reasons why strict liability should apply to consumer products as a whole, without the requisite of privity."[16]

Cases 65-67, covering widely varying awards, were all decided in accordance with strict liability. The court's determination of the degree to which strict liability may be applied in calculating the award is derived from the magnitude of defects found in the product or service. Contemporary legal definition states a defect as "a condition not contemplated by the ultimate user, which would be unreasonably dangerous to him."[17] One condition is the duty to warn if the product is unreasonably dangerous without adequate warning, and no such warning is given (*Canifax* v. *Hercules Powder Co.,* California, 1975). The imminent danger must be of such a nature as not to be initially obvious in the intended use of the product. There could be hidden dangers, operational steps, and the like which should be readily explainable to the user by a label, instruction booklet, or warning sign on the product in large print. The Federal Model Code is especially strict in this area. Juries are asked to determine whether there was any likelihood that the product would be misused, ultimately resulting in serious harm. The greater the potential danger and more serious the harm, the greater the duty to warn. Professor Richard A. Epstein of the University of Chicago Law School notes, however, that even "the plaintiff who neglects a warning or disregards a safety precaution may still be able to recover full tort damages."[18]

Design that makes the product unreasonably dangerous will suffice for the court's interpretation of a product defect as was concluded in *Greenman* v. *Yuba Power Products, Inc.* (California, 1962). Greenman, the progenitor of the doctrine, specifically notes that a manufacturer would be responsible under strict liability in tort for design, as well as manufacturing defects. Defective design, by its very nature, embodies negligence principles despite the fact that liability is found regardless of the use of all possible care. The corporate defense in many liability cases has grown weaker with new interpretations by the courts of product (service) defects and negligence. With an increasingly complex array of technology being introduced to the market, chance of design-related injuries have proliferated.

In the view of some, the pendulum has swung over too far to the side of the consumer and several reform possibilities are now up for debate. One reform involves limiting the useful and safe life of a product to ten years if no unauthorized alterations have been made to the product. Another limits the manufacturer's liability to strict adherence to state and federal standards for all aspects of the product, from design to marketing. Yet a third reform involves the return to comparative fault laws as mentioned before, which reduces award amounts in proportion to the amount of negligence exhibited by the plaintiff. Professor Aaron D. Twerski of Hofstra University Law School believes that this would defeat the very premise of strict liability: "We shouldn't cut a plaintiff's recovery by X percent because he's a *Schlemiel*, when the reason for saying there's a design defect in the first place is that it didn't protect the *Schlemiel*."[19]

Optimal function, low cost, and simple use are the ideal situations in a successfully marketed product. Adequate guards and safety devices must be part of the design whenever the product poses a danger to the average user and the danger is hidden to a significant extent. The key here in determining manufacturer's negligence is the court's decision on whether a reasonable person could detect and take preventive measures against the product's inherent danger points, for example, an exposed rotating chain, exposed blades, wires, and so on. As Dooley puts it, "one outstanding difference between defect in design measured in terms of negligence and strict liability in tort is the absence of safety devices. The almost universal rule is that a product manufactured or sold without a recognized safety device may be unreasonably dangerous."[20]

Furthermore, manufacturers have often been found negligent on the basis of deficient safety features at the time of the accident rather than at the time of manufacture of the product and thus a plaintiff was able to claim injury almost on an *ex post facto* basis. Indeed, product improvement itself could lead to claims resulting from troubles with earlier models. However, some new state laws are designed to put a check on this, by providing that new progress in safety design will not be held against the manufacturer, if in fact, it was not possible to use this knowledge earlier.[21] This does not excuse the company from exercising all possible care in preventing any obvious or foreseeable dangers, but does close an unjust gap in the manufacturer's defense. Strict liability is still strongly enforced. A large number of cases (numbers 68-87) illustrates the workings of strict liability. Again, they cover a wide range of accidents and of interpretation but the paramountcy of consumer or user interest is clearly demonstrated.

Liabilities of Utilities

Because their monopoly position reduces their incentive for product improvement as well as consumer choice, the courts have tended to impose stricter rules on utilities than on other businesses. This has also expressed itself in relatively high awards, as in cases 88-90. Most utilities are large corporations and so may be expected to be the target of more suits and for higher awards than smaller defendants. While the *Corpus Juris Secundum*[22] clearly stipulates that the wealth of a defendant should not be a criterion in setting awards, a wealthy defendant would also typically have greater resources for defending itself. Actually, many cases are settled out of court. Table 3.2 gives the experience of Long Island Lighting Co. (LILCO) in settling major suits in 1977. The wide range of percentages at which claims were settled is especially noteworthy.

Table 3.2
A Sample of Injury Claims against Long Island Lighting Company, 1977

Plaintiff	Claim	Settlement	Percentage of Original Claim
Farrantello	$ 56,000	$ 22,500	40
N.Y. Telephone	13,547	13,547	100
Boone	200,000	235,000	118
Fallance	750,000	140,202	19
Munder	175,000	20,000	11
Lyman	75,000	25,000	33
McGuaran	500,000	20,381	4
Hoofran	380,000	37,500	10
Durka	1,350,000	50,000	4
Miner	1,000,000	45,000	5
Jackson	1,000,000	600,000	60
Holst	100,000	30,000	30
Cinelli	715,000	60,000	8
Wolfson	350,000	300,000	86
Caputo	150,000	110,000	73

Source: Long Island Lighting Company, New York.

Liability Insurance

Stricter standards of business responsibility have resulted in substantially increased premiums for liability insurance. As table 3.3 indicates, they have risen consistently but the rate has accelerated sharply in recent years, almost doubling in the period 1975-1979 and before then in the period 1970-1975. These premiums also cover business risks other than product liability but reflect the strong upward trend in claims experience. As to the latter, a study by Insurance Services Offices,[23] a sample of 24,452 product liability claims against twenty-three major insurance companies between July 1, 1976, and March 15, 1977, shows that the average product-related injury claim was settled for $13,911 with 97 percent of the cost covered by insurance. Additional expense to the insurer involves attorney and witness fees, traveling expenses, and other costs that are directly related to the claim. No matter who wins the case, for every claim paid the insurer also incurs an additional expense of thirty-five cents on a dollar to cover defense costs. The high premiums now charged have led to consideration of tax incentives to help alleviate the problem and thus, by reducing tax receipts, turn it in part into a social cost.

Table 3.3
Business Liability Insurance Premiums Written, 1952–1976

	($ Millions)		($ Millions)
1952	420.9	1966	1,205.3
1953	510.6	1967	1,326.4
1954	571.7	1968	1,462.0
1955	607.6	1969	1,713.0
1956	669.6	1970	2,139.7
1957	726.5	1971	2,381.0
1958	775.4	1972	2,555.2
1959	862.1	1973	2,701.3
1960	962.8	1974	2,936.0
1961	1,022.9	1975	3,980.7
1962	1,058.9	1976	5,384.1
1963	1,090.9	1977	6,793.8
1964	1,110.8	1978	7,705.9
1965	1,136.7	1979	7,816.8

Source: Insurance Information Institute, as reported in *Insurance Facts*, 1980–1981 ed., "Products, Liability, Marine, Surety," p. 23.

Factors in Awards: A Statistical Analysis

The ninety cases cited above form an interesting pattern when they are analyzed with respect to seven factors: (1) amount of award, X_1 which was set as dependent variable; (2) physical pain and suffering, X_2; (3) mental anguish, X_3; (4) financial loss, X_4; (5) personal inconvenience, X_5; (6) death, X_6; and (7) year of award (1965 = 0), X_7.

Factors X_2 to X_5 were weighted individually for each case with a maximum of ten points depending on the severity of this particular variable. Factor X_6, death, was given a maximum of fifteen points with severity interpreted as the amount of negligence in the case. Factor X_7 was included as an indicator of time trend due to inflation and changes in legal provisions and philosophies.

A linear multiple correlation analysis shows a coefficient of multiple correlation of 0.2335 with an F ratio of 4.21 which has a significance level of about 0.001 meaning that such a result could occur by chance only with probability 0.001 or less. When the size of the awards, X_1, is correlated in turn with each one of the independent variables X_2 through X_7, the resultant simple coefficients of correlation (table 3.4) are all found to be significant at the 0.01 level,

Table 3.4
Simple Correlations of Size of Award with Gravity Factors and Time

Variables	r	t
X_2 Physical pain	0.3003	2.95
X_3 Mental anguish	0.4097	4.21
X_4 Financial loss	0.3251	3.23
X_5 Personal inconvenience	0.1791	1.71
X_6 Death	0.3434	3.43
X_7 Year of award	0.2602	2.53

except for personal inconvenience, X_5, and for X_7, which is significant at the 0.02 level. The values of r^2, indicating the proportion of the variation of X_1 accounted for by each of the independent variables in isolation, may appear low but, given the sample size of 90, they are still statistically significant.

However, the partial coefficients of correlation (table 3.5) tell a somewhat different story. They are a measure of the explanation that each added variable contributes after the others have done their share. Here, none is found to be significant at the 0.05 level, which indicates that no single factor predominates. Furthermore, if the independent variables are correlated with each

Table 3.5
Coefficients of Partial Correlation for Gravity Factors and Time

Variables	r_p	t
X_2 Physical pain	0.0920	0.84
X_3 Mental anguish	0.1807	1.67
X_4 Financial loss	0.1479	1.36
X_5 Personal inconvenience	0.0270	0.25
X_6 Death	0.1118	1.03
X_7 Year of award	0.0764	0.70

other, as in table 3.6, it is shown that, with two exceptions, all the simple correlations turn out to be significant since the calculated t's exceed the critical value of 1.99. This suggests that the gravity variables used measure rather similar phenomena, and that severities of injury in one category are strongly related to the others. The independent variables X_2 through X_6 (excepting X_7, years) are thus, to a degree, surrogates for each other and, accordingly, a

Table 3.6
Calculated t-Values for Simple Correlations of Independent Variables X_2 through X_7

Pairs of Variables		t
X_2	X_3	4.56
X_2	X_4	3.7
X_2	X_5	5.0
X_2	X_6	1.89
X_2	X_7	4.26
X_3	X_4	3.8
X_3	X_5	3.49
X_3	X_6	5.84
X_3	X_7	3.13
X_4	X_5	4.50
X_4	X_6	2.81
X_4	X_7	2.72
X_5	X_6	0.98
X_5	X_7	4.29
X_6	X_7	2.7

degree of multicollinearity is probable. When X_2 through X_6 are added together and the simple correlation with X_1 is calculated, the result gives $F = 24.7$ and a high degree of significance; its level is effectively zero.

Conclusion

This chapter has summarized recent trends in the interpretation of the responsibilities of business for its products and processes and the reaction of the legal system to accidents resulting from malfunctions of one kind or another. These trends have shown increasing tendencies to favor the plaintiffs in such cases and these have been expressed both in interpretations of the laws and in the greater size of the awards.

A selection of ninety cases was used to illustrate these developments. A correlation analysis shows that many factors related to the gravity of the accidents influence the size of the awards but that a substantial degree of variation and randomness still exists. Nevertheless, a rising trend over time is clearly in evidence; that variable is determinable with certainty and is not subjective, as indicators of gravity may well be, at least in part.

The results indicate that the rise in this sector of social costs will continue to put a premium on careful product design, warning labels, and the like. Developments in tort law, as described, may call into question whether it is realistic for business to expect that the current political climate will lead to a reversal of these trends.

Notes

1. *Alabama Digest*, vol. 7A, 1977 Cumulative Pocket Part: "Measure of Damages, (A) Injuries to Persons" (St. Paul Minn.: West Publishing Co., 1978).

2. *Corpus Juris Secundum*, no. 64 (New York: American Law Book Co., 1977), p. 457.

3. *Illinois Digest*, vol. 2, 1977 Cumulative Pocket Part (St. Paul, Minn.: West Publishing Co., 1978).

4. *Alabama Digest*, vol. 7A, 1977 Cumulative Pocket Part.

5. *California Digest*, vol. 18, 1978 Cumulative Pocket Part: "Damages" (St. Paul, Minn.: West Publishing Co., 1979).

6. *Maryland Digest*, vol. 1, 1977 Cumulative Pocket Part: "Damages" (St. Paul, Minn.: West Publishing Co., 1978).

7. *Florida Digest*, vol. 4C, 1977 Cumulative Pocket Part: "Damages" (St. Paul, Minn.: West Publishing Co., 1978).

8. S. M. Speiser, *Recovery for Wrongful Death* (Rochester, N.Y.: The Lawyer's Cooperative Publishing Co., 1975), p. 139.

9. J. E. Ullmann, *Quantitative Methods in Management* (New York: McGraw-Hill, 1976), pp. 36, 43.

10. Speiser, *Recovery for Wrongful Death*, p. 139.

11. *Alabama Digest*, vol. 7A, 1977 Cumulative Pocket Part.

12. "More Punitive Damage Awards," *Business Week*, January 12, 1981.

13. J. A. Dooley, *Modern Tort Law, Liability and Litigation*, vol. 2 (Chicago: Callahan and Co., 1975), p. 31.

14. Ibid., p. 154.

15. "The Devils in the Product Liability Laws," *Business Week*, February 12, 1979, p. 77.

16. Dooley, *Modern Tort Law*, p. 287.

17. *Reinstatement of Torts*, 2d ed. (New York: American Law Book Co., 1977), p. 435.

18. "The Devils in the Product Liability Laws," *Business Week*, p. 73.

19. Ibid. Twerski is coauthor of a major text on product reliability. A. D. Weinstein, A. D. Twerski, H. R. Piehler and W. A. Donaher, *Products Liability and the Reasonably Safe Product* (New York: Wiley, 1978).

20. Dooley, *Modern Tort Law*, p. 32.

21. "The Devils in the Product Liability Laws," *Business Week*, p. 73.

22. As cited in *Reinstatement of Torts*, p. 435.

23. Insurance Services Office, Product Liability Closed Claim Survey, *Highlights* (New York: American Law Book Co., 1977).

4
Production of Electricity

DONNA RAE MARTORELLA

How many things are judged impossible
before they actually occur!

Pliny the Younger, *Historia Naturalis*

The social costs of converting energy mainly arise from various problems in
the production and subsequent treatment of fuels. While this holds true if
fuels are burned directly and for any purpose, it is in the production of
electricity that the greatest problems arise. So far, there are no methods for its
large-scale production that do not have some impact on society in the form of
pollution and risks to its workers and their communities. These risks may be
long or short term and the problems may be protracted or sudden, or definable in detail with some difficulty. Yet their extent and the possibilities of vast
calamities that tend to be downplayed within the industry have given this part
of technology the highest degree of controversy outside the military sector.

This chapter reviews the hazards and social costs of producing electricity
from fossil fuels, in nuclear plants, and by other means, focusing on those that
so far have not proved preventable or have only been partially eliminated. In
the latter case, the steps taken by the utility become part of the cost of doing
business. The cost, therefore, is borne by those using the product and thus
ceases to be a social cost. On the other hand, all pollution, work risks, and
similar effects remaining after preventive efforts create social costs. It is these
social costs that have called into question the use and economic feasibility of
most of the processes involved, notably nuclear power. These challenges have,
in turn, brought about governmental attempts simply to impose the costs and
risks upon the public in the name of national need and have thereby led to

serious political confrontations here and abroad. Opportunity costs are also involved since the use of energy is linked directly to social and technical inefficiencies that give rise to them. Optimal energy use would clearly confer a great social benefit but is far from reality today.

Coal Combustion

Though experimentation continues on other methods, coal is mainly burned by blowing it in powdered form into a furnace. This produces a large volume of particulates and of waste gases such as carbon dioxide, nitrogen dioxide, and sulfur oxides.

Carbon dioxide is a serious pollutant in that it gives rise to a "greenhouse effect." As energy produced by coal (or combustion of carbon fuels generally) keeps increasing, the inevitable accumulation of carbon dioxide will cause an increase in temperature twice that which melted the glaciers that covered Scandinavia and Canada in the last Ice Age.[1] This is an estimated change of eleven degrees by the year 2200.[2] Carbon dioxide also depletes the ozone layer and this will allow more of the sun's radiation to reach the earth and thus increase its temperature further. The resultant melting of the polar ice caps and glaciers would cause a rising sea level, eventually flooding much of the land surface. On the other hand, a reduction in the ozone level could also allow more of the earth's heat to escape causing a decrease in atmospheric temperature. This would have the opposite effect on the earth and could bring about another ice age. Which scenario is more likely or whether the two effects will somehow balance each other are matters of scientific controversy. Their extremes would, of course, pose global problems of social cost far beyond any others so far identified. Either way, the emission of carbon dioxide cannot be prevented.

Nitrogen oxides also deplete the ambient ozone levels in the atmosphere and also contribute to photochemical smog. This causes severe health threats, especially to the old; it causes eye irritation, aggravates asthma and other respiratory diseases, and reduces lung tissue elasticity. Nitrogen dioxide also increases the acidity in rainfall, which in turn increases the acidity in waterways. This is responsible for large fish kills, especially in lakes, and has the potential for agricultural damage. Acid rain from the American Middle West has brought about sharp controversy within the Northeast and Canada over the damage caused to lakes and fisheries, notably the Atlantic salmon—all of it clearly a social cost. The current cost of damage done is estimated at \$5 billion a year, which is a true social cost.[3]

Another serious air pollutant is sulfur oxide, primarily sulfur dioxide. Sulfur dioxide becomes sulfurous acid, which is highly corrosive and eventually produces sulfates which are known to cause respiratory illness and affect the larynx, trachea, bronchi, and heart. They are also a lung irritant which may lead to lung disease, including cancer. They also severely stunt the growth of vegetation and, even more than nitrogen dioxide, cause acid rain; the two pollutants appear to be even more destructive when both are present. Contaminated rain and air pollution damage waterways as well as metals and stonework and have led to the accelerated destruction of historic buildings and art treasures in many parts of the world.

Fifty percent of all sulfur pollutants come from coal-fired plants and 30 percent more from oil users. In addition, coal- and oil-fired plants account for 40 percent of the particulate pollution and 55 percent of the nitrogen oxides.[4]

There are also toxic trace elements (mostly metals) which are being sent into the atmosphere. These particles are too small to be caught by the scrubbers or filters in the stacks. They include arsenic, beryllium, chromium, manganese, nickel, lead, antimony, lithium, selenium, thallium, vanadium, zinc, and cadmium. When inhaled, they are irritants and may cause lung disease, cancer, and a variety of other toxic effects.

Another air pollutant that escapes into the atmosphere from coal-fired plants consists of organic substances. An example of this is benzopyrene which is a known cancer-producing agent. The body's natural immunity to benzopyrene is destroyed by ozones, another of the pollutants emitted by the coal-fired plants.[5] Finally, there is fly ash which causes photochemical smog that is not easily dispersed and brings the same type of respiratory problems as sulfur and nitrogren oxides.

Sulfur dioxide and other pollutants are removed by scrubbing, which is the spraying of water into the coal gases before they leave the stack. The resultant sludge is a mixture of water and minute particles of coal, fly ash, and other pollutants (notably sulfates) and itself presents a disposal problem. Scrubbers are expensive and also consume between 5 and 7 percent of the energy produced; nevertheless, although they are strongly resisted by U.S. utilities and other coal users, they are required by the laws of most other industrial countries, especially in new plants.

The cost of cleaning the emissions from fossil-fueled plants accounts for a large percentage of the capital expenditures for air and water pollution controls. For all nonfarm businesses, pollution abatement took $9.2 billion in 1980, which was 3.1 percent of total spending for plant and equipment. Public utilities spent $2.9 billion or 31.3 percent of that sum, which accounted for 8.1 percent of their total capital spending. Air pollution abatement accounted for 60 percent of the amount spent.[6] Nevertheless, most fossil fuel plants are still at least technically in violation of the standards set by the Clear Air Act; only about 15 percent of new power plants employ scrubbers.[7]

The pollution and other environmental problems of coal combustion thus have a substantial uncompensated element of social cost.

Coal Mining

Both methods—underground and strip mining—raise the issue of the prudent exploitation of natural resources; premature depletion is clearly a social cost. In underground mining, almost complete removal is possible, but the room-and-pillar method mostly used in the United States leaves as much as a third of the coal in the ground. Later, small mines may attempt to salvage the remainder, but this usually leads to more costly and dangerous operations. As to strip mining, the feasibility of digging the coal significantly depends on the costs of restoring the land. Therefore, more rigorous standards set for reclamation have the effect of reducing the economically feasible area of exploitation.

The environmental impact of coal mining has been drastic, as has the related socioeconomic deterioration of its regions.[8] Coal extraction has resulted in the degradation of 19,000 miles of surface streams and 15,000 acres of impounded water.[9] Approximately thirty-three tons of solid wastes per ton of coal mined are produced by coal mined in Appalachia and seventeen tons per ton of coal mined in the West.[10] Furthermore, what with mine accidents and chronic lung ailments, miners have the highest health risks of any class of industrial workers.[11]

Underground Mining

The human costs of underground coal mining are made up of sickness and mine accidents due to explosions, rock falls, and the machinery used. The effects of coal and rock dust on miners' lungs have been known since 1813, the major ones being black lung and silicosis (pneumoconiosis). About 10 percent of all miners have black lung and even more suffer from silicosis.[12] When the Coal Mine Health and Safety Act of 1969 (see below) went into effect, 229,000 claims for lung disease were filed in an industry that at the time only employed about 200,000 miners.[13]

Each year 1 man in 10 working in the mines has a disabling accident and a miner is killed every two days, with more than 100,000 miners killed during this century.[14] Between 1952 and 1968 there were 5,500 deaths, 220,000 severe accidents, and an additional 250,000 miners who suffered from lung ailments. If projected (though uncertain) increases in the use of coal take place, by the year 2000, it is estimated that there will be 2,100 deaths, 49,000 injuries, and over 4 million man-days lost, in addition to the "normal" deaths and injuries that could have been expected without an increase in the use of coal.[15]

The death of seventy-eight miners in the explosion at the Consolidated Coal Mine in Farmington, West Virginia, in 1968 led to the Coal Mine Health and Safety Act of 1969. It set up the Mining Safety and Health Administration (MSHA) which started work in 1970; the Occupational Safety and Health Administration (OSHA) also enforces some of the safety rules.

As table 4.1 shows, deaths in general had been on a rising trend for the period 1966-1970, after having fallen consistently for sixty years. After 1970,

Table 4.1
Deaths in Coal Mines since 1906

Before MSHA		After MSHA	
Five-Year Period	Average Annual Deaths	Year	Number of Deaths
1906–1910	2,657	1970	260
1911–1915	2,517	1971	178
1916–1920	2,410	1972	172
1921–1925	2,215	1973	N/A
1926–1930	2,235	1974	132
1931–1935	1,240	1975	152
1936–1940	1,265	1976	N/A
1941–1945	1,311	1977	139
1946–1950	870	1978	106
1951–1955	522	1979	N/A
1956–1960	380	1980	N/A
1961–1965	174	1981	153
1966–1970	246	January-February 1982	22

Sources: Accidents and Unscheduled Events Associated with Non-Nuclear Energy Resources and Technology, Interagency Energy-Environment Research and Development Program Report, February 1977.

U.S. Bureau of Mines, *Mineral Yearbook* (Washington, D.C.: Supt. of Doc., various).

A. Abrams, "Mine Deaths Bring Funding Reversal," *Newsday,* February 10, 1982.

deaths showed a generally declining trend. However, in 1979 the budget for MSHA was cut and a hiring freeze on staff was imposed; this led to a rise in deaths once again. The Reagan administration cut funds further (from $152 to

$149 million); meanwhile, the number of inspectors had fallen from 1,400 in 1979 to 1,200 in 1981, by which time there were 5,000 fewer inspections than in 1980. The very poor record of 1981 and early 1982 led to sharp political demands for a reversal, backed up by a clause in the miners' collective bargaining agreement that provided a ten-day "mourning period" after an accident. That, in effect, threatened a legal coal strike, and faced with this possibility, the Reagan administration did a political about-face (rare in issues of this kind) and agreed to provide $15 million more in the 1983 budget, most of it in order to hire several hundred more inspectors.[16]

Even so, U.S. rates are alarmingly high. In Britain, which has about the same number of miners (225,000), 39 were killed and 555 seriously injured in 1981. The corresponding U.S. figures were 153 and 6,350. Moreover, British mines use the long-wall method rather than room and pillar because their relatively accessible coal is long gone and seams are also more convoluted geologically;[17] their methods allow more complete recovery of the coal.

There is a dreary regularity in the details that come out in inquests on coal mine disasters. Sloppy and irregular inspections, failure by managements to install safety equipment, poor housekeeping, risky operating methods, failure of miners to obey safety rules, negligibly small fines for violations—the record is indeed melancholy.

Further dangers come from slag piles, including those from abandoned mines. In many places the unusable rocks and earth removed are piled into mountains not far from the actual coal mine. These "tips" which may be several hundred feet high pose a dangerous hazard since they are open to the elements and can become waterlogged. They then lose their cohesive force and may begin to move, as happened in the disaster on October 21, 1966, in Aberfan, Wales. Without warning, a waterlogged tip moved and within minutes destroyed everything in its path, including seventeen homes and a school where over 200 young children were attending classes. The final death toll reached 144, 116 of whom were children.[18]

In the United States, there have been several cases where mine debris created an artificial dam in a stream which later gave way during high rainfall or spring thaws. Enormously destructive floods have been the result, and only the fact that many occurred in sparsely settled country avoided huge death tolls. Furthermore, mine run-off is a notorious polluter of streams and water supplies in coal areas.

Finally, in some areas, old mines have caught fire, in some cases spontaneously and, in one notorious case, that of Centralia, Pennsylvania, it has lasted for twenty years without sign of ending. Poisonous gases, including carbon monoxide, ground subsidence, and other damage are the result. So far,

$3.5 million has been spent on it; an estimated $90 million or more would be needed to "dig it out."[19]

Coal mining thus exacts enormous social costs, because as further noted in chapter 6, occupational disability is never fully compensated, let alone human suffering and pain. The environmental impact likewise is enormous and no real measure exists for it. In a real sense, it is also an opportunity cost representing the difference between what coal country looks like and what it might have been.

Strip Mining

Strip mining is less hazardous than deep mining, but can destroy the land. Coal stripping has disturbed 1.7 million acres of land (twice the area of Rhode Island), with 1 million acres of land still needing reclamation. According to plans, approximately 100,000 acres of this land will be reclaimed each year (in addition to those acres being reclaimed because of the present stripping).[20] Strip mining leaves the land barren without topsoil, which means that no vegetation can grow. In addition, most coal seams are aquifers and the stripping of coal causes serious problems with the water tables and ground water supplies.

If the land is not reclaimed, there is a high degree of erosion and silting. Spoil banks are formed by the excavated ground being pushed into a pile, making reclamation extremely difficult. The erosion of the stripped land and the spoil banks cause damage to homes, mountains, and rivers. However, the number of deaths caused by slides and so on or by machinery malfunctioning is much less than the number of miners lost in deep mines. No separate statistics are available on work casualties in strip mining.

The Surface Mining and Reclamation Act of 1977 requires the land to be restored to approximately the original contours with native or introduced vegetation. The yield of the land must be equal to or greater than that before stripping. The Act also set up a federal fund for the restoration of already stripped land which will be funded by the coal operators at the rate of thirty-five cents per ton of stripped coal and fifteen cents per ton of deep-mined coal. Reclamation of land presently being stripped costs about one cent per ton.[21] Reclamation usually takes three to four years to start and may take up to ten years to complete; there is doubt whether it can be done at all in some of the arid areas of the West.

This legislation took a long time to enact and caused much controversy. Its implementation promises to do likewise. Heeding allegations of inflationary impact on costs of coal, President Carter decided in 1979 to postpone the effective date of regulations to carry out the purposes of the law. Under James G. Watt, President Reagan's secretary of the interior, the administration moved to settle legal challenges to the regulations by the National Coal Association and the American Mining Congress, meanwhile holding state regulations in abeyance. The third-party intervention of environmental groups stopped a "sweetheart" agreement for a while but, as of 1982, the matter was still under appeal.[22] At issue is the nationwide uniformity of standards, rather than letting state regulations prevail; their variation in adequacy and enforcement was what had prompted federal action in the first place.

Another toll of strip mining is the dislocation of often small and remote communities by the temporary influx of strip miners. With deep mining, employment is over a long period of time, but strip mining is short-lived and relatively labor intensive. The introduction of outsiders into the strip-mining towns has caused problems such as high job turnover, crowded and unpleasant living conditions, unqualified and few teachers, shortages of housing and public services, an increased number of suicides and mental hospital admissions, and a worsening of public finances, transportation, and pollution. In one town being studied, both welfare and crime increased by 400 percent.[23] There was also an increase in drug addiction, alcoholism, child abuse, and wife beating.

Finally, in coal generally there is a toll from transporting the very large tonnage involved. For example, coal transportation accounts for 41 percent of all work-days lost on railroads.

Oil Refining

Oil is a fossil fuel and thus its use in the production of energy causes the same type of air pollutants (that is, sulfur dioxide, carbon dioxide, nitrogen oxides) as coal.

In oil refining, gases are emitted that cause explosions and fires. Thus, every sizable refinery in the Delaware Valley has had a fire of major proportion.[24] As in coal mining, most of these were caused by violations of OSHA requirements. For example, on October 11, 1971, the local union requested an inspection at the Mobil Oil plant in Paulsboro, New Jersey. The result was a twenty-eight-day check that cited 354 violations. However, the management had been given advance notice of the inspection and they cut back operations in order to clean up, removing the evidence of many problems. The fine was $7,350—an average of $20 per violation. Again, early in 1972 there was a fire at the plant and one death. For a serious violation of the law there is a maximum fine of $10,000, yet the actual one was only $1,215. In October 1972 there was another fire; however, this time the man was able to crawl out from

under the rubble. The fine was $900. OSHA did not even investigate the inci-
dent until days after the fire and then only at the union's insistence.[25]

Some of the gases emitted in oil refining are toxic. They include ketone,
ammonia, and hydrogen sulfide, which is deadly if inhaled. If death does not
occur, it can cause sensory loss, retardation, headaches, and dizziness. Air pollution from refineries is a major cause of smog and has been identified as a
principal cause of problems in such notorious areas as Los Angeles. Water pollution, both chemical and thermal, is also significant.

Oil Spills

While the most publicized ones occur on the international waterways, it is
on inland waterways, in coastal waters, and in ports that most spills happen—
75 percent, according to one study. It is here that the human loss and pollution are greatest;[26] collisions are often involved.[27]

When an oil spill occurs, the oil lies on the surface and it does not mix easily
with water. A recent study found that after being exposed to the sun for
twenty-four hours, several types of crude and refined oils (including no. 2 fuel
oil) become radioactive.[28]

Petroleum also contains a number of carcinogenic hydrocarbons with
benzopyrene being the most dangerous.[29] About 5 tons of it come from the 5
million tons of oil per year which are estimated to be spilled into the water
either accidentally or intentionally; 1.5 million of it are spilled into waterways
by tankers.[30] During 1975 alone, there were 10,141 reported spills in U.S.
waters, involving 14.4 million gallons of oil products.

In a spill, marine life may be all but eliminated or at least destroyed as part
of the human and animal food chain. Fish may die or be contaminated by
several hundred times the normal levels of benzopyrene. Birds die from losing
their buoyancy and the insulating properties of their feathers and from ingest-
ing the oil.[31] A wide range of sublethal ill effects has been observed in marine
organisms from plankton to large fish; they include stunted growth, irreg-
ularities in reproduction and feeding, tumors, and birth defects.[32] Table 4.2
gives a listing of some typical oil spills, stressing the major ones but also draw-
ing attention to the calamitous effects that even a "small" spill can have, such
as the one in Buzzards Bay, Massachusetts. In some areas, oil spills have led to
the destruction of coral reefs and consequent dangers to ports and shorelines.
Nor are spills limited to those caused by accidents; many tankers flush their
tanks into the ocean. Laws and international conventions to prevent this exist,
but are hard to enforce.[33]

The social costs of oil transportation are difficult to assess in that the total
physical extent of the damage is very hard to measure, not least because one

Table 4.2
Recent Large Oil Spills

Year	Tanker	Spillage	Results
1967	Torrey Canyon	118,000 tons of crude	Killed over 50,000 birds. Used a previously untested detergent in clean-up efforts.
1969	Drilling rig	12,240 to 124,190 tons of crude	Brought national attention to the oiling of waterfowl. Clean-up cost over $6 million. Damages of over $17.6 million.
1969	New York Central no. 34 (tug), Florida (barge)	700 tons of no. 2 fuel oil	Destruction of wild harbor marsh, commercial shell fishing for seven years, shore erosion, long-term pollution by tar balls at bottom, and residual chemicals.
1971	Wafra	25,000 tons of oil	Organisms killed included crabs, snails, algae, octopi, abalone, and lobster.
1973	Arrow	4.5 million gallons of Bunker C industrial fuel	Polluted over fifty miles of Nova Scotia beach. Took twelve months to clean up. Caused the erosion of up to sixty-five feet.
1974	Metula	51,000 tons of oil (No clean-up was done since it was spilled in a remote area.)	Affected 1,000 square miles. Killed mussel beds, marsh life, fish, and birds. One year later the oil had not dissipated at all; eighteen months later the oil still persisted. Two years later the regrowth still had not started. All organisms that came into contact with the oil died.
1974	Oil tank rupture	43,000 tons of Bunker C	Clean-up expenses were over $100 million.

Table 4.2 (*continued*)
Recent Large Oil Spills

Year	Tanker	Spillage	Results
1976	Urquillo	100,000 tons of crude (spilled off Spain)	Two thousand tons of dispersants used were ineffective. Twenty-five thousand to 30,000 tons of oil were found on 130 miles of coastline, 40 of which were heavily covered. Killed over 70 percent of the commercial clam species.
1976	Sananiena exploded	(in Los Angeles)	Killed nine, injured fifty.
1977	Argo Merchant	7.6 million gallons of heavy industrial oil (off eastern seaboard)	Covered 3,000 square miles. Endangered cod, halibut, oysters, flounder, yellowtail, and other shellfish and their larvae affecting the $52.2 million industry.
1977	Blowout on Bravo 14	28,000 tons of oil (North Sea)	Lost revenue was $87 million; $8 million in lost oil; $58 million in lost taxes to the Norwegian government.
1978	Amoco Cadiz	55 million gallons (220,000 tons) of oil	Worst spill in history. Killed twenty-five species of fish. Ruined hundreds of miles of heavily used Brittany Coast Beach. Killed thousands of birds. Will affect the French and English coast and marine life for ten years.

Sources: E. Keerdoja, "Oil on the Waters," *Newsweek*, May 23, 1977, p. 12.
E. Gundlach, "Oil Tanker Disasters," *Environment*, December 1977, pp. 16–20.
"Pouring Troubled Oil on Atlantic Water," *Science News*, January 1, 1977, p. 6.
"Worst Oil Spill," *Newsweek*, January 10, 1977, pp. 74–75.
"Disaster off the Brittany Coast," *Time*, April 3, 1978, p. 64.
W. Wertenbaker, "A Small Spill," *New Yorker*, November 26, 1973, pp. 48–54.
M. Blimmer et al., "A Small Oil Spill," *Environment*, March 1971, pp. 13–21.

cannot always fully determine conditions before the accident. Furthermore, it would be hard to decide on a monetary loss, except from the viewpoint of the commercial utility of the damaged species. It has further been suggested that reducing the plankton population as the result of continuing oil spills would, in turn, impair photosynthesis enough to endanger the world's oxygen supply. Social costs of such an eventuality are beyond the bounds of estimation.

Nuclear Power

In its state at the beginning of 1983, nuclear power must be counted as a major disappointment among large-scale technological developments in this century. No new nuclear power plants are now on order in the United States; currently, seventy-two nuclear power plants are in operation and the Nuclear Regulatory Commission thinks that twenty out of the seventy-five now under construction will eventually be canceled; nor, according to the NRC, is any change likely. In large part, this development is the result of reduced projections of the demand for electricity. It is also, however, the result of an enormous cost escalation that came as a most unpleasant shock to the utility industry where, by requiring constant added financing at ever higher interest rates, it has caused wholesale distortions and difficulties in their financial situation.[34] The third major factor, however, is increasing and compelling evidence that the safety problems of nuclear power at all of its stages are far from solution and that the risks are substantially greater than had been claimed. The risks have always been considered too large for individual utility companies. Hence, by the Price-Anderson Act, government insurance or reinsurance was provided for. Thus, the difficulties clearly become a social cost depending on claim experience. In addition, long-term effects of exposure, even to relatively low levels of radiation, are also likely to be greater than had been claimed in the past. There are four general areas of concern: uranium mining, reactor operation, waste disposal, and water usage.

Uranium Mining

The mining of uranium presents radiation dangers in the mines themselves and in the tailings they generate. Tailings are piled into miniature mountains that are easily accessible and can be substituted for sand in buildings; for example, in Grand Junction, Colorado, many houses were built that way. The walls give off radion which may cause lung cancer, bone marrow abnormalities, and birth defects from gamma rays.[35] The cost of correcting the problems in Grand Junction alone will be about $12 million to $14 million.[36]

This kind of radiation is also a grave danger for the miners themselves. One study of uranium mining in Arizona revealed that many uranium miners in Arizona of Navajo background contracted lung cancer, which until recently had been almost unknown among their people. Other studies indicate an enormously increased risk factor, leading the United Mine Workers Union to estimate that 80 to 90 percent of uranium miners can eventually expect to die of lung cancer.[37] In addition, the normal risks of mining are present, such as accidents and dust from the hard rock which is a leading cause of silicosis.

Mine tailings have also contaminated river basins, notably that of the Colorado River. Dam failures, floods, and pipeline ruptures have swept radioactive tailings into rivers that later served as the water supply to wide areas. The largest of these was the rupture of a dam in Church Rock, New Mexico, which contaminated the Rio Puerco with a hundred million gallons of radioactive water that eventually wound up in Lake Mead and, thus, as part of the water supply of large areas of the southwest.[38]

Reactor Operations

The problems of steady, low-level radiation from nuclear reactors under normal operation, while significant, are not the principal public worry at present.[39] Rather, a succession of accidents and other operating problems has in recent years made their operation ever more problematic. By far the most conspicuous such example was the Three Mile Island accident on March 28, 1979. It served to demonstrate that even very unlikely events could in fact happen. A great deal has been written on the accident and on the trail of carelessness, unheeded warnings, poor design and workmanship, and untrained staff that led to it. Whatever the explanations, a succession of blunders was responsible for something that should never have happened.[40]

From the viewpoint of social costs, however, the following are the most relevant developments. First, General Public Utilities, the utility group that, through its Metropolitan Edison division, operated the plant, was thrown into financial difficulties from which it has yet to emerge. Nothing much has been settled about the ultimate cost of the clean-up as well as compensation to the people who were displaced temporarily from the site of the accident. Being located about ten miles from Harrisburg, Pennsylvania, some 140,000 people were forced to flee the area because at one point it was thought that a hydrogen bubble in one of the buildings might cause a major explosion.

The dismantling of the plant is expected to take many years, and by 1982 was barely on its way. The cost of the clean-up was estimated at $1.1 billion, with insurance paying $340 million, and uncertainty as to how much of the remaining $760 million the federal government will contribute. In late 1979, the company advertised for people to help in this rather unenviable task, promising "unprecedented opportunities for new scientific experience." Billions of dollars in negligence suits have also been filed, involving the utility, the government, the equipment suppliers, and the local people. There also was a public "strike" of sorts against paying the greatly increased utility bills (up 42 percent) that resulted from Three Mile Island.[41]

Furthermore, the reactor involved in the accident was one of two. The other reactor was shut down for maintenance at the time. Extensive corrosion prevented the restarting of the undamaged reactor, and startup was held up by lawsuits alleging inadequacy of the repairs and continuing lack of safety. A $4 billion dollar lawsuit was filed by General Public Utilities against the reactor's builder, Babcock & Wilcox. GPU claimed that an earlier accident, similar to that at Three Mile Island, took place at a Babcock-built plant in Ohio. Babcock took steps to correct it, but GPU alleges, did not inform other customers. Babcock & Wilcox responded that GPU had all the information it needed but was too inept to use it. In an editorial titled "Pot and Kettle," the *New York Times* suggested that, pending the outcome, "the public will have to live with the awesome possibility that both members of the nuclear establishment may be correct in their opinion of the other." The suit was settled for $37 million in January 1983.[42]

A second major problem concerns the nuclear power plant in Diablo Canyon. In fall 1981 a major antinuclear demonstration took place there that led to some violence. Shortly afterwards, it was found by the Nuclear Regulatory Commission (NRC) that a construction error had been made in the earthquake safety system. One of the opponents' major points had been precisely that the plant had been located on top of an earthquake fault. The license to operate was revoked, again with potentially enormous losses, some of which may well again be borne by society at large if a government subsidy can be secured. This matter too was still under discussion in early 1982. Similarly, construction of the William H. Zimmer plant of Cincinnati Gas and Electric Co. was ordered halted on November 12, 1982, by order of the Nuclear Regulatory Commission after gross violations of safety standards and after the $1.6 billion plant was almost complete. The FBI and a federal grand jury were reported to be looking into falsification of safety documents and harassment of safety inspectors.[43]

One general problem having to do with reactor accidents has been an attempt to establish safe standards for one aspect of it or another. The Rasmussen report of 1974, also called WASH 1400, attempted to quantify some of the risks. However, further analysis indicated that its estimates were very much lower than they should have been and that some risks had been virtually ignored; the Nuclear Regulatory Commission repudiated the study in 1979.[44]

In 1982, the NRC again attempted to set benefit-cost guidelines and stated, "the risk to an individual or to the population in the area near a nuclear power plant site of cancer fatalities that might result from reactor accidents should not exceed 1/10 of 1% of the sum of cancer fatality risks resulting from all other causes."[45] The problem of course remains that radiation emission is not easily and directly translated into added fatalities in this way. The proposal generated substantial dissent within the NRC and its fate appears uncertain. However, the NRC, under the chairmanship of Nuncio Palladino, has proved itself to be highly activist in safety matters, a rather unusual stance for an agency of the Reagan administration.[46] It has issued major reports on such perennial problems as neutron embrittlement of reactor parts[47] and questioned the safety of the operating plants. Its concern comes at a time when further, albeit less grave, incidents seem to happen almost weekly.

Finally, as the example of Three Mile Island itself indicates, decommissioning of reactors is likely to prove an enormously expensive item. The expected life of a nuclear reactor is only thirty years. As of 1978, none had ever been dismantled. However, Consolidated Edison Company of New York, when faced with the obsolescence of their Indian Point Plant no. 1, gave it to New York State, which has not done anything toward removing it. The Fermi Test Breeder Reactor near Detroit was abandoned; its irradiated building stands on a guarded site. It may well be that the job would cost more than the plant cost originally. Moreover, the radioactive metals in a reactor would have to be kept permanently safe because they remain hazardous for 1.5 million years.[48] The decommissioning problem thus is likely to pose a major social cost problem, closely linked to waste disposal.

Radioactive Wastes

The use of nuclear materials produces a large quantity of radioactive wastes; one large nuclear plant (1,000 megawatts) produces the same amount of radioactive waste in one year as a 25-megaton bomb.[49] The wastes stay radioactive for decades, centuries, or in some cases, millions of years. How to keep them contained and isolated from the environment is a problem that, although there has been much research done, has no viable solution.

The types of wastes produced include tailings, which are left exposed in abandoned sites in the West (with the results noted earlier); low-level wastes, which are stored at several burial sites throughout the United States; and high-level wastes, which are presently being held in temporary storage since there is no permanent storage facility.

The military has produced approximately 215 million gallons of liquid high-level wastes. As of January 1, 1976, there was an inventory of 75 million gallons, half of which is in solid form. Most of this waste is stored in Hanford, Washington; however, there are wastes stored at Savannah River and at Idaho Falls. By the time the solidification of these wastes is completed during the 1980s, it is estimated that there will be approximately 500,000 tons of high-level radioactive wastes stored at these three sites.

The commercial power industry has only produced 600,000 gallons of high-level wastes. While the nuclear power industry is unlikely to grow as much as expected at one time, that total is bound to grow. Some 3 billion cubic feet of radioactive material have accumulated thus far from all sources.

The record of managing these wastes is, by and large, one of failure of burial methods, leaks, deteriorating containers that were supposed to last forever, and poor and careless management.[50] Concentrating and calcining wastes, turning them into glass, and burying them in places like salt mines was long thought to be an ultimate solution, but increasing evidence shows that this method, too, is not wholly reliable. Sweden plans to bury its nuclear wastes in geologically stable granitic bedrock but even so, the wastes have to be stored for forty years before disposal in order to let them cool down sufficiently.[51]

As to specific disposal sites, troubles have plagued all of them, for example, Hanford and Idaho Falls.[52] In West Valley, New York, the plant of the Nuclear Fuel Services Corporation was to be the first of many commercial reprocessors of fuel. It went bankrupt, leaving the disposal of the waste and debris on the site to New York State,[53] with cost estimates of clean-up ranging from $500 million to $1 billion.

The storage at these facilities is not, in any case, supposed to be permanent but rather temporary until a way can be found to keep the material permanently safe. But not even this was done consistently. Some 50 million cubic feet of low-level wastes stored at six burial sites include about 950 kilograms of plutonium, 740 kilograms of which was buried before 1970 with no provisions being made for its retrieval. As a point of comparison, a 1,000 megawatt electric nuclear power plant contains about thirty kilograms of plutonium during its entire life of thirty years.[54]

The transportation of nuclear materials, and especially of wastes, is itself a matter of major controversy. In spring 1982, the Department of Transportation proposed new and much more lenient regulations, directing that it be trucked over interstate highways and through cities. These proposals were rejected in federal court in an action that upheld the right of New York City to bar such shipments.[55]

Water Usage

Because of the need for reactor cooling and condenser water, nuclear power is highly water-intensive. Therefore, most reactors are located near a sizable body of water. The heat they impart to the cooling water causes thermal pollution by increasing the temperature of the water near the discharge. This can deplete the oxygen supply, and increase the population of algae and the decomposition of sewage and organic matter. In addition, when there is an increase in the water temperature, the old balance of aquatic organisms is drastically disturbed and new ones appear. Unfortunately, the new fish population often comes to consist of "junk" fish, rather than the more desirable food species.

Nuclear power is not, of course, the leading cause of presently existing thermal pollution. The condition is a well-known corollary of industrial development in the United States and elsewhere. Wide seasonal variation of water flow often makes it much worse, and cases exist like the Cuyahoga River near Cleveland, Ohio, which sometimes reached temperatures over 100° F in summer, before industries along it were required to install more cooling towers. Still, the prospect of a nuclear power plant means much more environmental stress of this sort and so thermal pollution provides yet another inhibiting factor to nuclear power plants.

General Prospects

The foregoing extensive difficulties have led to substantially less optimistic estimates of the prospects of nuclear power than were current some years ago. Specifically, in 1979, the Committee on Nuclear and Alternative Energy Systems (CONAES) of the U.S. National Academy of Sciences and Engineering made an assessment of all major energy sources. With respect to nuclear energy, it concluded that the rate of discovery and production of uranium cannot sustain much more than the present rate of construction of nuclear power plants. One answer would be the breeder reactor or more advanced thorium fuel cycles. The breeder, however, presents even more severe environmental problems in its operation and the associated reprocessing and refabrication, notably the real possibility of diversion of nuclear fuels for explosives. During 1981 the so-called safeguards of the International Atomic Energy Agency (IAEA) were found to be severely lacking, especially in the wake of the Israeli air attack that destroyed the Iraqi nuclear reactor being built. Proliferation is likely to be accelerated by widespread construction of breeder reactors. The Reagan administration has resuscitated the Clinch River breeder reactor, which at this time represents the principal effort in the United States; operating facilities exist in France and the Soviet Union.

CONAES concludes that "it would be imprudent either to abandon the nuclear option or to promote it at present as the keystone of a future U.S. energy policy. Until the risks of nuclear accidents, proliferation of weapons material and management of high-level wastes are better understood by experts and the general public, it cannot be expected that the political consensus necessary for a large and rapid expansion of nuclear power will be achieved."[56] Since 1979 when this was written, the aftermath of Three Mile Island and further troubles and enormous cost escalations have exacerbated the situation even more.

Transmission

Regardless of how it is produced, electricity must be transmitted. If this is done at high voltage alternating current, electromagnetic waves are emitted. Animal experiments suggest that high fields may produce hormonal and biological changes similar to those caused by stress, a higher mortality rate, and stunted growth.[57] Other studies on humans suggest that there is little ground for apprehension. High voltage direct-current transmissions reduce these problems somewhat, but problems due to electric fields have likewise caused some preliminary concern. While these effects certainly are not comparable in magnitude to such problems as coal pollution or nuclear waste management, they are sufficient to bring forth sustained opposition to high voltage transmission lines, quite apart from their aesthetic or other environmental effects.

Some Other Methods

This chapter has focused on currently used methods of producing electricity. Several additional ones have been proposed. First, there are hydroelectric dams. It is generally considered that outside of Alaska, which would present major transmission problems, most of the best hydroelectric sites in the United States have been utilized. Over the years, in fact, some small older plants were abandoned in favor of large thermal power stations. In a few places, such as Paterson, New Jersey, old plants are being put into working order, and there is considerable interest, especially in the northeast, in tax concessions and other incentives for using hydroelectric power on a small scale. At present, such actions are inhibited by laws that reserve such plants for local public utilities. The proposed plants, however, are not environmentally neutral. They too affect the flows of rivers and some of the aquatic habitat. If properly designed, however, they can also fulfill the necessary function of flood control, which is still a problem in many of the areas concerned.

An allied process is that of pumped storage in which water is pumped into a large reservoir during off-peak hours and then drained out through turbines to provide added power at the highest peak. A notable plan of this kind was that of Consolidated Edison Co. of New York near Storm King Mountain along the Hudson River. Environmental concerns and escalating construction costs stopped that project.

Finally, tidal power has from time to time been put forth as a possibility in some areas; the site in the Bay of Fundy between Maine and New Brunswick appears to be the best North American possibility. Though a full-scale and successful installation of this sort exists in France, little effort along these lines can be expected in the current political and economic climate of the United States. The same must unfortunately be said of such projects as Ocean Thermal Energy Conversion (OTEC) or the use of wave energy.

Geothermal methods are also only in an experimental stage, but it is already becoming apparent that in some areas at least they would present quite substantial pollution problems, as a result of dissolved salts and at times low-level radioactivity from deep strata. Finally, though controlled thermonuclear fusion appears to have reasonable prospects in the long term, its feasibility has not yet been demonstrated.

The use of solar and wind power is also of interest. If they could be adopted they would materially reduce the kinds of environmental burdens discussed in this chapter. Solar energy is well established as a means of providing heat and hot water for domestic use. Using it to generate electricity is still at an experimental stage, with a developing conflict between small-scale generation by individual users and central plants feeding into the existing distribution network. This is also true of wind power.

One problem is that a proliferation of on-site generation of small quantities of electricity would cause the remaining users of the system to shoulder increasing per capita burdens of fixed costs. This has led to sustained objections by electric utilities to cogeneration of power from industrial waste heat, which is an excellent and, in the United States, largely unexplored source associated with conservation.[58]

The new methods discussed above generally share the characteristic of reducing environmental impact and thereby social costs. Their introduction, however, must await a more salubrious climate of investment and general societal priorities. In an atmosphere where one of the principal actions of the administration has been to eliminate encouragement of energy conservation, where research support for solar and wind power has been greatly reduced and where the 1983 budget proposes the elimination of specific business incentives for conservation equipment, the short-run prospects are hardly favorable.

Conclusion

In its current forms, the production of electricity and energy conversion in general exact considerable social costs in spite of substantial expenditures for pollution abatement and safety. In coal, its mining, combustion, and transportation all exact their toll. Though technical solutions exist for coping with most of the pollutants, the plants are for the most part, far from their legally mandated quality.

In nuclear power, uranium mining, reactor operation, and decommissioning and waste disposal all present dangers many of which have no technical solution in sight, quite apart from the economic constraints. Since responsibility for these problems tends to be turned over to government, business costs of power generation have a clear and sustained tendency to become social costs.

Notes

1. W. S. Broecker, "Hazards of Coal Dependence," *Natural History*, October 1977, p. 8.

2. "Carbon Dioxide Pollution May Change the Fuel Mix," *Business Week*, August 8, 1978, p. 25.

3. D. D. Danes et al., "Trace Gas Analysis of Power Plant Plumes via Aircraft—Measurement of O_3, NO_x, and SO_2, *Science*, November 22, 1974, pp. 733-36, see also V. Mohnen and M. Oppenheimer, "A Debate: Are Enough Data in Hand to Act Against Acid Rain?" *New York Times*, November 14, 1982.

4. A. M. Squires, "Clean Power from Coal," *Science*, August 28, 1970, pp. 821-28.

5. D. T. Gibson, "Oxidation from Carcinogens Benzo(a)pyrene and Benzo(a) antracene to Dehydroilsby, a Bacterium," *Science*, July 25, 1975, pp. 295-97.

6. *Statistical Abstract of the United States, 1981* (Washington, D.C.: U.S. Government Printing Office, 1981), p. 204.

7. PUR Business Letter no. 2333; *PUR Executive Information Service*, September 14, 1978; see also M. Oppenheimer, "America's Acid Rain Makers," *New York Times*, September 23, 1981.

8. H. M. Caudill, *Night Comes to the Cumberlands* (Boston: Atlantic Monthly Press, 1963).

9. "Up in Smoke," *Forbes*, December 15, 1975, pp. 28-30.

10. "Coal: Where Management and Labor Share the Blame," *Business Week,* November 2, 1974, pp. 76-77.

11. U.S. House of Representatives, Subcommittee on the Environment and the Atmosphere, *Environmental Challenges of the President's Energy Plan: Implications for Research and Development,* 95th Cong., October 1977.

12. E. Eckholm, "Unhealthy Jobs," *Environment,* August 1977, pp. 29-38.

13. R. Cassidy, "Life and Death Underground," *New Republic,* December 12, 1970.

14. L. T. Galloway and D. Cohen, "Washington Law, Kentucky Coal; Review of Federal Coal Mine Health and Safety Act," *New Republic,* September 11, 1976, pp. 14-16.

15. L. Angran, "Getting Cancer on the Job," *Nation,* April 12, 1975; pp. 433-37.

16. A. Abrams, "Mine Deaths Bring Funding Reversal," *Newsday,* February 10, 1982.

17. P. J. Sloyan, "Britain Strives for Mine Safety," *Newsday,* January 4, 1982.

18. E. England, *The Mountain That Moved* (Grand Rapids, Mich.: William B. Eerdmans Publishing Company, 1967).

19. S. Kalson, "Slow Burn in Centralia, PA," *New York Times Magazine,* November 22, 1981, p. 155.

20. "Impact of Stiff New Rules on Strip Mining," *U.S. News and World Report,* August 1, 1977, p. 43.

21. "Last of the West, Hell, Strip It!" *Atlantic,* September 1973, pp. 91-94.

22. "A Quiet Move to Relax Strip Mining Rules," *Business Week,* April 6, 1981, p. 31.

23. P. Franklin, "Craig, Colorado; Population, Unknown; Elevation, 6,185," *Audubon,* July 1977, p. 118.

24. R. Scott, *Muscle and Blood* (New York: E. P. Dutton and Co., 1967).

25. Ibid., p. 27.

26. J. Cameron, "Cracking the Tanker Safety Problem," *Fortune,* April 1977; pp. 150-52.

27. E. Gundlach, "Oil Tanker Disasters," *Environment,* December 1977, pp. 16-20.

28. "Our Shining Seas," *Chemistry,* June 1977, pp. 22-23.

29. J. Sullivan, "Powdering over Oil; Contamination of Seafoods by Benzopyrene from Spills," *Environment,* July 1975, p. 38.

30. "A Technology Assessed," *Scientific American,* November 1975; p. 58.

31. T. H. Watkins, "The Day the Birds Wept," *Audubon,* January 1976, pp. 16-21.

32. W. Wertenbaker, "A Small Spill," *New Yorker,* November 26, 1973, pp. 48-54.

33. M. Glazer, "The Shipping Industry," in *Waste Disposal Problems in Selected Industries,* ed. J. E. Ullmann (Hempstead, N.Y.: Hofstra University Yearbooks of Business, 1969), ch. 3.

34. "N-Power Industry Revival Unlikely Soon, NRC Says," *Newsday,* March 3,

1982; "A Dark Future for Utilities," *Business Week*, May 28, 1979, pp. 108-24.

35. "New Alarms about Old Wastes," *Business Week*, February 2, 1976, p. 17.

36. H. P. Metzger, "AEC vs. the Public: The Case of the Uranium Tailings," *Science News*, July 13, 1974, p. 31.

37. F. C. Shapiro, "Nuclear Waste," *New Yorker*, October 19, 1981, p. 53; see also the testimony of Governor Bruce King of New Mexico in U.S. Senate Committee on Labor and Human Resources, *Asbestos Health Hazards Compensation Act of 1980*, 96th Cong., August 26-27, 1980, pp. 186-93.

38. Shapiro, "Nuclear Waste."

39. E. L. Salinger et al., "Radiation and Leukemia Rates," *Science*, March 19, 1971, p. 1069; see also Interagency Energy-Environment Research and Development Program, *Potential Radiation Pollution Risks from Expanded Progress* (Washington, D.C.: U.S. Government Printing Office, 1977), p. 16.

40. D. Ford, "Three Mile Island," *New Yorker*, April 6, 1981, p. 49; and April 13, 1981, p. 46; "The Ordeal at Three Mile Island," *Nuclear News*, April 6, 1979; TMI Ad Hoc Nuclear Oversight Committee, "One Year after Three Mile Island," 1980 (mimeographed).

41. Ford, "Three Mile Island"; B. A. Franklin, "Three Mile Island Marks Third Year of Bad News," *New York Times*, March 26, 1982.

42. "Pot and Kettle" (Editorial), *New York Times*, November 9, 1982; see also *Business Week*, February 7, 1983, p. 46.

43. D. Burnham, "U.S. Orders Construction Halt on Ohio Atom Plant," *New York Times*, November 13, 1982.

44. U.S. Atomic Energy Commission, *Reactor Safety Study*, WASH 1400, August 1974 and October 1975 (Washington, D.C.: Government Printing Office); see also R. Gillette, "EPA Cites Errors in AEC's Reactor Risk Study," *Science*, December 13, 1979.

45. "Proposed Nuclear Power Regulatory Policies," *New York Times*, February 12, 1982.

46. J. Miller, "Nuclear Panel Is Changing under Firm New Chief," *New York Times*, December 15, 1981.

47. M. L. Wald, "Steel Turned Brittle by Radiation Called a Peril at 13 Nuclear Plants," *New York Times*, September 27, 1981.

48. U.S. House of Representatives, Committee on Government Operations, *Decommissioning Nuclear Reactors*, Report 95-1090, 95th Cong., 1978; see also "Nuclear Dilemma: What Does It Cost to Dispose of an Old Nuclear Plant?" *Business Week*, December 25, 1978.

49. J. W. Gofman and A. R. Tamplin, *Poisoned Power* (Emmaus, Pa.: Rodale Press, 1971), p. 14.

50. Shapiro, "Nuclear Waste."

51. T. O'Toole, "New Problems with Atomic Waste," *Newsday*, February 10, 1979; see also R. Siever, "Radioactive Waste Disposal: Burial under Land or Sea?" *Annals of New York Academy of Sciences*, 368 (1981): 81; and B. Allard and J. Rydberg, "Nuclear Waste Storage in Sweden," *Chemtech*, April 1980, p. 211.

52. M. Wilrich and R. K. Lester, *Radioactive Waste Management and Regulation* (New York: The Free Press, 1977).

53. R. Severo, "Hearing on Nuclear Waste Is Set for Tomorrow Upstate," *New York Times*, January 12, 1979; see also J. F. Shea III, "Formulating Nuclear Waste Management Policy," *Annals of New York Academy of Sciences*, 368 (1981): 81. For an account of the legislative history, see *Newsletter* of Senator Daniel P. Moynihan, May 1982.

54. Wilrich and Lester, *Radioactive Waste Management and Regulation*, p. 50.

55. Council on Economic Priorities, "Waste Shipment Peril Explored," *Newsletter* no. 82-1, January 1982. For a report on the court decision, see T. J. Collins, "U.S. Judge Upholds City's Ban on Shipment of Nuclear Waste," *Newsday*, February 20, 1982.

56. U.S. House of Representatives, Committee on Science and Technology, *National Academy of Sciences Report: Energy in Transition, 1985-2010*, Report 119, 96th Cong., January 25, 1980, p. 111.

57. R. Becker and A. Marino, "Electromagnetic Pollution," *The Sciences*, January 1978, p. 144.

58. U.S. House of Representatives, Subcommittee on Energy Development and Applications, *Cogeneration*, no. 155, 96th Cong., July 22, 1980, especially pp. 104-43.

5
Industrial Pollution

GEORGE J. RUSSO

> It seemed a world from which vegetation had been banished; nothing existed except smoke, shale, ice, mud, ashes and foul water. . . . And the stench! If at rare moments you stop smelling sulfur, it is because you have begun smelling gas.
>
> George Orwell, *The Road to Wigan Pier*

Introduction

This chapter deals with the social costs of pollution in industries other than the utilities discussed in chapter 4. A deplorably great array of pollutants, as diverse as the industries that create them, exacts a steady toll in all industrial societies and, at least on a localized basis, in those that aspire to that stage of economic development. After a general review of water, air, and noise pollution, the problems of specific industries are examined, mainly focusing on paper, primary metals, chemicals and food processing, and waste disposal. These industries are also in the forefront of controversy over what part of the abatement cost is to be borne by them rather than simply left for society in general to cope with.

Water Pollution

Water pollution can be defined as the introduction into water of a substance in such quantities that it seriously hinders or precludes use of the water for a desired beneficial purpose. Because of multiple uses of water, what is pollution to one may be beneficial to another. For example, large quantities of phosphorus and nitrogen in irrigation water would be welcomed by the farmer as fertilizer, but could prove disastrous to a lake. Further, almost any material is innocuous in water if present in "acceptable" amounts and, indeed, what would be pollutants in large concentration are in some cases present naturally as well. To some degree, therefore, pollution is relative and is a matter of social values as well as mere chemistry. Deciding what is acceptable is very much one of these "sociochemical" judgments.

Organic residue is one principal water pollutant. Oxygen utilization during its aerobic heterotrophic decomposition in water may reduce oxygen concentrations to such low levels that normal aquatic organisms are severely stressed or completely eliminated if anoxic conditions develop. The level of organic pollution is usually measured by determining the quantity of oxygen used in the aerobic degradation of the organic material and is, termed biochemical oxygen demand (BOD).

A second type of water pollution is caused by coliform bacteria. Coliform bacteria counts are commonly used to evaluate the sanitary quality and possible presence of pathogens in waters. Coliforms are nonpathogenic and ubiquitous in the terrestial environment but are present in very large numbers in the feces of warm-blooded animals.

Dissolved solids are another major type of water pollution. The total quantity and types of dissolved minerals (salts) in water determine its acceptability for many uses. In natural waters, the most common cations are calcium, magnesium, sodium, and potassium with traces of iron, manganese, and other cations; the most common anions are bicarbonate, chloride, sulfate, and nitrate with traces of phosphate, carbonate, fluoride, and other anions.

Drinking waters are generally required to contain less than 500 mg/l TDS (total dissolved solids) but healthy humans and other animals can tolerate up to 5,000 mg/l or more in their drinking water if necessary. Larger fresh-water aquatic organisms, such as fish, seem to be little affected up to about 5,000 mg/l. Water is generally unacceptable for irrigation if above a TDS level of 2,000 mg/l; type of crop, soil conditions, and irrigation practices determine usability between 1,000 and 2,000 mg/l. Below 1,000 mg/l TDS, the water is generally usable.[1] Sea water (which is unsuitable) contains about 35,000 mg/l TDS.

Excessive quantities of fine sand, silt, and clay in water give it a discolored, turbid appearance, fill in ponds and lakes, clog stream bottoms, and interfere with many beneficial uses. Streams and lakes vary widely in natural suspended solids (sediments) and this variation is often the major factor determining the quality of the aquatic habitat. Human activities frequently increase sediment loads, usually resulting in a degradation of aquatic habitat.

Excessive photosynthetic productivity in waters often results in nuisance conditions with increased turbidity, discoloration, odors, unsightly clumps of debris, and decreased aquatic habitat quality as the main consequences. It is caused by a nutrient-rich condition called eutrophication.[2]

Various trace elements (nutrients) restrict the growth of plants and small aquatic habitat and sometimes exogenous factors, such as temperature, turbidity, sunlight, and toxicity also have this same effect. Nitrogen or phosphorus or both in waters are frequently found to be the limiting nutrients. Of these, phosphorus is usually the more manageable. Finally, thermal pollution, as described in chapter 4, also results from many industrial operations where water is used as coolant, wash water, or otherwise heated.

Expenditures for the abatement of water pollution have risen steadily since the Water Pollution Control Act of 1956 and especially with further legislation in 1972 and later. The Environmental Protection Agency (EPA) has been charged with enforcing new federal standards for water purity. In 1978, $19.2 billion were spent nationally for pollution abatement of which 44.4 percent was spent by government at all levels and nearly all the remainder by business. There is, unfortunately, no reliable indicator of how much pollution is still exacting its toll, but the fact of the steady rise in expenditures, a very large part of which is in the form of fixed capital, suggests that a great deal still remains to be done.[3] This view is strengthened by the fact that the obligation of federal construction grant funds has not progressed with either the facility or the efficiency that Congress intended. In short, the job was not done as fast as it should have been, and the original appropriations took a long time in being translated into viable projects.[4] By the statutory deadline in 1982, a major portion of the nation's publicly owned waste water treatment systems had not met secondary or higher treatment levels. Primary treatment consists of simple settling and screening; secondary treatment involves extensive removal of pollutants; tertiary treatment means the restoration of water to drinking water quality. As a result, the Reagan administration proposed a substantial scaling down of quality standards and objectives.

Adequate sewers are another important ingredient of pollution control. The estimated cost of constructing needed public sewerage facilities is $60.1 billion, according to a survey the EPA conducted in 1973.[5] This survey is based on the cost of building new facilities and inflation will have more than doubled that amount since then.

Air Pollution

Air pollution has a multitude of deleterious effects on human behavior, on property, and on the environment, such as increased human morbidity, accelerated deterioration of structures, and diminished agricultural output. The effects of air pollution typically occur external to the emitter. A national estimate for 1970 of air pollution damage to property gave a range of $3.4 to $8.2 billion with a "best" estimate of $5.8 billion. Damage to human health, materials, and vegetation was estimated within a range of $3.0 billion to $11.0 billion, with the "best" estimate of $7.0 billion.[6] If these effects put a cost on society but not on the emitters, the tendency exists to produce more pollution than is economically efficient. It has been advocated on economic grounds that pollution should be reduced to the level at which marginal savings effected by pollution abatement equal the marginal cost of that abatement. Thus, savings in the cost of pollution are equivalent to the benefits that accrue from pollution reduction.

The earliest published attempt at estimating the cost of impaired health from air pollution is that of Ridker, who estimated the total national cost of morbidity and mortality for diseases associated with the respiratory system.[7] The Lave-Seskin study expanded the number of diseases covered by Ridker. In particular, it included such suspected results of air pollution as increased heart disease and cancer of the stomach, esophagus, and bladder.[8] Lave and Seskin consider the evidence relating air pollution and health to be quite good in the case of bronchitis and lung cancer, and, although evidence correlating air pollution with heart disease and nonrespiratory cancers is not as good, they believe that a consideration of all factors suggests causality for these diseases as well. They estimated that the total annual cost for increases in human morbidity and mortality caused by air pollution was $2.08 billion for 1963.[9]

Air pollution has a variety of effects on materials, including corrosion of metals, deterioration of materials and paints, and fading of dyes. In many parts of the world, historic structures and art treasures have suffered enormously accelerated deterioration after having survived unscathed for centuries. Damage to vegetation as a result of air contaminants has been recorded in the United States since the turn of the century. What was once associated only with point sources has evolved into widespread problems generated by proliferating urban expansion. It is severe enough for commercial and noncommercial production of crops and forests in many areas to be jeopardized and in some cases discontinued. The particularly grave problem of acid rain was discussed in chapter 4.

An estimate of air pollution by source is presented in table 5.1. The distribution by percentage of each of the principal pollutants varies considerably by origin. If it is noted that fuel combustion is also partly industrial, other than power generation, it is clear that industrial operations account for a substantial portion of the total. A tabulation over the period 1970-1979 shows some improvements, though in nitrogen oxides there has been marked deterioration.[10]

Table 5.1
Air Pollutant Emissions, by Source: 1970 and 1979

Pollutant	Total Emissions (mil. sb. tons)		Moving Transportation		Moving Fuel Combustion		Stationary Industrial	
	1970	1979	1970	1979	1970	1979	1970	1979
Carbon monoxide	124.4	100.7	97.7	82.1	2.0	2.1	9.9	6.9
Sulfur oxides	31.2	27.0	0.8	1.1	23.3	21.6	7.1	4.5
Hydrocarbons	30.5	27.1	13.3	9.7	0.3	0.2	11.4	13.7
Particulates	23.1	10.5	1.4	1.5	8.0	2.8	11.2	4.7
Nitrogen oxides	21.0	24.9	7.9	10.1	11.4	13.6	0.9	0.9

Source: Statistical Abstract of the United States, 1981, p. 205.

The national health costs due to air pollution for mortality and morbidity in 1970 were estimated to be $4.6 billion;[11] Lave-Seskin put it at $4.3 billion.[12] Most health studies relate health effects to particulates, sulfur dioxide, and sulfur oxide pollutants. These have been studied most often because (a) generally there is more information on dose-response for these pollutants than for any others; (b) generally more and better air quality data are available for these pollutants than for any others; and (c) the measurement of particulates in many cases seems to be a fairly good index of overall air quality. Therefore, assuming that the health costs of air pollution stem mainly from particulates and sulfur oxides, about 59 percent or $2.7 billion of the $4.6 billion in health losses is attributable to particulates and the remaining $1.9 billion, or 41 percent, to sulfur oxides.[13] Other health impairments are associated with carbon monoxide, hydrocarbons, and oxides of nitrogen. The above are medical costs, with no further allowances for suffering and discomfort.

In connection with materials, pollution damage of $700 million to elastomers and dyes are attributed to oxidants and nitrogen oxides; $400 million of damage by sulfur oxides; and because of the difficulty of separating the pollutant interactions, the remaining $200 million is shared equally between particulates and sulfur oxides; the remainder of the total materials cost estimate, $400 million, is allocated in proportion to the emissions of pollutants, except for carbon monoxide, which according to present knowledge is not damaging to materials.

The above estimates again refer to actual damage and take no account of the steady deterioration of all kinds of structures which is only too readily observable in many communities. This imposes a substantial social cost in that individuals have to pay for uncorrected industrial pollution by having to have their houses painted more frequently and, as for problems elsewhere, they are not only aesthetically disagreeable but frequently involve much higher expenditures when the damage has reached the point of requiring extensive repairs that can no longer be postponed.

Noise Pollution

The increasing noise level of modern life is exacting an ever more significant toll in terms of damage to health, deterioration of property values, and of the general quality of modern life. TV sets and hi-fi's, including those blasting forth from neighbors or passersby in the street, air-conditioners, and traffic are becoming ever more insistent. Ear phones have introduced a further new and damaging element, especially among young listeners who may suffer hearing deterioration much beyond chronological aging. In central cities in the United States and elsewhere, the once desirable hotel rooms facing a street or public square are often avoided by visitors in favor of quieter rooms in the back. Kitchen noise may rise as high as ninety decibels which is substantially higher than the usual television or hi-fi sounds (eighty decibels).[14]

In an industrial environment, workers can lose efficiency, resulting in accidents and absenteeism. The clinical details of how hearing loss is induced by repeated noise are well established. The Surgeon General has estimated that between 6 and 16 million Americans today are going deaf from occupational noise.[15] Chapman estimates that if city noise increases at its present level, by one decibel a year, everyone will be stone deaf by the year 2000.[16] In addition to hearing loss, a variety of health effects, including irreversible conditions, have been observed, ranging from dizziness and nausea to impaired coordination of limbs, multiple psychological disorders, depression, ulcers, and hypertension. By increasing the level of stress, moreover, excessive noise aggravates the conditions caused by it. In industrial operations and construction, the level of noise is often so high that shouts of warning cannot be heard. Some government appropriations have been made to reduce noise. In 1975, $80 million was spent for that purpose.[17] However, regulatory attempts at reducing noise in various kinds of machinery have become engulfed in the general dismantling of product safety controls by the Reagan administration.

Specific Industries

It is a characteristic of pollution that its worst problems are concentrated in a small group of industries. The social cost issue is whether they pay for all the damage caused by their pollutants or whether society at large bears some of the cost. Industry spends a great deal on pollution abatement and solid waste disposal. However, as noted previously, much remains to be done.

Table 5.2 shows expenditures by various industries in 1979; at $7.1 billion it accounted for 4 percent of total capital spending by business. It is note-

Table 5.2
New Capital Business Expenditures for Pollution Abatement, by Industry: 1979

Industry	Pollution Abatement Expenditures ($1 Million)			Percent of Total Capital Outlays by Business[1]	
	Total	Air	Water	Solid Waste	Total	Air
All industries	7,143	3,915	2,664	564	4.0	2.2
Manufacturing	3,977	2,103	1,493	381	5.1	2.7
Durable goods[2]	1,585	936	540	109	4.2	2.5
Primary metals	811	558	227	26	12.4	8.5
Electrical machinery	115	27	82	6	2.3	0.5
Machinery, except electrical	88	36	39	13	1.1	0.4
Transportation equipment	261	122	97	42	3.3	1.6
Stone, clay, and glass	145	116	22	7	5.0	4.0
Nondurable goods[2]	2,392	1,167	953	272	5.9	2.9
Food, including beverages	148	51	84	13	2.9	1.0
Textiles	32	21	10	1	3.0	2.0
Paper	297	133	124	40	6.1	2.8
Chemicals	440	203	184	53	5.2	2.4
Petroleum	1,385	708	530	147	8.4	4.3
Rubber	62	38	12	12	3.3	2.0
Nonmanufacturing	3,167	1,811	1,172	184	3.2	1.8
Mining	187	59	105	23	3.4	1.1
Railroad	20	2	17	1	0.5	0.1
Air transportation	13	7	5	1	0.4	0.2
Other transportation	24	11	11	2	0.8	0.4
Public utilities	2,763	1,653	975	135	8.3	5.0
Communication, commercial, and other	160	79	59	22	0.3	0.2

[1] Based on outlays reported in source.
[2] Includes industries not shown separately.

Source: Statistical Abstract of the United States, 1980, p. 216.

worthy that this share has declined materially since 1975 when it was 5.8 percent.[18] Petroleum, primary metals, and chemicals account for some 67.2 percent of expenditures in the manufacturing sector and, as evident from the
right-hand portion of the column, there is substantial variation in the ratios of
pollution abatement expenditures to total capital outlays in the individual
industries. Here, too, a look at earlier data indicates a general falling off in percentages since 1975, indicating that some industries appear to be on the way
to accomplishing the major part of the new investment legally required of
them.

As to specifics, certain of the industries have had to face some highly significant technical problems and it is generally true that most of them resisted
strongly the imposition of the new federal standards. The paper industry, for
example, had to deal with a great deal of water pollution in particular. Many
of the plants had substantial discharges of pulping liquor and other chemicals
that were not only lethal to aquatic life but also gave streams a bad odor,
especially in seasons when the water flow was low. A second major source of
pollution came from burning of wood wastes and lignin. The latter is a natural
plastic material that binds the fibers and must be eliminated during pulping; as
yet the industry has found no way of directly utilizing what might well be an
excellent plastic, derived from sources other than petroleum. At any rate, the
disposal of these wastes has accounted for a major part of the expenditures
required.

The primary metals industry includes steel as well as nonferrous metals and
thus many economically troubled and uncompetitive facilities. In some of
them the need to comply with environmental regulations as well as those of
occupational safety and health was followed by the closing of several plants
with industry attempting to place the blame for the closure on the new
requirements. However, the indications are that this was only an excuse; steel
industries in most parts of the world are required to follow even more stringent environmental restrictions. When the German Federation of Industries
(BDI) tried to establish that jobs are lost as a result of environmental and
related improvements, the result of the study proved negative, and so did
similar ones in the United States.[19]

The specific problems of the primary metals industry include piles of slag
and ore tailings, water pollution, and air pollution from furnaces and fabri-
cation units. In most of these the technology for abatement is clearly available,
even though in the case of furnaces a major problem arises in that most of the
pollution takes place when they are tapped, resulting in large volumes of
pollutants during a short period.

Water pollution consists of the leaching of metals as discussed earlier. Also,
particularly in the steel industry, pickling liquor has traditionally been a prob-

lem. In the United States, until very recently, steel makers used sulfuric acid pickling which makes for a difficult disposal problem, rather than the hydrochloric acid method used in Europe and Japan in which the acid is recycled.

It is in the chemical industry and related sectors of the petroleum industry that some of the most serious industrial pollution problems are to be found. They encompass not merely air and water pollution of all kinds during manufacture, including powerful toxins such as dioxin, but also particularly the disposal of hazardous wastes.

An emission of dioxin in Seveso near Milan, Italy, caused the evacuation of a sizable sector of the community and brought in its train an extensive catalog of health problems for the population. The total losses to the community and its people were enormous and eventually had to be met in part by the owners of the plant, which happened to be a subsidiary of the large Swiss conglomerate Hoffman-LaRoche. So large a company was able to meet its obligation, but clearly a smaller enterprise might well have gone bankrupt and left public authorities holding at least some of the bag. As it was, even the settlement of the Seveso case left many of its victims inadequately compensated or without anything.[20] Other noted cases were the contamination by polychlorinated biphenyls (PCBs) of the Hudson River and many cases in which insecticide manufacture led to contaminated waterways. The PCBs in the Hudson River destroyed a fishing industry that had been making a tentative comeback as sewerage systems in upstate New York cleaned up the river; as a result the fish were judged to be unfit for human consumption.

One of the most serious cases of industrial pollution in the United States occurred at Love Canal in Niagara Falls, New York. It is an abandoned waste material dump that contaminated surrounding air and water, leading to the forced abandonment of property and serious health damage to many of the inhabitants. Initial costs to New York State were $21 million, of which $11 million were for evacuation and relocation and $10 million for remedial work. Additional claims of $42 million in damages were filed by the local population.[21] The case moved near a final settlement in 1981 in which again a compromise had to be arrived at.

The site had originally belonged to the Hooker Chemical Company which had deeded it to New York State and thereafter tried to disclaim all knowledge and responsibility. The problem of dump sites that have been abandoned, whose ownership is not clear or whose owners simply do not know what lies buried under their property, have posed a very extensive and disheartening problem. Indeed, a sizable part of dumping of waste materials is done illegally. Truckers are simply instructed to dump barrels or containers of stuff wherever possible, perhaps camouflaged as other kinds of garbage. Barrels and drums leak and eventually contaminate the soil and aquifers, foul the air, and may in fact be the cause of explosions. In some cases, potentially useful materials are discarded rather than reprocessed, salvaged, or recycled because it is cheaper at present to throw them away, especially when this can be done illegally. Encouraging salvage and related research by subsidy would again turn a business cost into a social cost.

Professor William R. Ginsberg, an authority on the legal aspects of the matter, suggests that the problem has not yet been properly addressed.[22] The latest law on the subject is the Comprehensive Environmental Response, Compensation and Liability Act of 1980 (Superfund), which is directed toward remedial action at disposal sites, particularly where no responsible party is solvent or identifiable. These are usually abandoned sites ignored by the earlier Resource Conservation and Recovery Act of 1976 (RCRA), which set minimum standards for the transportation, treatment, storage, and disposal of hazardous wastes. However, the Superfund makes no provision for victim compensation for personal injury, lost earnings, or property damage.[23] The Superfund is mostly generated by charges on the raw materials used by those industries that generate most hazardous wastes and will be used mainly to clean up long neglected sites. Thus a business cost takes the place of part of a social cost but the rest will still be borne by the individual victims.

One of the most serious contaminants at present is asbestos. Quite apart from the suffering of those who work with it, a topic discussed in chapter 6, asbestos is almost ubiquitously present in buildings, factories, homes (where, for example, boilers used to be covered with asbestos), machines (for example, hairdryers some years ago), and elsewhere. The hazards are well documented[24] and the very spread of the material makes its disposal a difficult problem even where it is no longer used in new work; the demolition of old buildings, for instance, creates significant local hazards. The asbestos industry, as will be seen, has predictably responded by seeking to have its potentially enormous liability turned into a social cost.

Finally, food manufacturing also exacts its toll, most notably in water pollution, due to food washing and processing, highly putrescible effluents that cannot be stored for long, and coloring of waterways by food pigments; animal blood, if dumped, is a prime example of the last two kinds of pollution. In addition, there are solid wastes from unusable parts of materials as well as natural and processing wastes and raw material containers. The food industry shares with many other manufacturing industries the characteristics that its operations may be on a small or seasonal scale and that it is therefore possible to make use of sewers and local garbage disposal in getting rid of the wastes. This may raise problems as to the equitability of user fees because clearly in smaller communities the presence of several sizable industrial customers may result in the need to provide facilities of much greater capacity.[25] The important point in the matter of handling of food is the speedy and sanitary disposal of liquid and solid wastes so as to minimize the propagation of insects and rodents and to eliminate odors. Food processing plants are highly unwelcome for these reasons in most neighborhoods. Again, the presence of such facilities may well lead to social costs in depressing property values and causing a general degradation in the quality of life of the community. The total social cost problems of food production are further addressed in chapter 13.

A Time of Regression?

The Clean Air Act was up for renewal in 1982 in an atmosphere that, given the politics of the Reagan administration, promised sustained attacks upon its provisions in addition to drastic cuts in the budget of the Environmental Protection Agency (EPA). As one statement of what is in store, one might note the recommendations of Chilton and Penoyer in a publication of the Center for the Study of American Business, a group formerly under the direction of Murray Weidenbaum, later Mr. Reagan's chairman of the Council of Economic Advisers.[26] They propose first that standards should not be set by the EPA but by "an *independent* scientific body" (emphasis in original). But of course, the EPA, not having a direct interest in the outcome, was supposed to be exactly an independent scientific body. The process is thus transformed into a "we versus they" situation with prospects of "splitting the difference" —but surely this would take much more time, which one would have supposed from past protests was exactly what business was anxious to avoid. In any event, the Act was extended with few changes. Congressional sentiment had turned against gutting the Act.

The authors further suggest that some standards should be set by states and that states should be allowed to substitute emission fees for current offset procedures. Only national park areas should be kept free from significant deterioration of air quality; translated, this means that everywhere else a little pollution is acceptable. It is of course doubtful whether national parks can ever be insulated in this way when their surroundings are contaminated. Once the best available control technology is installed, there should be a ten-year ban on the specification of new emission sources; in other words, new scientific information is to be disregarded. Finally, it is proposed that automobile emission standards be drastically revised downward since "the costs appear to far outweigh potential health benefits." The recommendations finally disclaim any intention of "advocating trading lives for dollars," claiming that they will provide "the same level of benefits at a greatly reduced cost to the American consumer." One could, one supposes, comment on ill winds and muddy waters.

The proposal that states should set pollution standards is based on the old belief that the kind of pressure that industry has traditionally been able to apply to state governments will lead to lower standards and sloppy enforcement. It is a belief well founded in fact. Enforcement of current environmental laws is sporadic and, in some places, derisory. In a review of the situation in Louisiana, for instance, Kedia and Young comment:

> It is not uncommon to hear the remark that "the South is soft on pollution," the implication being that the movement of industry (particularly the chemical sector) towards the South is due to less stringent or less stringently enforced regulations in the region. In the case of Louisiana, there seems to be some truth in such allegations. . . . [In a survey of mainly chemical plants] the vast majority of executives . . . felt either that the laws were no worse than elsewhere or were implemented less severely in the state than elsewhere.[27]

Yet Louisiana, among other high risk factors, is one of five states with thirty or more hazardous chemical waste dumps, including three especially toxic ones, one of which has already led to at least one death. Clearly, more rather than less enforcement is needed and the "downward auction" in standards that would inevitably follow a state takeover would have calamitous results for the future, as well as undoing the real progress of the past fifteen years or so.

Conclusion

This chapter has shown that as a result of successive legislation, a substantial share of the costs of pollution has been turned into business costs of the industries responsible for them. Nevertheless, the continuing need for these facilities and remaining levels of pollution suggest that a good deal of this work still remains to be done. How the costs of future expenditures compare to the actual damage suffered is not something that can be readily determined; furthermore, there is not even agreement that everything is being done to remedy the increment of deterioration that is still found year by year.

A major part of the problem consists of dealing with abandoned dump sites of a variety of materials. In no area of concern is the consequence of past mismanagement and, unfortunately, at times of present inadequate law enforcement, so distressingly clear as in the continued dumping of waste products of all kinds and the task of cleaning up what has come before. Continued social costs are unfortunately probably unavoidable in many of these cases. The technical possibilities of dealing with pollutants are by and large solved, although individual problems still exist. As we noted in chapter 1, moreover, industrial manufacturing is one area in which multinational corporations have the choice, at least in part, of transferring some of their operations to countries less fastidious than the United States, when its laws are enforced—or, with an eye to the budding scandals at the EPA in 1983, perhaps one should say, "if its laws are enforced."

Notes

1. U.S. Environmental Protection Agency, *Quality Criteria for Water* (Washington, D.C.: U.S. Environmental Protection Agency, 1977); K. M. Mackenthum, *Toward a Cleaner Aquatic Environment*, U.S. Environmental Protection Agency (Washington, D.C.: U.S. Government Printing Office, 1973); *Clean Water: Report to Congress 1975-76* (Washington, D.C.: U.S. Government Printing Office, 1976), p. 25.

2. EPA *Quality Criteria for Water.*

3. *Statistical Abstract of the United States, 1980*, p. 214.

4. U.S. Environmental Protection Agency, *The Staff Report to the National Commission on Water Quality* (Washington, D.C.: U.S. Government Printing Office, 1976), pp. 1-61.

5. U.S. Environmental Protection Agency, *The Economics of Clean Water* (Washington, D.C.: U.S. Government Printing Office, 1973), p. 21.

6. U.S. Environmental Protection Agency, *The Economic Damages of Air Pollution* (Washington, D.C.: U.S. Government Printing Office, 1974), p. 124.

7. U.S. Environmental Protection Agency, *Cost of Air Pollution Damage: A Status Report* (Washington, D.C.: U.S. Government Printing Office, 1973), p. 10.

8. L. B. Lave and E. P. Seskin, *Air Pollution and Human Health* (Baltimore: Johns Hopkins University Press, 1977), p. 224.

9. EPA, *Cost of Air Pollution Damage*, p. 10.

10. *Statistical Abstract of the United States, 1981*, p. 205.

11. EPA, *Economic Damages of Air Pollution*, p. 128.

12. Lave and Seskin, *Air Pollution and Human Health.*

13. EPA, *Economic Damages of Air Pollution*, p. 128.

14. T. L. Chapman, Bureau of Elementary and Secondary Education, *Sounds and Noises: A Position Paper on Noise Pollution* (Washington, D.C.: U.S. Government Printing Office, 1975), p. 20; see also U.S. Environmental Protection Agency, *Noise Pollution* (Washington, D.C.: U.S. Government Printing Office, 1972), p. 50; J. E. Brody, "Noise Poses a Growing Threat, Affecting Hearing and Behavior," *New York Times*, November 16, 1982.

15. Chapman, *Sound and Noises*, p. 26.

16. Ibid., p. 24.

17. *Statistical Abstract of the United States, 1976* (Washington, D.C.: U.S. Government Printing Office, 1976), p. 185.

18. *Statistical Abstract of the United States, 1980*, p. 216.

19. "Geld Rausgeworfen," *Der Spiegel*, May 7, 1979; see also R. Kazis and R. Grossman, *Fear at Work* (New York: Pilgrim Press, 1982).

20. T. Whiteside, "The Herbicide 2-4-5T," *New Yorker*, July 25, 1977, p. 30; "The Accident at Seveso," *New Yorker*, September 4, 1978, p. 34.

21. A. F. Palazzetti, "Chemical Dump's Residue of Anger," *Newsday*, November 19, 1978.

22. W. R. Ginsberg and L. Weiss, "Common Law Liability for Toxic Torts: A Phantom Remedy," *Hofstra Law Review* (Spring 1981), 9: 859.

23. W. R. Ginsberg, "A Public Policy for Hazardous Waste Disposal," Paper to Hofstra University Public Policy Workshop, March 24, 1981 (mimeographed).

24. P. Brodeur, *The Asbestos Hazard* (New York: New York Academy of Sciences, 1980); see also I. Selikoff, "Practical Questions for Politicians," *Annals of the New York Academy of Sciences*, 387 (1982): 1.

25. National Industrial Pollution Control Council, *Pollution Problems in Selected Food Industries* (Washington, D.C.: U.S. Government Printing Office, 1971); for an analysis of related economy of scale, see J. E. Ullmann, *Waste Disposal Problems in Selected Industries* (Hempstead, N.Y.: Hofstra Yearbooks of Business, 1969), pp. 277-82.

26. K. W. Chilton and R. J. Penoyer, Making the Clean Air Act Cost Effective, pub. no. 42 (St. Louis: CSAB, 1981), pp. 32-34.

27. B. L. Kedia and S. Young, "Foreign Direct Investment in Louisiana: Employment and Environmental Impact," *Louisiana Business Review*, Summer 1981, p. 12.

6
Occupational Disability

BRIAN DAHM

> Work-work-work
> Till the brain begins to swim;
> Work-work-work
> Till the eyes are heavy and dim . . .
> Oh God, that bread should be so dear
> And flesh and blood so cheap!
>
> Thomas Hood, "The Song of the Shirt"

Introduction

Each year, several million American workers become sick, are injured, or die as a direct consequence of their employment. The frequency of these occupational disabilities, their economic effects, and their implications for social justice led to the establishment of an insurance system to alleviate the problem. Workers' compensation was thus one of the first major attempts to shift what had been the social cost of work-related casualties to a business cost, for business was required to finance the system.

At present, however, this objective is far from being fulfilled. Analysis of its workings reveals that burdens of proof, especially for diseases rather than accidents, still fall disproportionately upon the workers, that amounts actually paid out are grossly inadequate to sustain those affected, that there is wide and quite untenable geographic variation in the treatment of claims, that public assistance of one kind or another must make up for these shortcomings, and that, therefore, what should have been turned into a business cost is still, to a great extent, a social one. This is especially so at a time when, as will be shown, strong attempts are being made to make the public pay for even more of the more serious industrial dangers.

The Workers' Compensation Insurance System

The first state workers' compensation laws in the United States were enacted in 1911. Prior to that time, sick or injured workers seeking to gain relief from the physical and financial hardships imposed by their disabilities were forced to bring common-law suits against their employers. The well-established common law principle that negligence was the only ground on which employers could be held liable for the injury or death of their employees required disabled workers to prove such negligence. At the same time, employers had several common-law defenses which could be cited: that negligence by the employee or fellow employee led to the disability or that it resulted from a hazard normal to the employee's occupation, which hazard was assumed by the employee upon taking the position. As a result, a slow, costly, uncertain legal process developed that operated too harshly on the disabled, and new legal provisions were demanded.

The final result of these demands was the enactment of the various state, federal, and territorial workers' compensation laws, which are based on the general principle that industrial employers should assume the cost of occupational disabilities without regard to whether they are responsible for them. Workplace accidents and illnesses are to be insured as is any other potential hazard. Economic losses to industry resulting from the incidence of worker disability are to be considered costs of production and included in the price of goods and services. Losses are spread over the consuming public, rather than being absorbed solely by the affected worker or employer.

There are six basic objectives of workers' compensation:[1]

1. To provide sure, prompt, and reasonable income and medical benefits to the occupationally disabled, or income benefits to their dependents, regardless of fault

2. To provide a single remedy and reduce court delays, costs, and work loads that arise from personal-injury suits

3. To ease the financial drain on public and private charities of uncompensated industrial accidents

4. To eliminate payment of fees to lawyers and witnesses as well as time-consuming trials and appeals

5. To maximize employer concern with safety and rehabilitation through adjustment of insurance rates

6. To reduce preventable accidents and human suffering through a frank study of accident causes

Two major evaluations of the effectiveness of the workers' compensation insurance system were undertaken in the 1970s: in 1972 by the National Commission on State Workmen's Compensation Laws and in 1979 by the Interdepartmental Workers' Compensation Task Force, composed of members from several federal agencies. As will be shown, the results show serious problems with the system.

Wage Replacement and Income Loss Under Workers' Compensation

For purposes of payment of income benefits in cases of work-related disability, the workers' compensation insurance systems of the fifty states, the District of Columbia, U.S. Virgin Islands, Guam, Puerto Rico, and the federal government classify each case into one of five groups. They are occupational death and four kinds of disabilities that are judged to be temporary or permanent, partial or total. *Temporary total disabilities* are reported most frequently and are about 70 percent of annual "incident" (new) disabilities. *Permanent partial disabilities* account for almost 30 percent of the total number of incident disabilities, but the greatest share (over 60 percent) of income benefits is for incident cases. "Schedule" permanent partial disabilities involve the loss of, or loss of use of, a specific member of the body, such as an arm, a leg, a hand, a foot, fingers, toes, or loss of sight or hearing, and are so called because income benefits are paid subject to a schedule which varies with the injury. *Temporary partial disabilities* are often treated as permanent partial disability, subject to later revision. *Permanent total disabilities*, which prevent the disabled worker from ever returning to any form of labor, are the least prevalent group, but the amount paid per case is the highest. The average per case benefit in work-related death cases is also high but is somewhat lower than that of permanent total cases since the death of the worker leaves one less family member to support.

There is little uniformity among the jurisdictions in their treatment of injuries. Almost all usually pay 66 2/3 percent of wages in temporary and permanent total disability cases. However, there are great differences in the maximum and minimum payments allowed, time and amount limits on total benefits, waiting period to qualify for benefits, and retroactive periods required to allow benefits to be paid from the first day of disability. A summary of some of these differences is presented in tables 6.1 through 6.4.

The wide variations in income benefits make estimation of wage loss and wage replacement under workers' compensation a complicated process. Estimates must be made on a state-by-state basis, using data on lost work days, wages, and benefit payments supplied by each jurisdiction. The National

Table 6.1
Summary of Statutory Maximum Weekly Payments of Temporary Total Disability Income Benefits under Workers' Compensation as of January 1, 1978

Dollar Range	Number of Jurisdictions
$225 and above	6
$200–$224	8
$175–$199	8
$150–$174	12
$125–$149	8
$100–$124	7
$ 75–$ 99	4
Less than $75	2
	55

Source: U.S. Chamber of Commerce, *Analysis of Workers' Compensation Laws* (1978 ed.).

Table 6.2
Summary of Statutory Maximum Awards under Workers' Compensation as of January 1, 1978, for Selected "Schedule" Permanent Partial Disabilities

Part of Body	High	Low	Median
Hand	$165,493	$8,736	$20,500
Foot	139,041	6,000	17,000
Eye	108,520	6,000	17,000

Source: U.S. Chamber of Commerce, *Analysis of Workers' Compensation Laws* (1978 ed.).

Safety Council performs such an analysis of wage loss annually, and for 1976 estimated that the total wages (or in cases of permanent disability or death, present value of total wages) lost by workers who became injured on the job during the year amounted to approximately $3.6 billion.[2]

A study of recipients was made by Monroe Berkowitz as part of the *Supplemental Studies for the National Commission on State Workmen's Compensation Laws.*[3] He estimated that for a thirty-five-year-old worker with a wife and two children who became partially (50 percent) disabled while earning the average weekly wage in the worker's jurisdiction, the most that the injured worker could expect to recover under the laws in effect at the time of the study

Table 6.3
Summary of Statutory Waiting Periods for Receipt of Income Benefits under Workers' Compensation as of January 1, 1978

Number of Days	Number of Jurisdictions
7	23
5	5
3	26
2	1
	55

Source: U.S. Chamber of Commerce, *Analysis of Workers' Compensation Laws* (1978 ed.).

Table 6.4
Summary of Statutory Retroactive Periods* under Workers' Compensation as of January 1, 1978

Number of Days	Number of Jurisdictions
More than 28	3
28	6
21	7
14	23
7–10	9
3–6	6
No provision	1
	55

*Number of days disability must last before income benefits are also received for waiting period.

Source: U.S. Chamber of Commerce, *Analysis of Workers' Compensation Laws* (1978 ed.).

(1971), regardless of the jurisdiction, was 30 percent of lost wages on a present value basis. Had the same worker become permanently and totally disabled, wage replacement was somewhat more effective. In twenty-two out of fifty-two jurisdictions examined, workers' compensation replaced at least 40 percent of the present value of lost wages, and when combined with Social Security disability income (DI) benefits (see chapter 8), replaced between 40 and 80 percent in every jurisdiction. For death benefits, theoretical wage replacement was even greater—in excess of 100 percent of lost wages in some jurisdictions due to the lack of an offset provision limiting the total of workers' compensation and DI benefits to 80 percent of prior weekly wages, as is the case for permanent total disability. Note, however, that these figures apply to new successful claimants, not recipients or applicants.

Whatever the theoretical limits and entitlements, in practice the system fails to compensate in most cases for occupational illness and pays long-term compensation to only 15 percent of the estimated 410,000 workers severely disabled by occupational injuries. The average award for a person totally disabled for life is 30 percent of lost wages.[4]

The inadequacies of the programs in meeting the needs of the disabled are further made clear when incomes of household units having one or more disabled persons are broken down by source. Table 6.5, based on 1970 incomes, shows that the principal shares are still borne by the injured person and by the spouse in the more severe categories. It is especially noteworthy that workers' compensation benefits make up only $0.6/9.3 = 6.5$ percent of the public programs and that they provide only 0.6 percent of income. However, the table refers to all kinds of disabilities, whereas workers' compensation is limited to job-related cases.

Still, in 1978, Social Security DI and the welfare system disbursed a total of $2.7 billion to about five times as many severely disabled workers as workers' compensation. It is also estimated that some 280,000 workers were without any form of financial assistance.[5] While the ratios are not comparable, both surveys indicate the relatively minor role played by workers' compensation in the total problem of the disabled. The public assistance provided is not a pure social cost because it includes contributions by the worker to social security; however, the social security system presently uses all current contributions to meet current benefit payments. In any case, what takes place here is a shift of part of the cost of job-related accidents and sickness to other sectors of society.

Medical Benefits and Related Legal Issues

Medical coverage has always been an important element in workers' compensation. From the start, it provided for some medical treatment. In only fifteen states, however, were the benefits not limited either in duration of coverage or dollar total.[6] By the 1970s, unlimited treatment was available in every jurisdiction either through statutory or administrative authority although that too, as will be shown, is not necessarily so. There is no waiting period for receipt of medical benefits, as there is for income benefits. In many temporary disability cases, the injured worker receives medical expense coverage while not disabled for a length of time sufficient to qualify for cash benefits. It follows that for the short-term injured in particular, the availability of medical care is now the greatest advantage of workers' compensation.

Table 6.5
Source of 1970 Disability Unit Income, by Severity of Disability:
Percentage Distribution of Mean Income of Recently Disabled Adults Aged
18–64 with Income from Specified Source

	Severity of Disability			
Source of Income	Total	Severe	Occupational	Secondary Work Limitations
Mean income	$7,682	$6,762	$7,537	$9,342
Total percent	100.0	100.0	100.0	100.0
Earnings	81.0	76.0	81.0	87.0
Disabled person	38.6	28.5	36.7	52.0
Spouse	42.2	47.4	44.0	34.8
Children	0.2	0.2	0.3	0.2
Assets	3.0	3.3	1.6	3.5
Public income maintenance	9.3	13.7	7.2	5.0
Social insurance programs	7.4	10.0	6.5	4.8
Social Security	3.9	5.3	2.7	2.8
Railroad retirement	0.1	0.1	0.3	0.1
Veteran's payments	0.9	1.2	0.9	0.6
WORKERS' COMPENSATION	0.6	0.8	0.8	0.3
Government pensions	0.9	1.7	0.4	0.2
State temporary disability	0.4	0.4	0.8	0.1
Unemployment compensation	0.6	0.5	0.6	0.7
Public assistance	1.8	3.7	0.7	0.2
Private pensions	2.3	3.4	2.5	0.7
Other private source	2.5	2.7	4.5	1.1
Relatives	1.3	1.0	3.5	0.3
Private insurance, etc.	1.2	1.6	1.1	0.8
Not reported	1.9	0.9	3.2	2.6

Source: P. Frohlich, "Income of the Newly Disabled: Survey of Recently Disabled Adults,"
    Social Security Bulletin, September 1975, p. 11.

Medical care under workers' compensation has been subject to the great
increases in the cost of medical care generally, but statistics on medical costs as
a proportion of total benefits paid reveal that their share actually fell slightly,
from 37.1 percent in 1940 to 32.0 percent in 1977.[7]

Full coverage of occupational diseases has lagged behind that of job-related
injuries because of a belief that (1) a flood of claims would swamp the system;
(2) workers' compensation would tend to become a system of health insurance due to the difficulty in distinguishing between occupational and non-

work-related diseases; (3) problems of administration and benefit abuse would result from this difficulty; and (4) the assumption of responsibility by employers for long-developing diseases would be unfair,[8] even though cancer and other major industrial diseases may have latency periods of decades. The results are predictable. Of the estimated 650,000 victims of asbestosis, silicosis, and other occupational diseases, only 5 percent receive workers' compensation and the few who get these benefits only get about one eighth of their lost income.[9] Another estimate, by S. Posner, a member of the New York State Workers' Compensation Board, puts the recipients of aid at only 3 percent of a total of almost 2 million workers.[10]

Several major reasons for this obvious shortfall and, indeed, for the general inadequacies of the system, lie in certain legal provisions that served to make the original "no-fault" objective of workers' compensation rather one-sided. First, the burden of proving entitlement still rests on the claimant. It is only by the establishment of presumptions and definitions that the burden is shifted, even in part, to the employer,[11] but such presumptions may in turn be lengthily challenged in the courts. Second, the insurer of the employer has the right to challenge any claim and according to the Labor Department does so frequently in serious cases.[12] Third, it is virtually impossible to provide incontrovertible evidence that a disease was directly caused by a job-related factor. Causation is hard to prove, especially in still inadequately understood diseases like cancer or those with contributory factors, such as an aggravation of the risk when the claimant has been a smoker. When a claim is challenged, the worker must cope not only with legal costs in some cases, but with delays that can stretch into months. The insurers then may offer a "compromise and release" settlement in which, in return for a modest lump-sum payment, the worker waives all future claims against the insurer, including medical payments. These "settlements" offered to a worker who, as a rule, is becoming ever more desperate, are sanctioned in that they are supposed to "encourage" workers to return to work rather than "malingering." However, studies to test that claim have proved inconclusive.[13]

Other studies have pointed to the severe effects of industrial accidents and sicknesses on the families of the direct victims.[14] Such conditions have never been compensated and are borne by those affected or by often inadequate social services; again social costs ensue. The quality of medical care is also crucial. There are two main problems: The first is the choice of a physician and who is to make that choice, the worker or the employer. Workers may not be able to judge the qualifications of physicians in specific areas, and could thus select a doctor who would render substandard treatment. On the other hand, employers might pick a physician mainly for the low fees he charges, rather than his qualifications. Some jurisdictions have compromised by requiring the employer to put forth a panel of qualified physicians from which the employee can choose.

A further problem involves the establishment by several jurisdictions of fee schedules for the performance of certain medical procedures and operations. While ostensibly a means of holding down the cost of medical care under workers' compensation by keeping fees artificially low, fee schedules have in some instances resulted in excess costs, as physicians have had to overtreat patients in order to make up for the low fees.[15] Other doctors simply will not handle workers' compensation cases because there is no money in them. In New York, one of two states in which fee schedules under workers' compensation are consistently lower than those of Blue Shield,[16] 258 physicians have given up their authorizations to treat compensation patients since the adoption of the workers' compensation fee schedule by the state's no-fault automobile accident insurance system in 1977. The mass resignations prompted an inquiry which led to the indictment of eight physicians under the antitrust statutes for conspiring to refuse treatment to those injured on the job or in automobile accidents.[17]

One long-time point of resistance of employers was refusing employees access to the records kept by the employers' medical departments. These records include not only employees' medical histories but chemical, environmental, and other tests. These have in practice often proved embarrassing in that they showed that companies often knew about and ignored the hazards. Finally, the Occupational Safety and Health Act of 1970 (OSHA) provided for release of the data to the employees but not before the hearings[18] during which company physicians argued against employee access to their own medical files, chiefly on the grounds that laymen cannot understand the medical terminology, and besides, if they find out how sick they are, they will panic. Among those opposing that view, one sad point was that a dying person is entitled to get his wordly affairs in order.

Employers' Costs

Workers' compensation is financed by employer contributions. Much of it ($6.2 billion out of $11.9 billion in benefits paid in 1979) is carried by large private insurance companies. A further $1.5 billion was paid into state and federal insurance funds, with the rest mainly self-insurance, which is permitted to large companies who cannot otherwise get insurance, or find it more effective to set up a fund of their own.[19]

More important than how the money is raised, however, is the share that ultimately gets to the injured worker. In 1976, the private carriers paid out about half their premiums.[20] By 1978, $13 billion was paid into the program, but about $5.5 billion (42.3 percent) went for administrative and legal costs. Additionally, some companies provided supplementary disability payments to their employees, but these payments varied widely.[21]

The most significant current development, however, is a systematic attempt to have compensation for the most serious industrial conditions paid for by the taxpayer. The matter has received the most sustained attention in connection with the hazards of asbestos and polyvinyl chloride. The hazards of both are well covered in the literature and need not be reiterated here.[22] Congressional hearings were held on the subject in 1980.[23] One source of concern is a different legal attitude that for the first time burdened the asbestos industry with substantial punitive damages. The problem has spawned a specialized journal, *The Asbestos Litigation Reporter*, which estimates that 10,000 to 12,000 law suits involving 25,000 persons are pending.

The result has been to throw the industry into turmoil and to calls for government intervention. The main event was the filing for bankruptcy under Chapter 11 of the Johns-Manville Corporation, the largest producer, in August 1982. This temporarily halted suits against the company but it shifted the problem into the public arena, that is, into the realm of social costs, as proposals were made to make the government responsible. One reason was that much of the exposure had taken place in government shipyards during World War II; this may have been a reasonable argument for some of the earlier cases but is certainly much weaker when the consequences of asbestos exposure in the postwar building boom and other activities result in asbestos diseases. Another aspect of the legal tangle are the lawsuits that Johns-Manville and other affected companies in the Asbestos Compensation Coalition (the coordinating industry group) have filed against their various insurance companies which, not surprisingly, are trying to disclaim responsibility. Various proposals for resolution are now before Congress.[24] Such intervention might also clarify and make more uniform the somewhat haphazard pattern of compensation awards to date. Wide variation is found in them and tort law itself is found to be a somewhat problematic and unreliable remedy.[25]

A second important decision was that of *American Textile Manufacturers Institute* v. *Donovan*[26] in which the U.S. Supreme Court decided that workers' safety must be protected despite the high cost. The majority of the Court held that the Occupational Safety and Health Act of 1970 was "to place preeminent value on assuring employees a safe and healthful working environment. Congress itself defined the basic relationship between costs and benefits by placing the 'benefits' of worker health above all other considerations, save those making attainment of this 'benefit' unachievable."

As a result, the current industry view is that beyond the asbestos problem itself, the government should provide compensation for all occupational and environmental diseases. This is strongly resisted by others who claim that "the true asbestos story is one of asbestos industry fraud and insurance industry incompetence," and that the true question is "whether we are dealing with another industry bail-out such as Chrysler, Penn Central, or Lockheed."[27] In the context of this volume, what is intended here is a clear shift of these costs to the social sector.

Preventing Occupational Disability

Industry still must bear the prime responsibility for making workplaces safer. This became plain particularly after the passage of the Occupational Safety and Health Act referred to earlier. Few items of legislation, however, have engendered more frenzy on the part of business than OSHA. To be sure, not all of its standards, especially at the beginning of its operation, were well founded technically but the neutralization of OSHA was a prime business objective as the Reagan administration began, Mr. Reagan having at one time proposed its abolition. Under its new head, Thorne G. Auchter, the regulatory activism of Dr. Eula Bingham, its previous head, is a thing of the past. The titles of two articles in the business press, "OSHA's Latest Recall of Carter Era Rules,"[28] and "The Door at OSHA Opens Up to Industry,"[29] are typical indications. OSHA's budget was slashed, thus impairing even further its already inadequate inspection program. An organization called "Stop OSHA" is funded by the U.S. Chamber of Commerce, and the whole issue has become bound up in deregulation. A study by the Sierra Club and associated groups has sharply criticized the new regime for failure to make progress against occupational accidents and diseases and lax enforcement of rules.[30]

The developments in tort law in the asbestos and other cases appear to presage sustained conflict in this area which, in the last analysis, is basic to the topic of this chapter. OSHA rules have at least a potential as an adequate defense in such cases, provided they are based on technically defensible judgment. Eliminating OSHA or compromising its operation may paradoxically leave less rather than more protection for business.

Conclusion

Starting with the laudable intention of compensating workers injured or made ill by their jobs, the system that has developed appears to be floundering That this is not inevitable in an industrial society among other things is attested to by the fact that in Ontario, Canada, compensation for industrial diseases is awarded four and one-half times as often and in Sweden eleven times as often as in the United States. Uniform standards, with federal administration, would also considerably reduce the demonstrated inequalities that the state-based system now has.[31] This, for one thing, would have vitiated the thus far successful defense of the U.S. government against Vietnam soldiers who were affected, together with their offspring, by Agent Orange, the notorious defoliant used in Vietnam, in which they were forced to sue in their states of residence, under state law, in spite of the fact that they were clearly on federal business while soldiers and that the statute of limitations had long run out in several jurisdictions. That matter still awaits a final resolution, and it is expected that legislative relief, once more involving taxpayers' funds, will eventually be sought.

One point often cited against OSHA is that its advent has done nothing to stem what is quite obviously a sharply rising accident rate. There was a 40 percent decline between the late 1940s and 1963. Since that time, however, the rates have almost doubled. Gordon and Naples[32] put this down to the "disinvestment" in plant and equipment by many companies that had spent their liquid capital on mergers, commercial speculation, and overseas operations. In short, the trouble is the general deterioration of the American industrial establishment. They suggest that union pressure particularly would be effective in reversing the trend, but unions have not always been as keen on safety issues as they might have been.

In sum, then, the process of transfer from social costs to business costs has never worked well in the system and whatever flow has been in that direction is in danger of being ended or reversed. The lead is being taken by industries that, for all too long, had chosen to ignore the burdens they had placed upon the health of their workers and on broader reaches of society.

Notes

1. U.S. Chamber of Commerce, *Analysis of Workers' Compensation Laws*, 1978 ed., p. 3.

2. National Safety Council, *Accident Facts*, 1977 ed., p. 5.

3. M. Berkowitz, "Workmen's Compensation Income Benefits: Their Adequacy and Equity," *Supplemental Studies for the National Commission on State Workmen's Compensation Laws*, vol. 1 (Washington, D.C.: U.S. Government Printing Office, 1973), pp. 189-274.

4. M. Reutter, "The Shame of Workmen's Compensation," *The Nation*, March 15, 1980, p. 298.

5. Ibid.

6. M. and R. Somers, *Workmen's Compensation* (New York: John Wiley & Sons, Inc., 1954), p. 87.

7. "Current Operating Statistics," *Social Security Bulletin*, September 1978, tables M-1, M-3.

8. F. Cheit, *Injury and Recovery in the Course of Employment* (New York: John Wiley & Sons, Inc., 1961), p. 46.

9. Reutter, "Shame of Workmen's Compensation."

10. S. Posner, letter to *New York Times*, January 6, 1982.

11. A. Larson, *Workmen's Compensation*, (New York: M. Bender, 1972), par. 80.33.

12. Reutter, "Shame of Workmen's Compensation."

13. B. Russell and J. Schramm, "Three Issues in Compensation Medical Care," *Supplemental Studies for the National Commission on State Workmen's Compensation Laws*, vol. 2 (Washington, D.C.: U.S. Government Printing Office, 1973), p. 275.

14. P. A. Franklin, "Impact of Disability on the Family Structure," *Social Security Bulletin*, May 1977, p. 18.

15. L. B. Reed, *Medical Care under the New York Workmen's Compensation Program* (Ithaca, N.Y.: Sloan Institute of Hospital Administration, Cornell University, 1960), pp. 58, 108.

16. Russell and Schramm, "Three Issues in Compensation Medical Care," p. 279.

17. "State Accuses 8 L.I. Doctors of Conspiracy," *New York Times*, December 7, 1977.

18. *Federal Register*, vol. 45, no. 102, May 23, 1980, pp. 35212-303.

19. D. Price, "Workers' Compensation: Coverage, Benefits and Costs," *Social Security Bulletin*, March 1979, p. 30; see also *Statistical Abstract of the United States: 1981*, p. 338.

20. Reutter, "Shame of Workmen's Compensation."

21. D. R. Simpson and M. S. White, Jr., "Employer Supplementation of State Required Workmen's Compensation," *Supplemental Studies for the National Commission on State Workmen's Compensation Laws*, vol. 1 (Washington, D.C.: U.S. Government Printing Office, 1973), p. 293.

22. E. C. Hammond and I. J. Selikoff, eds., "Public Control of Environmental Health Hazards," *Annals of the New York Academy of Sciences*, vol. 329, 1979.

23. U.S. Senate, Committee on Labor and Human Resources, *Asbestos Health Hazards Compensation Act of 1980*, 96th Cong., August 26-27, 1980.

24. "Suits That Are Searing Asbestos," *Business Week*, April 13, 1981, p. 166. W. E. Schmidt, "Manville Asserts U.S. Must Share Costs of Asbestos Damage Claims," *New York Times*, August 28, 1982; K. B. Noble, "Hearings Are Planned on Risks Faced by Asbestos Workers," ibid.

25. W. R. Ginsberg and L. Weiss, "Common Law Liability for Toxic Torts: A Phantom Remedy," *Hofstra Law Review*, vol. 9, Spring 1981, p. 860.

26. L. Greenhouse, "Justices Decide U.S. Must Protect Workers' Safety Despite High Cost," *New York Times*, June 18, 1981.

27. See the debate in Hammond and Selikoff, "Public Control of Environmental Health Hazards," p. 399; see also P. MacAvoy, "You Too Will Pay for Asbestosis," *New York Times*, February 14, 1982, and R. E. Sweeney, "Asbestosis," *New York Times*, February 21, 1982.

28. "OSHA's Latest Recall of Carter Era Rules," *Business Week*, April 27, 1981, p. 48.

29. "The Door at OSHA Opens Up to Industry," *Business Week*, April 6, 1981, p. 32.

30. "Environmental Group Assails Reagan on Worker Protection," *New York Times* October 31, 1982.

31. Reutter, "Shame of Workmen's Compensation."

32. D. M. Gordon and M. I. Naples, "More Injuries on the Job," *New York Times*, December 13, 1981; see also Posner, letter.

7

Unemployment

JOHN A. INNES

> And the roads were crowded with men
> ravenous for work, murderous for
> work. . . . On the highways the people
> moved like ants and searched for
> work, for food. And the anger began
> to ferment.
>
> John Steinbeck, *The Grapes of Wrath*

Introduction

On March 3, 1982, CBS News presented a lengthy set of interviews with a growing group of Americans who were searching vainly and with increasing desperation for jobs in western states like Colorado and Wyoming. They had mainly come from Michigan, Texas, and, like the people in Steinbeck's Depression epic, from Oklahoma. "When did you eat last?" the interviewer asked one young man. "Three days ago," was the reply. All of it was a forceful reminder of an economy gone wrong, the more so since John Ford's famous movie, which he made from the book in 1939, had been shown on another New York station only three days previously.

It was, as before, a harbinger of other changes. Back in 1958, the then secretary of defense, Charles E. Wilson, advised a group of unemployed people in Michigan to go "bird-dogging around the country" in search of work. The remark later was widely believed to have been responsible in part for the Republican reverses in that year's congressional election which cleaned out a lot of conservatives who had been elected in a widely heralded conservative swing a short time earlier. Unemployment is regarded as a main factor in a similar outcome of the 1982 Congressional elections.

Not that Wilsonian "bird-dogging" would do much good. The despair of
the job seekers in the broadcast was plain enough. Moreover, California, the
destination of Steinbeck's "Okies," was finding that it too was not immune to
slumps. In much of 1982, its unemployment rate was somewhat higher than
the national average; the state, hobbled as it is in tax policy by Proposition 13,
not only cannot respond appropriately, but expects a $3 billion shortfall in
budgeted revenue.[1]

Nationally, The Department of Labor reported an unemployment rate of
10.1 percent in October 1982, reflecting a total of about 11.1 million people
out of work. This is the highest rate since the Depression. It continued well
into 1983 and hopes for abatement faded, even amid the somewhat anemic
"recovery." The distinction between recession and depression, never too
clear, was in danger of disappearing, what with unemployment rates and business bankruptcies at the highest levels since World War II and becoming
truly disastrous in communities with major plant closings.

The reasons for the persistence of unemployment are complex and some
aspects are beyond the scope of this volume. The effect of military spending
on it is discussed in chapter 15. The alleged responsibility of pollution controls
and safety measures were referred to in chapters 1, 5, and 6. The present
chapter concentrates on determining the social costs of unemployment itself.

Social Cost and Unemployment Insurance

The loss of output that results from the millions of unemployed creates a
very large opportunity cost to society. If a worker's output can be measured
by the wage he would receive if employed, then the loss in wages gives an
approximate dollar value of the social cost. In calculating this cost, three
separate classes of the unemployed will be considered: (1) those who meet the
government's definition of being unemployed—they are not working, are
looking for a job, and are available for work if they find a job; (2) those
workers who are underemployed, that is, workers who want a full-time job
but are now working part-time for economic reasons; and (3) discouraged job-
seekers who have dropped out of the labor force and are not looking for a job
and consequently are not considered in the government statistics on unemployment.

For these reasons, the government statistics on unemployment are often
questioned and alleged to produce a systematic undercount. Essentially, they
are the result of a sample survey of households. But households with unemployment are often so troubled and disorganized that they inhibit contact.
Secondly, the extent to which people are able and willing to work, or discouraged, is associated with eligibility for unemployment compensation (see

below) and, even if anonymity is promised in the sample survey, respondents often do not believe it. Third, there is now a substantial "underground" economy that is dependent on barter and cash transactions and bordering in some cases on the criminal, and that is, almost by definition, very hard to assess.

Before proceeding, it is necessary to consider the cost of unemployment insurance. In 1980, a total of $17.9 billion was paid out in unemployment insurance.[2] Since unemployment insurance is paid for by employers who, in turn, pass all or part of the cost on to consumers, the cost of unemployment insurance is a business cost rather than a social cost. As Joseph Becker notes: "In the absence of unemployment benefits, the cost of unemployment resembles such other social costs of production as the expense of purifying—or enduring—industrially polluted water and air. A system of unemployment benefits financed by a payroll tax operates to transform a social cost into a business cost, changing a part of the hidden cost of unemployment into a more visible and measurable magnitude capable of being related more directly to market prices."[3]

Unemployment insurance is a true insurance in the sense that contributions to it are adjusted in line with claims experience. Moreover, firms are treated on an individual basis, so that those with high labor turnover are charged up to four times as high a rate as those with stable employment.

While it may at first appear logical that the amount of unemployment insurance paid out should be deducted from the opportunity cost of unemployment, this is in fact questionable. The opportunity cost is lost output, that is, goods and services lost to society, whereas no tangible addition is made by the recipients of unemployment benefits. On the other hand, one could argue that if the opportunity cost is viewed as foregone purchasing power and thus a viable input to society, that is indeed restored at least in part by unemployment insurance. In the present chapter, both methods are presented, thus yielding both kinds of findings.

One other point is relevant here. It has been variously charged that the availability of unemployment insurance extends the duration of unemployment because workers have more on which to fall back. Studies by Ehrenberg and Oaxaca,[4] Marston,[5] Chapin, and others[6] have tested this proposition and found that though there appears to be a slight lengthening of the period, the amount is on the order of half a week, certainly insignificant in relation to how long people stay unemployed. For instance, in 1980, median duration was 11.4 weeks for white-collar workers, 13.2 for blue-collar workers and 10.8 weeks for service workers,[7] when the overall rate was 7.1 percent.

Although approximately 90 percent of the labor force is covered by unemployment insurance, only about half the unemployed actually receive it. To qualify for benefits, an unemployed worker must (1) be able and available for work and actively seeking it, (2) not have refused suitable employment, (3) not be unemployed because of a labor dispute, (4) not have left his job voluntarily or have been fired for misconduct in which case there is a statutory waiting period before benefits, and (5) have been employed previously in a covered industry or occupation for a minimum length of time and have earned a minimum amount as prescribed by state law. State requirements as to eligibility, maximum payments, and so forth vary widely.

Unemployment insurance enables workers to be more selective in the jobs they choose; this may well result in some cases in higher postemployment wages. In the absence of unemployment insurance, they might have chosen a job that would have put them in the underemployed category, that is, people working part-time when they would rather work full-time. Any net effect on social cost cannot be estimated from available data.

Lost Earnings

In this section, an estimate is first presented of the opportunity cost of unemployment in terms of labor time wasted. In this way, it is possible to obtain a cumulative indication of the impact of unemployment. This is followed by a more detailed analysis of 1976, including an estimate of the monetary cost.

Table 7.1 presents the historical trends in size of civilian labor force, unemployment, and unemployment rate. From 1960 to 1969, there was a steady decline to a minimum of 3.5 percent in that year. The rate rose again, reaching a top of 8.5 percent in 1975, declining to 5.8 percent in 1979, and rising to its new peak of 8.8 percent in February 1982. At that point, 91.2 percent (100-8.8) of the labor force was employed, or 98.7 million.

Assuming that the monthly total for 1982 is also the annual average, the total of unemployment of 1960 to 1982, obtained by summing the third column of table 7.1, is 117.6 million labor years (that is, 117.6 million working 1 year). Thus, in the twenty-three years listed, enough wasted labor time has accumulated to be 1.19 times the total expected to be worked in 1982 ($117.6/98.7 = 1.19$).

A more conservative approach would be to consider that about 3 to 3.5 percent is about the minimum that the United States has experienced since 1946. Thus, in the data set presented, one could consider separately the excess over that amount since 1969 when the rate previously was that low. The total would be $\Sigma N_t(r_t - 0.035)$, the summation being from 1969 to 1982, N_t the number of people working in year t, and r_t the corresponding unemployment rate. This results in a total of 43.0 million labor years, which is 43.7 percent

Table 7.1
Civilian Labor Force, Unemployment, and Unemployment Insurance, 1960–1982

Year	Total Civilian Labor Force (Millions)	Unemployed (Millions)	Unemployed as Percent of Civilian Labor Force	Payments of Unemployment Insurance ($ Billions) Basic	with Supplements	Difference
1960	69.6	3.9	5.5	2.8		
1961	70.5	4.7	6.7	4.3		
1962	70.6	3.9	5.5	3.9		
1963	71.8	4.1	5.7	3.4		
1964	73.1	3.8	5.2	3.3		
1965	74.5	3.4	4.5	3.0		
1966	75.8	2.9	3.8	2.7		
1967	77.4	3.0	3.8	2.8		
1968	78.7	2.8	3.6	2.9		
1969	80.7	2.8	3.5	2.9		
1970	82.7	4.1	4.9	3.8	4.2	0.4
1971	84.1	5.0	5.9	5.0	6.1	1.1
1972	86.5	4.8	5.6	4.5	5.4	0.9
1973	88.7	4.3	4.9	4.0	4.5	0.5
1974	91.0	5.1	5.6	6.0	6.9	0.9
1975	92.6	7.8	8.5	11.8	19.6	7.8

Table 7.1 (*continued*)
Civilian Labor Force, Unemployment, and Unemployment Insurance, 1960–1982

Year	Total Civilian Labor Force (Millions)	Unemployed (Millions)	Unemployed as Percent of Civilian Labor Force	Payments of Unemployment Insurance ($ Billions) Basic	with Supplements	Difference
1976	94.8	7.3	7.7	9.0	16.2	7.2
1977	97.4	6.9	7.0	8.4	13.0	4.6
1978	100.4	6.0	6.0	7.7	9.0	1.3
1979	102.9	6.0	5.8	8.6	9.4	0.8
1980	104.7	7.4	7.1	N/A	N/A	N/A
1981	106.4	8.1	7.6	N/A	N/A	N/A
February 1982	108.2	9.5	8.8	N/A	N/A	N/A

Source: U.S. Bureau of Labor Statistics, "Employment and Unemployment: A Report on 1980," *Special Labor Force Report 244* (Washington, D.C.: U.S. Government Printing Office, 1981); *Historical Statistics of the United States to 1970*, Series H-55, *Statistical Abstract of the United States, 1980*, pp. 351–52; 1977, pp. 341–42.

of the total estimated to be worked in 1982. Clearly, all these are substantial losses, even if one conceded the 3.5 percent minimum an unavoidable rate. That, incidentally, would still have been considered very high in those countries of Western Europe with effectively negative unemployment among their own citizens, the shortfall being made up of millions of guest workers from Southern Europe, Turkey, and North Africa.

Column 5 of table 7.1 gives the totals paid out in unemployment insurance by the regular programs which are, as noted, financed by employer contribution. Since 1970, the federal government has also made contributions for supplementary benefits, for example extended benefit periods and coverage, especially for those losing public sector jobs that had not been hitherto covered by unemployment insurance. As column 6 shows, these contributions were very large in the recession years 1975 and 1976. At present they would certainly have to be large again, even though the Reagan budget plans their end. At any rate, these supplements were true social costs, and from 1970 to 1979, they totaled $25.5 billion, of which 76.9 percent was incurred in 1975-1977.

The above total losses are only those due to the officially unemployed. The following more detailed analysis based on a special study in 1977, tries to give a comprehensive measure. In 1976, an average of 7.3 million people were unemployed each month; of them, 5.9 million were looking for full-time work, and 1.4 million were looking for part-time work.[8] Assuming that the average part-time worker works twenty hours a week, this means that the equivalent of 8.0 million people were looking for full-time jobs each month.

Table 7.2 gives a breakdown of unemployed persons by industry of last job from which earnings are calculated. Column 1 shows the number of unemployed persons who want full-time jobs by industry of their last job, and column 2 gives those who want part-time jobs. Column 3 gives the equivalent number of people seeking full-time jobs, which is derived by adding column 1 and one-half of column 2. It was assumed that the proportion of unemployed workers seeking full-time jobs was the same for each industry and was equal to the proportion for the entire population of employed, or 80.6 percent.

Column 4 gives the average weekly earnings for each industry. If it could be assumed that the previous wages of the unemployed were approximately equal to the average wages in their last job, then the dollar amount of lost wages for the year *could* be obtained by multiplying columns 3 and 4 and then multiplying the result by 52. However, since the workers with less seniority are usually the first to be laid off, it would be expected that the previous wages of the unemployed are lower than the average wage for their particular industry. In fact, a study by the Bureau of Labor Statistics of those unemployed five

Table 7.2
Lost Earnings of Unemployed Workers by Industry, 1976

	Average Monthly Unemployed Seeking Full-Time Work (Thousands)	Average Monthly Unemployed Seeking Part-Time Work (Thousands)	Average Monthly Equivalent Seeking Full-Time Work (Thousands)	Average Weekly Earnings (All Workers) (dollars)	Average Weekly Earnings for Previously Employed (c) (dollars)	Earnings Lost by Unemployed ($ Millions)
TOTAL	5,873.3	1,412.7	6,579.7			38,844.7
Mining	29.4	7.1	33.0	274.35	178.33	306.0
Construction	557.2	132.9	623.7	284.56	184.96	5,998.6
Manufacturing	1,351.0	325.2	1,513.6	208.12	135.28	10,647.5
Transportation and Public Utilities	193.8	46.7	217.2	257.11	167.12	1,887.5
Wholesale and Retail	1,210.0	291.3	1,355.7	134.13	87.18	6,145.9

Finance, Insurance, and Real Estate	158.6	38.2	177.7	159.58	103.73	958.5
Service Industries	875.6	210.7	981.0	146.01	94.91	4,841.5
Agricultural Wage and Salary Workers	141.0	33.9	158.0	98.37 (a)	63.94	525.3
All Other Classes of Workers	646.1	155.6	723.9	175.93	114.35	4,304.5
No Previous Work Experience	710.6	171.1	796.2	120.00 (b)	78.00	3,229.4

(a) Based on 1974 monthly average salaries of $334 with board and $423 without board.
(b) Assumed wage.
(c) Column 4 × .65.

Source: U.S. Department of Labor, *Special Labor Force Report No. 199* (Washington, D.C.: U.S. Government Printing Office, 1977), table 10, p. A-12; table 15, p. A-15; table 3, p. A-38.

weeks or more in 1961 found that, on the average, they had earned about $70 per week on their last job, whereas the average weekly earnings adjusted for fringe benefits in 1961 were $89.87.[9] This means that the average previous wage of the unemployed was 77.9 percent of average hourly earnings.

Because the composition of the unemployed has shifted toward women and teenagers in the years since 1961, the ratio of the average previous wage of the unemployed to average weekly earnings would presumable be even lower than the 77.9 percent of 1961. For 1971, Robert Gordon[10] calculated the previous wage of the unemployed to be 69 percent of the average weekly earnings of the employed. Since 1971, the same demographic shift of unemployment to women and teenagers has continued, and so it can be assumed that for 1976 a figure of 65 percent would be reasonable.

Therefore, to determine the previous wages of the unemployed for each industry, column 4 is multiplied by 65 percent to obtain column 5. Now, 52 × column 3 × column 5 gives the amount of lost earnings for each industry per year. For example, the total lost earnings of all officially unemployed workers give a $38.8 billion net opportunity loss. The net loss in spending power is thus $38.8 billion minus the $11.8 billion in basic unemployment insurance paid all that year, or $27.0 billion.

The Underemployed

In 1976, there was a monthly average of 2.9 million nonagricultural workers who were working part-time for economic reasons. In table 7.3 the social costs of these underemployed workers for each industry is calculated by finding the difference between the number of hours worked on a full-time schedule and the number of hours worked by the average part-time worker in that industry and multiplying this difference by the average hourly earnings for the industry. This figure gives the weekly lost earnings of the part-time worker and when multiplied by fifty-two, and by the number of workers (col. 1), gives the lost earnings for the year, assuming that all part-time workers remain in that status for the entire year.

The total figure of $16.0 billion is only $5.9 billion less than the lost output of the unemployed, after adjustments for unemployment insurance. This underscores the fact that although the unemployed receive most of the economic and political attention there is also a serious problem of underemployment. The total of $16.0 billion is, of course, greatly affected by the assumption that all part-time workers are so employed for the entire year. But there are also two other classes of the underemployed that have not been considered: those who earn less than an arbitrary minimum and those who are working below their highest skill level.

Table 7.3
Lost Earnings of Involuntary Part-Time Workers, 1976

	No. Part-Time Workers for Economic Reasons (Thousands)	Average Hours, Total at Work	Average Hours, Workers on Full-Time Schedules	Difference (Col. 3–Col. 2)	Average Hourly Earnings	Lost Earnings for Year (Millions)
TOTAL	2,889	20	40.0(a)	20.0	6.41	16,031.0
Mining	12	21.0	41.2	20.2	7.67	80.0
Construction	301	23.3	41.7	18.4	5.19	2,425.0
Manufacturing	542	20.7	42.6	21.9	6.46	2,691.5
Transportation and Public Utilities	142	19.9	43.4	23.5	3.98	1,044.6
Wholesale and Retail Trade	879	20.1	41.5	21.4	4.36	4,275.1
Finance, Insurance, and Real Estate	68	17.9	42.1	24.2	4.36	329.9
Service	945					5,184.9

(a) Estimated.

Source: U.S. Department of Labor, *Special Labor Force Report No. 199* (Washington, D.C.: U.S. Government Printing Office, 1977), table 30, p. A-25; table 3, p. A-38.

Establishing what is the proper minimum wage is difficult since local economic factors would have a great bearing. What would not be considered an acceptable minimum wage in New York, for example, may be acceptable in other parts of the country. Similarly, it would be difficult to quantify the cost of those who are working below their highest skill level. The probable substantial costs of these two classes of underemployment are not included in the total.

Unemployed Workers Not in the Labor Force

Table 7.4 shows that in 1976 a monthly average of 59.1 million people were not considered to be in the labor force. Of this total, 5.1 million or 8.7 percent wanted a job but were not looking for a variety of reasons, such as school attendance, ill health, home responsibilities, and job market and personal factors. Assuming that those 5.1 million unemployed would earn at least $120 per week if they were gainfully employed, the lost earnings of this group comes to $32.1 billion.

This may be an overstatement in that not all of the 5.1 million may really be looking very hard or effectively for a job. But restricting this category to only the 910,000 people who think they cannot get a job would be much too small, since a lot of people who say they do not want a job now should also probably be in that group. Half the group, or 2.6 million, might be a useful estimate and, indeed, that is the number that is often used for this purpose. Note that including it would raise the real number of unemployed to 13.1 million, or 12.3 percent of the labor force, as of June 1982. Using this 1976 estimate later for a 1982 update is thus conservative.

Table 7.5 summarizes the lost earnings for the three groups, that is, the officially unemployed, the underemployed, and the discouraged workers who want a job but are not considered part of the labor force. The total of $70.2 billion represents the social cost that results when everyone who wants a job is not able to find one. Revising the lost earnings of discouraged workers from $32.1 billion to $16.2 billion would give a total amount of lost earnings of $54.3 billion.

Wherever the true cost lies, it is very plausibly within this range. Turning now to an estimate for 1982, the midrange point of $62.2 billion may be translated by multiplying it by an inflation factor at an average rate of 8.5 percent for 1976-1982, or 1.67, and an allowance for the greater number of people affected. Taking the official number of unemployed of 10.5 million, plus the 2.6 million discouraged workers, plus one quarter full-time equivalent, that is, 10.54 = 2.6 million underemployed, gives a total of 15.7 million affected. Related to the 7.3 million unemployed in 1976 (see table 7.1), this

Table 7.4
Job Desire of Persons Not in Labor Force and Reasons for Not Seeking
Work, 1976

	Thousands	Percent
Total not in labor force	59,125	100.0
Do not want a job now	53,984	91.3
Current activity:		
Going to school	6,386	10.8
Ill, disabled	4,713	8.0
Keeping house	30,763	52.0
Retired	8,596	14.5
Other	3,526	6.0
Want a job now	5,141	8.7
Reason not looking:		
School attendance	1,441	2.4
Ill health, disability	648	1.1
Home responsibilities[a]	1,171	2.0
Think cannot get job	910	1.5
Job market factors:	643	1.1
Could not find job	367	0.6
Think no job available	276	0.5
Personal factors:	267	0.5
Employees think too young or too old	146	0.2
Lacks education or training	78	0.1
Other personal handicap	43	0.1
Other reasons	971	1.6

(a) Includes small number of men not looking for work because of "home responsibilities."

Source: U.S. Department of Labor, Special Labor Force Report No. 199 (Washington, D.C.:
U.S. Government Printing Office, 1977), table 35, p. A-29.

gives a factor of $15.7/7.3 = 2.15$. The opportunity cost of unemployment for 1982 is thus an estimated $62.2 \times 1.67 \times 2.15 = \$223.3$ billion. Putting it more conservatively, that is, accepting a 3.5 percent unemployment rate as an inevitable minimum, the number of excess unemployed changes to $10.5 - 3.5 = 7$ million and the 2.15 factor to $(7.0 + 2.6 + 2.6)/7.3 = 1.67$, so that the cost then becomes $62.2 \times 1.67 \times 1.67 = \$173.5$ billion. This is about 81 percent greater than the $96 billion deficit originally expected in the 1983 federal budget. If this rate turns out to be correct, moreover, then assuming an

Table 7.5
Lost Earnings of Unemployed and Underemployed (in Billions), 1976

	Highest	Lowest
Officially unemployed	21.9	21.9
Underemployed	16.2	16.2
Unemployed and not in labor force	32.1 (max)	16.2
Total	70.2	54.3

Source: See Tables 7.2, 7.3, and 7.4.

effective federal income tax rate of 21 percent, this is a revenue shortfall of $36.4 billion, or 38 percent of the deficit; the latter, of course, has had to be revised sharply upwards. Clearly, whatever the details, very substantial amounts are involved here, especially when one considers the leverage effects of deficits on other aspects of the economy.

More immediately, the sharp rise in unemployment, beginning in 1981, has increased once again the social cost component of unemployment insurance. As of February 28, 1982, the unemployment insurance trust fund had a cumulative deficit of $7.3 billion. The trust fund is a way by which states can borrow from the general Treasury funds when they have exhausted their own funds and can no longer pay benefits. About nineteen states were in that situation. While these funds are only loans that are expected to be repaid when business improves, unemployment falls and premiums paid by business increase, there is no way of predicting when this will come about. Moreover, the federally financed extended benefits of thirteen weeks beyond the basic twenty-six maximum in most of the states may exhaust the $4 billion budgeted for them in fiscal 1982, which is a true social cost. About thirty-seven states now have unemployment rates high enough to qualify for this program[11] which, though scheduled to end, was extended in 1983.

Other Consequences of Unemployment

The social costs of unemployment go beyond those defined above. The deepening recession also bankrupts businesses which then, of course, are unable to furnish employment once conditions ease. Savings of individuals are drawn down, so that effective purchasing power is reduced much longer than might otherwise happen, to say nothing of buyer confidence.

There is also a link between unemployment and the environmental and safety issues discussed in chapters 3, 4, and 5. When conditions are bad, unions appear willing to compromise on these other matters to save jobs, even though, as noted, there is no evidence that environmental concern "eats jobs." Rather, inability to meet the standards for the environment and safety set in the current laws is a reflection on the competence of managements.[12] Nevertheless, as the Clean Air Act was up for renewal in 1982, unions were divided over it, the automobile workers wanting eased automobile pollution rules and the construction workers wanting eased standards in general (except for cars), all to create jobs. Other unions supported the straightforward extension of the Act.[13]

Conclusion

This chapter deals with the social cost of unemployment; it is especially timely when, as this is being written, very high rates are again being encountered. The analysis has taken into account not only those officially reported as unemployed, but also the underemployed (those working part-time who would like to work longer hours) and those too discouraged from looking for work by failure to find jobs. The estimate of total cost is very large in relation to several rather crucial financial variables such as deficits and tax receipts. Thus, the social costs of unemployment represent a substantial tragedy, which deserves more compassionate and effective attention than it appears to be receiving at this time.

Notes

1. R. Lindsey, "Dismayed Californians Find State Not Immune to Slump," *New York Times*, March 3, 1982; idem, "California Facing $3 Billion Budget Gap," *New York Times*, November 14, 1982.

2. *Statistical Abstract of the United States, 1981*, p. 322. The total includes extended benefits payments made under regular state and federal unemployment insurance and the temporary "Federal Supplemental Benefits Program" and the "Special Unemployment Assistance Program."

3. J. M. Becker, *Experience Rating in Unemployment Insurance* (Baltimore: The Johns Hopkins University Press, 1972), p. 48.

4. R. G. Ehrenberg and R. L. Oaxaca, "Do Benefits Cause Unemployed to Hold Out for a Better Job?" *Monthly Labor Review*, March 1976, pp. 37-39.

5. S. T. Marston, "The Impact of Unemployment Insurance on Job Search," *Brookings Papers on Economic Activity*, 1 (1975): 13-48.

6. G. Chapin, "Unemployment Insurance, Job Search, and the Demand for Leisure," *Western Economic Journal*, vol. 9 (March 1971), pp. 102-7; C. A. Lininger, Jr., *Unemployment Benefits and Duration: A Study of the Effects of Weekly Unemployment*

Benefit Amounts on the Duration of Unemployment Benefits (Ann Arbor, Mich.: Institute for Social Research, University of Michigan, June 1963).

7. U.S. Bureau of Labor Statistics, *Employment and Unemployment: A Report on 1980, Special Labor Force Report 294* (Washington, D.C.: U.S. Government Printing Office, 1981), p. A-19.

8. U.S. Department of Labor, *Special Labor Force Report No. 199* (Washington, D.C.: U.S. Government Printing Office, 1977), table 10, p. A-12.

9. Earnings on last job of the unemployed is from R. L. Stein, "Work History, Attitudes, and Income of the Unemployed," *Monthly Labor Review*, vol. 86 (December 1963), p. 1410. Average hourly earnings adjusted for fringe benefits is from *Economic Report of the President Together with the Annual Report of the Council of Economic Advisers, January 1973*, table C-31.

10. R. J. Gordon, "The Welfare Cost of Higher Unemployment," *Brookings Paper on Economic Activity*, 1 (1973): 133-205.

11. "Unemployment Deepens the Jobless Fund Deficit," *Business Week*, March 22, 1982.

12. J. E. Ullmann, "See What You Made Me Do," in *Private Management and Public Policy*, ed. L. Benton (Lexington, Mass.: Lexington Books, 1980), p. 189.

13. P. Shabecoff, "Unions Divided on Revision of Clean Air Act," *New York Times*, March 8, 1982.

8
Old Age

ROBERT H. CHESNEY

> The notion that the working class
> have been absurdly pampered, hopelessly
> demoralised by doles, old age pensions,
> free education, etc., is still widely held.
>
> George Orwell, *The Road to Wigan Pier*

Introduction

This chapter discusses the social cost aspects of income security, health care, shelter, nutrition, and tax relief for the aged. In general, the "old age" bracket consists of persons aged sixty-five or over, although some statistics may include some early retirements between ages sixty-two and sixty-five. The central problem is to assure an adequate level of sustenance for the old and try to keep the elderly out of poverty.

What portion of the effort required is a social cost is, however, not as easy to determine as may at first appear. The principal issue is the way in which social security is financed. On the one hand, its income is in the form of contributions, not taxes. This is not mere semantics. Social security contributions are placed in a special trust fund and may not be used for other purposes. They are not insurance premiums, however. So far, what with inflation and cost-of-living adjustments, most recipients collect a great deal more than they paid in. While their actual checks do depend on how much people earned and for how long, their amount is adjusted upward on a regular schedule as long as inflation persists. Once the basic entitlement has been set, later changes in payments are thus independent of the contributions of the individual.

The effect is that current contributors do not pay into an insurance fund of the conventional variety but rather pay the current benefits. They in turn believe that when they retire those then working will pay their benefits. All this would make sense as long as the economy performs satisfactorily. Unfortunately, it has not done this and so one aspect of the current controversy on social security is whether its benefits will some day have to be met in part from general tax revenues. In that case one could argue that a social cost is incurred, if one were to view social security as an independent enterprise remote from other government operations. Since aside from Medicare B (see below) there have been no infusions of general tax funds into the system, there are thus no social costs in the strict sense associated with social security.

However, there are two cautionary points, the first of which is mainly of historical interest. It is that general funds have always been envisaged as at least a potential source of funds if the system ran into trouble. From 1943 to 1950, such supplementation was legally permitted though never used.[1] In November 1982, the system was forced to borrow from the Treasury, because of cash-flow problems. The second point is the way in which government spending is now reported. Before the 1968 budget, social security was excluded from the general budget because, as noted, it had its own funds. Thereafter, all expenditures were consolidated and social security appeared as government spending, just like the defense budget, agricultural subsidies, debt service, and so on. At the time the change was first made, it afforded the government a way of claiming that military expenditures were only a small part of its total spending, whereas, when social security was excluded, wars past, present, and future (including the mainly war-caused debt service) took about half of what was left. The habit of consolidating all spending, however, persisted and, as the battle for the 1983 budget opened, social security cutbacks or other manipulations of the system were part of it, just like the many questions of what else was to be supported or cut.

Private pension plans also normally do not involve social cost questions. They are instituted by businesses and normally do not involve public funds explicitly. Their effectiveness is being widely questioned, notably with respect to their integrity, eligibility of employees, and vesting. These are matters of regulatory policy and practices as in the Employee Retirement Income Security Act of 1974 (ERISA). The social cost involved, and in old age generally, is the need for the public sector to make up in welfare or similar programs for the inadequacies of pension plans, social security, and other sources of income of individuals. To the extent that the income of the retired comes from employer or employee contributions, they are part of recognized fringe benefits, that is, of employee compensation, and are thus a business rather than social cost.

Demographics and Economic Troubles

The current troubles of the social security system stem essentially from two sources. First, when benefits were linked to the consumer price index in 1972, contributions were based, both with respect to amount of earnings subject to tax and percentage tax rate, on a wage index. For as long as wage rates keep ahead of inflation, this system serves to increase social security funds. However, beginning in 1973, real income began to decline and it has continued to do so, gradually producing a cash-flow problem for the system. This change is also responsible for the proposals being made to tie both contributions and benefits to the same index, to base cost of living indexes on the lower of consumer price index (CPI) and wage rate changes, and others.

Deficits so far have been made up by reserve funds but these were exhausted by fall 1982. The Social Security Administration predicts deficits for the rest of the decade as follows:

Year	1982	1983	1984	1985	1986	1987	1988	1989	1990
$Billion	(7.8)	(10.5)	(15.0)	(7.9)	(10.4)	(13.6)	(16.8)	(19.5)	7.0

In 1990 and later, surpluses will again prevail, because the very small Depression generation will then retire. A long-term problem, however, will arise, beginning in 2010 when the "baby boom" generation begins to retire. From about 3.2 workers per retired person in 1981, the ratio will drop to about 2.5 by 2015 and 2 or even less in 2025.[2]

In response to these problems, the Reagan administration proposed a series of cuts in benefits and modifications of entitlement, the principal ones of which were the elimination of a $122 monthly minimum and cutting the benefits from 80 percent to 55 percent of regular amounts for early retirement. Protests mounted quickly and neither of these proposals was enacted.

On the social cost issue, Consumers Union proposes that "as a pay-as-you-go system indexed to wages and prices, social security is highly dependent on the performance of the economy. Money from the general fund should be borrowed to make up for fluctuations in revenue collections caused by adverse economic conditions."[3] Note that borrowing is envisaged, since in the 1990s the system will again run at a surplus. Of course, major economic changes, both favorable and unfavorable, would change these projections drastically.

Whatever the troubled present and future problems, social security has been the chief element in reducing the proportion of elderly poor from 35 percent in 1959 to 14.6 percent in 1974 and around 15 percent since then.[4] Two-thirds of elderly households rely on social security for at least half their income. The change wrought by social security is well summarized by Wilbur

J. Cohen, a former secretary of the Department of Health, Education and Welfare:

> At the end of 1934, about half of all persons aged 64 or over were estimated to be mainly or wholly dependent on relatives and friends for their support. Except for the development of the public income-maintenance programs for the aged, the burden of such dependency would have increased rapidly as the aged population grew at the average rate of 3 percent a year, twice as rapidly as the total population.[5]

R. J. Myers notes that social security and other governmental (railroad, civil service, states) retirement plans cover about 97.5 percent of all wages and salaries paid.[6]

In addition to the old age and survivors' benefits, which are the best known of the system's programs, it also provides disability income, as discussed in more detail in chapter 7. In addition, from the earliest times on, it has operated a supplementary income program designed to maintain certain minimum benefits. Originally called Old Age Assistance (OAA) and, since 1974, Supplementary Security Income (SSI), it first greatly exceeded regular benefits at a time when few workers were eligible. Beginning in 1952, however, the benefits under this program began to decline relative to the main one, and by 1980 were 6.2 percent of it.[7]

Health Care

Over the decade 1966-1978, the total amount spent on medical care for the elderly rose at an average annual rate of 15.5 percent from $8.2 billion in 1966 to $41.8 billion in 1978. About 50 percent of the increase was due to the increases in the price of medical care, 36 percent to increases in services, and 14 percent to population increases.[8]

The estimated per capita health care expenditures for persons aged sixty-five and over for fiscal years 1966-1978, by type of expenditure, are given in table 8.1. These have also shown sustained increases as shown in the columns for rates of change. The data for 1975-1980 give changes for the whole population and not merely for those aged sixty-five and over. However, there is an accelerating trend; the rates for 1975-1980 are uniformly higher than those for 1966-1978. They are led by huge increases in nursing home and hospital care.

After July 1966, Medicare became the major single source of health care funds for the aged. This part of the Social Security Administration consists of

Table 8.1
Estimated per Capita Health Care Expenditures for Persons 65 Years and Over, Selected Years 1966-1978

	1966	1969	1972	1976	1978	Rates of Increase 1966-1978	1975-1980
		Dollars per Capita*				Percent per Year	
Total	445	717	967	1,521	1,821	11.7	13.2
Hospital care	178	313	417	689	795	12.5	13.4
Physicians	90	131	158	256	321	10.6	11.7
Dentists	13	16	18	32	50	11.2	11.8
Other health professionals	12	14	17	23	40	10.0	10.2
Drugs	62	78	92	121	124	5.8	8.3
Eyeglasses and appliances	15	19	19	19	23	3.6	11.0
Nursing homes	68	133	238	351	456	15.9	16.5
Other health services	7	12	9	31	14	5.8	12.4

*Totals may not add due to rounding.

Source: U.S. Department of Health and Human Services, *Health: United States, 1981,* pp. 204, 211.

two benefit packages: Hospital Insurance (HI) and Supplemental Medical Insurance (SMI, Medicare B). HI is supported by employed persons and their employers. SMI is financed by those persons covered by HI who elect SMI coverage and is also financed, as noted below, by the Treasury. Medicaid is a separate assistance program for needy and low-income persons of all ages.[9] Its primary contribution to the needs of the aged is for nursing home care (48 percent or about $6.9 billion in 1980).

The tax and premium rates for HI have increased by 668 percent during 1966-1978 and are scheduled to increase an additional 118 percent between 1979-1982, that is, at a total annual rate of 17.6 percent. Indirectly, U.S. society is also paying an additional sum of over $900 million (1977 and 1978 costs) for HI coverage. These indirect costs represent federal government transfers from general funds appropriations to meet costs of benefits for persons not insured for cash benefits under Old Age Survivors' and Disability Insurance (OASDI) or railroad retirement and for costs of benefits arising from military wage credits.[10]

Table 8.2 presents total expenditures of Medicare and Medicaid from 1967 to 1978. Medicaid is welfare-based, that is, subject to a means test, and is therefore not part of the program connected to social security. However, it is noteworthy that the two programs are converging in cost, Medicaid having started out at a substantially lower level. Medicare includes SMI. The costs of the latter are covered by two sources. The premiums paid by those insured by SMI establish an initial amount in the fund. This premium increased 157 percent over the period 1966-1978. The second source of SMI funds is the general fund of the federal government; from 1966 to 1973, they matched approximately those of the SMI beneficiaries. In 1974, however, general fund contributions began to increase and by 1977 had reached a level of about 70

Table 8.2
Total Expenditures for Medicare and Medicaid (in billions of dollars)

Year	Medicare	Medicaid
1967	4.6	2.8
1970	7.1	5.5
1976	18.4	14.9
1977	21.7	16.7
1978	25.0	18.4
1979	29.3	20.5

Source: Statistical Abstract of the United States, 1981, pp. 335, 337.

percent ($4 billion) of the total annual SMI trust fund income.[11] It now finances most of it.

Finally, table 8.3 projects the costs for HI and SMI for the years 1980, 1990, and 2000, at what should be considered a conservative rate of increase compared to historical figures. The prospective increases are clearly very high indeed and so is the public share of it, if the present organization of health care continues.

Table 8.3
Projected Costs of Medical Care for Those 65 or Older: 1980, 1990, 2000

	1980	1990	2000
Population aged 65 or over (000) (a)	24,927	29,824	31,822
Per capita expenditures ($) (b)	2,163	5,126	12,149
Total ($ billion) (c)	53.9	152.9	386.6
Private share (d)	31.2	88.4	223.4
Public share	22.7	64.5	163.2

Notes: (a) From *Statistical Abstract of the United States, 1978*, p. 327.
  (b) Extrapolated from table 8.2, using an annual rate of increase of 9 percent.
  (c) Line (a) × line (b).
  (d) Based on a private share of 57.8 percent, as in 1980. U.S. Department of Health and Human Resources, *Health: United States, 1981*, p. 200.

Shelter

Basically, the aged of America have four possibilities for shelter: as homeowners, renters (house or apartment), dependents as relative or nonrelative, or as residents of long-term care institutions. According to a government survey,

> Many people in this age group rely on long-term institutional care at some point. According to the 1970 census, 5 percent of the people 65 years and over were residents of institutions, and by 85 years and over, 19 percent were residing in institutions at any given time (Census Bureau, 1973). The risk of being institutionalized at some point is high. . . .
>
> [However,] in the past decade the proportion of the elderly maintaining their own household has increased and the proportion classified as living with "other relative" (i.e., residing in families of which they are neither

the head nor the wife of the head) has decreased. Of the 21.3 million elderly not in institutions in 1975, some 5.8 million lived alone, 11.4 million were married and living with a spouse, and 4.1 million lived with other relatives or nonrelatives.[12]

In metropolitan areas of the urban United States as a whole, retired home-owners consistently show a higher cost, as a percent of total budget, than all other homeowners. Some of these costs are publicly subsidized.

The Department of Housing and Urban Development (HUD) provides housing assistance to low-income families to improve their opportunity to secure decent housing. Housing assistance is currently provided through three major activities within HUD's subsidized housing programs: lower income housing assistance, public housing, and home ownership.[13]

Housing benefits for the aged, 1971-1979, are presented in table 8.4. These publicly funded payments, or subsidies, have increased from $233 million in 1971 to a projected expenditure of $1.257 million in 1979. This is a 5.39-fold increase in nine years. Comparable later statistics are not available.

The average percentage increase of housing benefits for the aged exceeds 23 percent over the 1971-1979 period. However, due to the somewhat unstable change in this increase from year to year only a 6 percent average

Table 8.4
Housing Benefits for the Aged: Benefits, Beneficiaries, and Average Payment, 1971–1979*

Year	Benefit Outlays (Millions of $)	Number of Beneficiaries (Thousands)	Average Monthly Payments (in Dollars)
1971	233	332	58
1972	230	304	62
1973	252	814	26
1974	244	625	33
1975	375	1,025	30
1976	405	1,085	31
1977	806	2,484	28
1978*	1,051	2,706	32
1979*	1,257	2,993	35

*Estimated, 1979.

Source: Executive Office of the President, Office of Management and Budget, *Special Analysis, Budget of the United States Government—Fiscal Years 1973, 1974, 1975, 1976, 1977, 1978, 1979*, Washington, D.C.

yearly increase is used to project future costs of housing benefits for the aged. The resultant cost for the year 2000 is $4,273 million.

Nutrition

As a major item in family budgets, food might be expected to bear the brunt of the adjustments that normally accompany a reduction in income following retirement. Many studies, however, have indicated that food expenditures are not very responsive to income changes. The decrease in income associated with retirement results in a proportionately much smaller decrease in expenditures for food.[14]

Given a reduction, sometimes dramatic, in income upon retirement many retired persons look to the federal government for assistance. The food stamp program was designed to assure needy families an opportunity to purchase food for an adequate diet[15] and is the major source of supporting aged nutrition needs through public funding.

Seventeen percent of food stamp households had one or more elderly persons (aged sixty-five or over), for a total of 1 million participants. Over 88 percent of the households with elderly persons were one- and two-person households.[16] The cost of this type of "in-kind" benefit for the aged is shown in table 8.5.

Table 8.5
Food Benefits for the Aged: Benefits, Beneficiaries, and Average Payment, 1971–1979*

Year	Benefit Outlays (Millions of $)	Number of Beneficiaries (Thousands)	Average Monthly Payments (in Dollars)
1971	163	2,448	6
1972	164	1,300	10
1973	126	810	13
1974	145	843	14
1975	959	3,846	21
1976	569	2,294	21
1977	558	1,490	31
1978*	591	1,544	32
1979*	468	2,494	16

*Estimated, 1979.

Source: Executive Office of the President, Office of Management and Budget, Special Analysis, Budget of the United States Government—Fiscal Years 1973, 1974, 1975, 1976, 1977, 1978, 1979, Washington, D.C.

The food stamp program is based on a mathematically structured net income and assets test which has changed since mid-1971, in line with generally rising family income levels, including those of social security beneficiaries. At the end of 1974, the average social security benefit for both a single person and a married couple happened to be at about the same level as the food stamp income standards.[17] However, no constant increase in the number of beneficiaries or average monthly payments is evident from table 8.5. In projecting future needs, if a 6 percent average yearly increase is used to project the costs for providing nutrition for the aged, the resultant costs for the year 2000 are $1.6 billion.

Table 8.6
Tax Expenditures for Income Security, by Type: 1974–1982

	Fiscal Year			
	1974	1977	1980	1982
		$ Million		
Federal				
Exclusion of social security veterans, and railroad retirement benefits	3,125	4,935	8,225	13,180
Net exclusion of pension contributions and earnings	5,020	10,105	21,710	30,210
Exclusion of capital gains on sales of houses by persons aged 65 and over	10	40	N/A	N/A
Additional personal exemptions	1,150	1,140	2,040	2,505
Tax credit for the elderly	100	230	130	120
TOTAL	9,405	16,450	32,105	46,015

Source: Office of Management and Budget, Special Analysis, Budget of the United States Government—Fiscal Years 1974, 1977, 1980, 1982.

Tax Relief

A 1975 study by the Federal Council on the Aging found that the elderly as a group are treated more favorably than the nonelderly by the federal individual income tax. They pay 6.2 percent of their incomes in federal income taxes while nonaged households pay 10.5 percent. However, this preferential treatment largely offsets other taxes that disproportionately burden the elderly (such as property tax) at other levels of government. Table 8.6 depicts the federal income tax provisions for the aged which, on both an individual and a corporate level, lead to a decrease in tax revenues.

In addition, house sales by those over sixty-five are not subject to capital gains tax ($125,000 maximum exclusion) and there are also veterans benefits, which are tax exempt. Finally, states grant some of the same concessions as well as others, so that the total should be increased by about 16 percent, a proportion that appears to have remained constant for some years. Thus, the total for 1982 is increased from $46.0 billion to $53.4 billion.

A projection of these costs utilizing 1982 as a base and increasing at a rate of 9 percent to the year 2000 yields a total tax expenditure of $217 billion in 2000. A 9-percent rate is quite conservative since the 1974-1982 increase was 19.8 percent per annum.

The term "tax expenditures" is popular with government budget planners, but rather less so among citizens in general. To many, it implies that all money is fair game for the tax collector and that somehow a favor is being done to the public by not collecting it; hence, the money is being "spent" in some way. Under the circumstances, however, this is hardly a properly defined social cost. To be sure, a totally unfair tax system is a detriment to society, but one would be hard put to define a "fair" system in that sense as well. This is again one of the many instances in which one's personal values determine the ultimate assessment of social costs.

Summary and Conclusion

This chapter has attempted to illustrate the many costs assumed by society for supporting its elderly population. Table 8.7 summarizes several of the figures previously discussed approximating the total social cost of supporting the aged in 1980 at $61.8 billion. Futher, these costs are increasing rapidly; projecting them to the year 2000 and under conservative assumptions gives a total of $386.1 billion.

These very large sums are *not*, however, social costs, except as noted. If one accepts the governmental definition of tax expenditures, the item "tax relief" is obviously a social cost. So are the relatively small items on housing and nutrition. Income security, however, is met entirely by earmarked contributions and health care is met to a large extent by such payments.

In making such forecasts, one must necessarily make rather drastic assumptions. The social security systems, Medicare, and social programs generally are now in limbo. They are fair game for reduction, as government funds are

Table 8.7
Total Costs of Old Age: 1975–1976, 2000, and 2020 (in billions of dollars)

Type	1980	2000
Income security (a)	—	—
Health care (public share)	22.7	163.2
Housing	0.5	4.3
Nutrition	1.4	1.6
Tax relief	37.2	217.0
Total costs	61.8	386.1

(a) Depends on whether the social security system will have to be supported from public funds. The cost of welfare programs in general are discussed in chapter 9.

diverted instead to an enormous military buildup. As to health expenditures in particular, attempts are constantly being made at "cost containment," that is, some way of limiting what is a very substantial increase.

As 1982 ended, a National Commission on Social Security Reform, composed of eight Republicans and seven Democrats, was trying to put together a package of measures that would tide the system over its current difficulties. Actually, as noted before, the problem is short range, unless the economy remains for a very extended time in its current miserable state. Various means of raising money were examined, from increased payroll taxes, taxing some of the benefits, various fomulas for cutting benefits, to raising the retirement age. It was widely expected that agreement would be difficult and that some basic political precepts would be called into question, particularly of Republicans, a fringe of which sometimes advocates making social security "voluntary," thus wrecking the system as it stands. In March 1983 a compromise incorporating elements of all the above steps was enacted under bipartisan sponsorship.

Finally, it is counterproductive to the solution of the support problems of old age to consider the job as a nuisance of some sort. Rather, it is a necessary and essential task of society to cope with the problems decently. As R. A. Lester put it:

Unfortunately one cannot arrive at the determination of the proper level of social insurance benefits by mathematical means or by scientific tests, or even by pure logic. The answer depends upon one's economic and social philosophy—the sympathy he has for human misfortune, the stress he places on preserving individual dignity, and the kind of society he envisions as desirable. The answer will also vary with the kind of economy in which the level is to apply (the general standard of living, the distribution of personal income, and the division between market and governmental determination of economic affairs) and with the traditions, history, and culture of the society in question.[18]

Notes

1. "Your Stake in the Fight Over Social Security," *Consumer Reports*, September 1981, p. 503.

2. Ibid.

3. Ibid.

4. Ibid.; see also National Retired Teachers Association and American Association of Retired Persons, *1978 Federal Legislative Program and 1978-79 State Legislative Program* (Washington, D.C.: National Retired Teachers Association, American Association of Retired Persons, Action for Independent Maturity, n.d.), p. 6.

5. W. J. Cohen, "Twenty-five Years of Progress in Social Security," in *Social Security Programs, Problems and Policies*, ed. W. Haber and W. J. Cohen (Homewood, Ill.: Richard D. Irwin, Inc., 1960), p. 88.

6. R. J. Myers, *Social Security* (Homewood, Ill.: Richard D. Irwin, Inc., 1975), pp. 28-29.

7. *Old Age and Survivors Insurance after 20 Years*, cited by W. Haber and W. J. Cohen, *Social Security Programs, Problems and Policies* (Homewood, Ill.: Richard D. Irwin, Inc., 1960), pp. 173-74; see also *Statistical Abstract of the United States, 1981*, p. 322.

8. U.S. Department of Health and Human Resources, *Health: United States, 1981*, p. 204.

9. C. I. Schottland, *The Social Security Program in the United States*, 2d ed., rev. (New York: Meredith Corporation, 1970), pp. 69, 70.

10. U.S. Department of Health, Education, and Welfare, *Social Security Bulletin*, July 1978, p. 42.

11. Ibid.

12. U.S. Department of Health, Education, and Welfare, *U.S. Health, 1976-1977*, p. 4.

13. Executive Office of the President, Office of Management and Budget, *The Budget of the United States Government, Fiscal Year 1979*, p. 200.

14. J. H. Murray, "Changes in Food Expenditures, 1969-73: Findings from the Retirement History Study," *Social Security Bulletin*, July 1978, p. 21.

15. *Budget of the U.S., 1979*, p. 201.

16. U.S. Congress, Senate, Select Committee on Nutrition and Human Needs, *Food Stamp Program Profile: Part 2—Appendix*, 94th Cong., 2d sess., 1976, p. 21.

17. R. J. Myers, *Social Security*, pp. 407-8.

18. R. A. Lester, "The Nature and Level of Income Security in a Free Society," in Haber and Cohen, *Social Security Programs*, p. 73.

9
Slums and Poverty

GARY KNOX

> Poverty does not produce unhappiness;
> it produces degradation; that is why it
> is dangerous to society. Its evils are
> infectious and cannot be avoided by any
> possible isolation of the rich. We
> cannot afford to have the poor always
> with us.
>
> Bernard Shaw, *The Intelligent Woman's*
> *Guide*

Introduction

The social cost of poverty and related conditions is in part defined by such statistics as welfare costs. However, most activities that try to alleviate poverty in other respects are part of the support of those not living in the poverty areas usually known as slums. The costs of extra police and fire protection, sanitation, health services, and education are not readily separated from those required in other areas,[1] and estimates of, for example, extra crime committed by the poor in nonpoverty areas are even more difficult to arrive at. Still, this chapter presents the results now available on this subject. To some extent, it overlaps several items discussed before. The various programs of social security and workers' compensation, for instance, provide sustenance to many slum dwellers although they are not sufficient to change their way of life to real advantage.

The term "slum" means the crowded, often dilapidated, and unsanitary dwellings of the poor. But slums are more than a description of housing stock; rather they are the places where broken down men and women and, increasingly, children wage an almost hopeless fight to live. Euphemisms abound; slums are "blighted areas," "deteriorated neighborhoods," "gray areas." But, as Dr. James B. Conant wrote: "In each [of the largest American cities], one can find neighborhoods composed of various minority groups. Many of these are areas now designated as culturally deprived or culturally different, but in my youth they would have been more simply designated as slums."[2]

Probably no American writer's historical reputation is based as solidly on his writing about slums as that of Jacob Riis. His angry writing about them had a marked impact on public policy for many years. In 1890 he wrote:

> In the tenements all the influences make for evil; because they are the hot beds of the epidemics that carry death to rich and poor alike; the nurseries of pauperism and crime that fill our jails and police courts; that throw off a scum of forty thousand human wrecks to the island asylums and workhouses year by year; that turned out in the last eight years a round half million beggars to prey upon our charities; that maintain a standing army of ten thousand tramps with all that implies; because, above all, they touch the family life with deadly moral contagion. This is their worst crime, inseparable from the system. That we have to own it the child of our wrong does not excuse it, even though it gives it claim upon our utmost patience and tenderest charity. What are you going to do about it? is the question of today.[3]

Slums in the United States, as in other countries, are often the homes of minority groups, but in America the time when they were the expected first homes of successive waves of immigrants lies in the past. As those earlier groups prospered, they moved out, and reminiscences of the old slum days are relegated to nostalgic writings, such as those of Harry Golden, Alfred Kazin, and others. Later identifiable immigrant groups, especially from Europe and Asia, did not pass through the first "slum generation."

As it is, American slums are nothing if not diverse in their makeup. They include Blacks, Puerto Ricans, Chicanos in the largest numbers, but also poor whites from Appalachia, American Indians, small Oriental enclaves, diverse immigrants from the Caribbean area and South America, and others.[4] Their problems are often complicated by their having lived in different climates and in the country; city life is unfamiliar and difficult, quite apart from the economic hardships.

Slums may consist of the multistory warrens that one might consider their "traditional" architectural form, or they may be dilapidated-looking suburbs, run-down formerly genteel neighborhoods, the mini-slums of rural areas, or the square miles of shantytowns that surround most of the world's major cities today.[5] Moreover, these conditions have a tendency to spread, engulfing formerly acceptable neighborhoods; suburban flight then accelerates and more areas are opened up for deterioration.[6] Whatever methods have been used to halt the spread appear to have been inadequate.[7] R. Vernon, writing in 1965, observes that only about three square miles of New York City had been improved in the preceding two decades when activity in slum clearance was strong.[8]

The way in which neighborhoods deteriorate is familiar. Poorer new inhabitants are housed at greater densities in buildings no longer properly maintained. Retail areas, already beset by the moves to shopping centers, find it difficult to maintain adequate levels of sales; they continue to be faced with high rents and an increasing level of crime. Ultimately, the merchants leave. The last stage is that of the fire epidemics in which the area is virtually burned out; trying to collect the insurance money on the structures is literally the terminal stage. Physical deterioration is thus an important hallmark of slum conditions, but these are widespread indeed. It is estimated that one out of four families lives in homes that are inadequate, deteriorating, and at least the seedbeds of slum areas.[9] Some 16 percent of urban families live in totally dilapidated housing.[10]

However, what makes today's slums so persistent and accelerating a phenomenon is the combination of poverty, ill health, deliquency, and crime, much of it related to drugs, with a growing lack of hope that anything better will be possible for future generations. It was that hope that had made earlier poor areas "slums of hope," rather than the currently prevalent "slums of despair"[11] in which, in many cases, a permanent underclass seems to have settled.

Education is no exit, as it once was for sizable groups of former slum dwellers. The schools are poor, overcrowded and beset by crime and delinquency. An additional problem is linguistic in that Spanish speakers particularly have established bilingual enclaves that resist assimilation. Spanish, being linked historically to the earliest postdiscovery settlement of the Western hemisphere, has been less prone to be supplanted by English than other languages as children entered American schools. The version of English spoken by Blacks and Appalachian whites has also produced cultural barriers.

For a variety of reasons, therefore, the communities tend to be insular and their poor self-image certainly is one clue to their condition:

> In some ways most important, bad housing affects the way poor people feel about themselves and the way other people feel about them. It's hard to have self-respect in a rat-infested, crumbling, crowded apartment. When someone leaves a place like that to try to get a job, he

already feels licked. Similarly, other people think of poor people in the same terms. Some of them mistakenly think that poor people are no good because they live in slums or because the streets are dirty. Of course, they've never lived in a place where the landlord didn't turn on the heat and where the city didn't collect garbage. But, they still feel that way, and their attitude represents an important effect of bad housing on poor people.[12]

The cost of a slum is a burden on all taxpayers. For one thing, the chief source of revenue for a city is its real estate. Better property can be taxed more. Slums obviously represent worn-out, run-down property. Because the buildings have deteriorated, they are less valuable. The result is that taxes on such property decline. Buildings that once produced a large amount of income for the city no longer do so. This lost income must be made up by charging higher taxes on other property in the city.

Making matters worse is the fact that slums require more, not fewer services. They require more garbage collection and more police, fire, and health protection, not less. These services must be provided and they must be paid for. Since the people living in the slums cannot pay for them, those living outside must. For every dollar needed to service the slum area, only ten cents comes from the area itself.[13] As the burden of taxes falls increasingly on middle-class residents, they move away. Some sell their homes to the less prosperous and the cycle of slum development is encouraged to begin again. Rising taxes must be borne by a smaller and smaller group who must pay for the services needed by the ever-increasing slum area.

The last stage of that process is the emergence of whole communities that are mostly slum or whose residential areas, at any rate, are heavily of that variety. Newark and Camden, New Jersey; Gary, Indiana; East St. Louis, Illinois; and Detroit are examples.

In some areas, a reversal of the process has taken place, leading to "gentrification"; deteriorated property that is often well located with respect to the more desirable attributes of the broader community is taken over by individuals who manage to remodel and restore the areas. Its incidence is limited, however, and, in any event, raises the question of where the displaced slum dwellers are then supposed to move. The same problem arose in many places where office and commercial construction and road building displaced poor neighborhoods. The result all too often was the spread of slums elsewhere while the restored neighborhood became a single-purpose area, deserted in the evening and at night, and, quite often, a more dangerous place than before for those in it.

Studies of the Costs of Slums

Though considerable work has been devoted in recent years to refining methods of identifying, counting, and characterizing the poor, little work has been done in deriving estimates of the benefits of eliminating poverty. This situation exists even though the federal government recognizes that expenditures for processes that remove diseconomies should be subtracted from the value added to society's output, rather than added as is presently done.[14]

There are a number of exceptions. Gary Becker, for instance, has written on the potential benefits of enhancing human capital generally.[15] Burton Weisbrod tackled the conceptual problem of accounting for neighborhood spillovers and spill-ins associated with education and, in doing so, has suggested a measurement technique that develops new criteria for the allocation of social welfare.[16] Others, such as Herbert Hill, have projected budgets required to eliminate slums but their figures are not based on any better estimates of what is required.[17]

The early empirical research on social costs dates from the mid-1930s. These studies compared the incidence of fire and crime and rates of mortality and morbidity in slum and nonslum areas to justify public housing and urban renewal. The hope was that public subsidies for housing would be more than compensated for by lower costs for fire and police protection, higher property values, housing code enforcement, and the improved health of the once slum residents. Levels of public expenditure in these early studies were typically obtained by applying an average cost per unit of service to the activity data. The work of Jay Rumney is one of the more detailed studies of this period. Rumney cites fifteen studies showing a pathology of high illness, fire, and crime in slums. He also presents data from thirteen cities (mainly during 1932-1935) showing a ratio of slum expenditure to revenue generated in the range of 2.2 to 9.0 with a median of about 5.0.[18]

A few studies have examined the effects of relocating slum families in improved public housing. The most comprehensive of these, a project costing $500,000, consisted of a sample of 1,000 families, which controlled for income.[19] No significant differences were found between the mortality rates of residents in slums and public housing. Reduced morbidity rates for persons under thirty-five were found, but not for persons over forty-nine. An earlier study made in 1947 found that relocation to decent housing did have significant effects on patterns of behavior.[20]

In 1964-1965, Charles Benson and Peter Lund studied neighborhood expenditures in Oakland, California, for several transfer services (welfare, public housing), household participation services (libraries, recreation, sanitation, schools, fire, police, code enforcement), and neighborhood maintenance services (fire, police, street maintenance, sanitation, building inspection, lighting); looked at the costs of specific supplying units; and allocated these costs to three areas of approximately 15,000 persons each.[21] Their findings tend to confirm much of earlier evidence that, quite apart from pure transfers, the utilization of public services is inversely related to socioeconomic level.

More recently, Marvin Berkowitz performed a comprehensive study of the social costs of human underdevelopment and their measurement in New York City neighborhoods. He developed a cost-accounting framework and associated data to estimate the utilization and costs of a selected set of public services in seven large residential areas of varying levels of effective human wealth in New York City. Three of the seven neighborhoods were established Black and Puerto Rican slums (Harlem Model Cities, South Bronx Model Cities, and Brooklyn Model Cities), two were declining transitional areas (South Jamaica, Queens, and Fordham/Concourse, Bronx), and two were upper-middle income White communities (Flatbush/Flatlands, Brooklyn, and Bayside/Central Queens). A summary of the results of his study is presented below.[22]

1. The findings for neighborhood expenditure liabilities reveal essentially the same ordering between levels of human underdevelopment for all services, regardless of the magnitude of the outlay. Neighborhoods having a relatively high dollar use of one social service or neighborhood maintenance service have a relatively high dollar utilization for others. Neighborhoods with a relatively low use of one service have a relatively low use of others.

2. The pattern of costs seems to be relatively invariant whether the neighborhood liabilities are deflated to dollars per capita, per adult, per household, per $1,000 of property market value, or some other consumption base.

3. Of the services explored, public assistance is by far the most costly ($200-$300 per capita in the poor areas to $10-$20 per capita in the soundest areas). The estimated percentages of residents receiving public assistance in 1969 were about the following: Harlem Model Cities, 25 percent; South Bronx Model Cities, 33 percent; Brooklyn Model Cities, 33 percent; South Jamaica, Queens, 33 percent; Fordham/Concourse, Bronx, 5 percent; Flatbush/Flatlands, Brooklyn, 2.5 percent; Bayside and Central Queens, 1 percent; citywide, 12.5 percent.

4. For two other social services, after-school recreation and adult education programs offered at schools in the target neighborhoods, and

drug addiction services, the soundest areas have per capita liabilities 12.5 percent to 33 percent as high as those in the high human under-development neighborhoods. The intervention of probation officers and the family court to help reconcile family difficulties, to deter-mine support and questions of paternity, and to give direction for child neglect and supervision is six to ten times more common for the poorer areas as for their sounder counterparts.

5. Neighborhoods with the largest proportions of public housing also make the greatest use of housing code enforcement services. Some 25 percent of the housing units in Harlem Model Cities are public or publicly aided. These receive a subsidy of nearly $25 per project resi-dent and $100 per target area resident in terms of payments for amor-tization and interest, operating deficits, city contributions for project police, and tax exemption.

6. The general findings for local law enforcement outlays show that the lowest human wealth neighborhoods have per capita expenditure liabilities of $100-$150—three to five times as high as their high human wealth counterparts. These costs include public outlays for police, the criminal courts, district attorneys, and that portion of pro-bation that could be associated with crime. The relative neighbor-hood burdens are borne out by examining who goes to state prisons and for which crimes. In 1968 about 47 percent of the persons sen-tenced to prison terms of more than one year for robberies in Brook-lyn lived in the Brooklyn Model Cities area; only about 2 percent of the sentenced offenders resided in Flatbush/Flatlands, less than two miles away, despite roughly comparable sizes of adult population. For burglaries, the respective rates were 37 percent and 3 percent. Two large residential areas in Queens showed the same skewing effect: 25 percent of that borough's felony convictions were residents from the declining transitional area, South Jamaica, while an adult population 1.5 times as large in nearby Bayside contributed only 1 percent of felony convictions. With an average cost in state correc-tional institutions of $4,200 per inmate during fiscal year 1968-1969, the social burden of crime approximates the disposable incomes after taxes and travel expenses of a large proportion of ghetto workers.

7. The high internalization of ghetto social costs is demonstrated by examining the relative victimization indexes for sixteen common crimes as simple counts and weighted by the Wolfgang-Sellin serious-ness scale. The Model Cities areas were found to have levels of vic-timization on a per adult or per household basis of three to four times

their sounder counterparts, despite significantly higher per capita levels of police patrol expenditures.

8. The costs of fire protection reflect the relative frequency and serious-ness of fires in the different neighborhoods as well as some historical reasons for the location of fire units. The Model Cities neighbor-hoods have per capita costs of about $30, whereas those in Flatbush and Bayside are about $15.

9. Estimated paid insurance losses were approximately four to five times higher on a per capita basis in the low human wealth areas than in the most sound areas over the period 1959-1968. The financial and psy-chological impact of these statistics for property owners also serves as a performance indicator of the city's housing and fire protection policies.

Elements of the Slum Problem

Each of the slum elements has a negative character, a character that makes the community at large regard it as a problem. In attempting to deal with these problems there are a number of direct and indirect social costs that are borne by either the slum community or society as a whole. These costs are listed in table 9.1.

An indication of the overall cost of the government component of direct services expenditures is suggested by table 9.2. By far the largest portion of these federal outlays benefiting low-income persons is in cash transfers for public assistance, social security, unemployment, and so on—$12 billion in 1974—and in-kind income outlays for consumption such as food stamps and housing subsidies—$3.2 billion in 1974. These outlays are made to supply minimum material wants. Expenditures for health, education, manpower and community action, and other areas raise the 1974 total to $27 billion. Most of these latter outlays are made to advance equal opportunity and enhance human resources. The food stamp program is discussed further in chapter 13.

When the Berkowitz data presented earlier is updated to reflect 1974 dollars, the average total dollar outlay per New York City slum resident is approximately $1,130. This represents expenditures in the areas of education, welfare, health, police protection, fire protection, and housing. Adjusted to produce an average national dollar outlay based on state and local government employees' salaries compared with New York City municipal employees' salaries, it is estimated that in 1974 state and local government expenditures alone benefiting slum residents were approximately $111.6 billion.

Table 9.1
Some Components of Slum Operating Costs

Direct Costs—expenditures traceable directly to economic poverty/human underdevelopment
  Internal Cost—borne by individuals within the slum
    Added treatment costs
    Higher rents, food prices, clothing, furniture, and credit costs
    Costs of premature death
  External Costs—borne by the whole of society, including adjustments of
  nonslum residents (social costs)
    Differential costs of local public services—added costs of police, courts,
      prisons, fire protection, health, public assistance, public housing
    Added health treatment costs due to contact with the poor of low health
      level
    Costs of special antipoverty programs
    Unusual costs to control civil disorders
    Undesirable neighborhood effects—net changes in urban and suburban land
      and property values
    Direct losses due to fire damage and crime—loss of income associated with
      added crime, delinquency, civil disorder resulting in damage to persons
      and property
    Higher business, residential, and personal insurance rates for fire and crime
    Costs of relocation and commutation to suburbs—congested highways,
      use of time
    Precautionary costs to prevent crime—private guards, locks
    Expenditures for private school for children
    Restricted availability of scarce physical, monetary, and human resources
    Psychic income; discrimination

Indirect Costs—losses in productivity due to an underdeveloped or under-
  utilized state of human resources
  Internal costs—borne by individuals within the slum
    Differential between actual and potential lifetime earnings of the slum poor
      (possibly net of consumption and taxes)
    Value of alienation and self-esteem, social and political awareness and
      commitment
  External Costs—borne by the whole of society, including individual adjustments
  of nonslum residents
    Inefficiency in business firms attributable to higher absenteeism and
      turnover of slum workers
    Scale effects of additional productivity on national growth, redistribution
      of taxes from earnings associated with additional production

Source: Marvin Berkowitz, *The Social Costs of Human Underdevelopment* (New York: Praeger
    Publishers, 1974), p. 46.

Table 9.2
Federal Outlays Benefiting Persons with Low Income, 1970–1974
(in Billions of Dollars, for Years Ending June 30)

Item	1970	1971	1972	1973	1974
Total	17.8	21.8	25.1	25.2	27.1
Human Investment (a)	3.6	4.4	5.1	5.0	4.8
Maintenance (b)	14.2	17.4	20.0	20.2	22.3
By program area:					
Cash payments	8.8	10.5	11.3	11.0	11.9
Social security and railroad retirement	5.2	5.9	5.8	6.0	6.3
Public assistance payments	2.2	2.8	3.6	3.2	3.8
Veterans pensions and compensation	1.0	1.1	1.1	1.1	1.0
Unemployment benefits	.3	.6	.7	.5	.6
Other cash payments	.1	.1	.1	.2	.2
In-kind transfers (food and housing)	1.1	1.8	2.3	2.7	3.2
Food stamps	.3	.8	1.0	1.2	1.6
Child nutrition (including commodities for schools)	.2	.3	.5	.5	.6
Other food programs	.3	.3	.3	.3	.2
Housing subsidy payments	.3	.4	.5	.7	.8
Health	4.1	4.6	5.4	5.4	6.2
Medicaid	1.7	2.1	2.7	2.7	3.2
Medicare	1.7	1.7	1.7	1.5	1.8
Veterans medical care	.2	.2	.2	.3	.3
Other health (excluding veterans care)	.5	.6	.8	.9	.9
Education	1.4	1.7	1.8	1.8	1.8
Early childhood education	.3	.3	.3	.3	.4
Elementary and secondary education	.8	1.0	1.1	1.0	1.0
Higher education	.2	.3	.3	.4	.3
Vocational and adult education	.1	.1	.1	.1	.1
Manpower	1.5	2.0	2.4	2.2	2.0
Skill training	.9	1.2	1.4	1.2	.9
Work support	.5	.6	.8	.8	.3
CETA—state/local programs	—	—	—	—	.6
Labor market services	.1	.2	.2	.2	.2
Other	1.1	1.4	1.9	2.0	1.9

Table 9.2 *(continued)*
Federal Outlays Benefiting Persons with Low Income, 1970–1974
(in Billions of Dollars, for Years Ending June 30)

Item	1970	1971	1972	1973	1974
Community action (including related programs and model cities)	.6	.7	.7	.8	.8
Miscellaneous human investment	.1	.1	.1	.1	.1
Social services, child care, and other miscellaneous maintenance	.4	.5	1.1	1.1	1.0
By funding agency:					
Health, Education, and Welfare	12.7	15.0	17.3	17.4	19.2
Agriculture	.7	1.5	1.9	2.0	2.4
Labor	.7	1.7	2.3	2.0	1.8
Veterans Administration	1.2	1.3	1.3	1.4	1.3
Housing and Urban Development	.3	.5	.7	.9	1.0
Office of Economic Opportunity	1.7	1.4	1.0	.7	.7
Economic Opportunity Programs	1.8	2.2	2.4	2.3	1.6
All others	.5	.6	.6	.6	.6

Notes: Figures represent estimated direct benefits to persons with income below low-income level through federal expenditures and direct-loan programs. Dash represents zero.

(a) Includes programs that actively promote education, the development of work skills, and community and economic development.

(b) Programs that provide income support and certain essential noncash support and services to meet basic needs of persons with low income.

Source: Marvin Berkowitz, *The Social Costs of Human Underdevelopment* (New York: Praeger Publishers, 1974), p. 48.

Poverty and Some Proposed Remedies

The poverty that lies at the base of slums and their spread has within the last generation led to a considerable variety of proposed remedies, some of which were implemented with mixed results. As disillusion with these projects spread and was extensively fostered in the political controversies of the time, it became fashionable to write all of these efforts off as failures. One could, however, just as clearly argue that President Johnson's War on Poverty was aborted by the need to divert great funds from these efforts to the Vietnam War. Furthermore, as with most major public efforts, money is not the only issue—motivation, interest, and commitment are equally important, and these too were no longer available once the Vietnam War escalated. This interpretation is hardly novel in American history. It is generally conceded that the social reforms of the New Deal of the 1930s likewise came to an end as a result of war preparations and America's entry into World War II.

While one cannot be sure that a lot more money would have produced a lot more results, it is true that for a variety of reasons the programs disappointed their sponsors and their importance has sharply diminished over the years. This applies particularly to areas such as education in which, for example, the Comprehensive Education and Training Act (CETA) led to a variety of difficulties including corruption, mismanagement, and, above all, selection of its beneficiaries from groups other than the poor for which it was originally intended.

Housing, likewise, started with the Model Cities program, but this too has been systematically starved of funds. The problem there has been quite simply that as interest rates soared and capital became scarce, housing starts declined precipitously. At the beginning of 1982 housing starts were down 59 percent from 1980, and an upturn in 1983, while significant, was hardly robust. Meanwhile the Reagan administration continued its policies of reducing or eliminating federal housing subsidies, and state and local governments proved generally unable to take up the slack, given their own straitened circumstances and the prevailing political atmosphere.

It is, moreover, of interest to place the Federal Housing Program in proportion. Mills[23] has calculated the total federal expenditures for housing for the period 1948-1972. A total of $41.0 billion was spent by government at all levels. Not all of it, or indeed most of it, however, was devoted to slum clearance but rather included subsidized middle-income housing and the reconstruction of blighted commercial or industrial areas.

On the other hand, it is important to realize that the principal governmental subsidy for housing went to individual homeowners, mostly in suburbia and in low-density, single-family housing in cities. Since real estate taxes and mortgage interest are deducted from taxable income, homeowners realize very substantial cash flow from this provision of the tax laws. These benefits aggregated $60.1 billion in 1948-1972, or about one and a half times that of the amount spent for public housing of all kinds. Clearly then, the focus of government policy has not been in the direction of slum clearance.

The aid that now goes to slum dwellers is primarily welfare and income-in-kind. The latter consists principally of rent supplements which are part of welfare allotments and are included in welfare funds, and food stamps which are discussed in more detail in chapter 13.

Welfare payments have become a very substantial item in governmental expenditures. Table 9.3 shows these payments and indicates particularly that

Table 9.3
Total Public Assistance Payments: Selected Years, 1960–1980*

Year	Supplemental Security Income (SSI)	Aid to Families with Dependent Children	Total
		$ Billion	
1960	N/A	N/A	2.31
1970	—	4.9	4.9
1975	5.7	9.2	14.9
1979	6.9	11.1	18.0
1980	7.7	12.5	20.2

* Includes state and local tax contributions.

Source: Statistical Abstract of the United States, 1981, p. 344; 1980, p. 334.

certain items, such as aid to families with dependent children, have increased by the largest margin. The program is currently state administered with some funds in some states locally provided. While in past years proposals have been made for federalizing welfare, President Reagan's "new federalism" program proposes to do just the opposite. Food stamps, which are now a federal program and aid for dependent children, would become entirely local responsibilities, whereas Medicaid would become an entirely federal one.

The problem with that approach is that although Medicaid has been a rapidly rising item, the fact remains that there is now enormous variation among the welfare levels of the states and territories. On the one hand it is possible for a whole new generation of welfare refugees to crowd the poverty areas of the more generous states, while at the same time there is a downward auction among the various jurisdictions as to who can get away with the least. Such policies in turn have serious consequences for local tax levels and all that implies in terms of advantages in seeking new business, industrial development, and the like. Once more, it is clear that what starts out as a social cost problem of relatively limited scope and concentration becomes a far more extensive one once its ramifications are critically examined.

Finally, with respect to education, very substantial sums were earmarked for remedial education, bilingual work, and so on. Head Start, bilingual education, adult basic education, college work study, and open enrollment were all developed in an effort to improve the education of the poorer people. However, all of these have since been cut back. In education particularly, the outlook was very clouded as 1983 began, with the administration trying to phase out the Department of Education altogether, reducing federal involvement in education as near to nothing as is feasible, and leaving most of the funds in the form of block grants rather than the form of earmarked funds for the needy.

The situation has been greatly exacerbated in the short run, quite apart from the longer term policies discussed above. For 1982, Congress cut funding for the much-criticized Comprehensive Employment and Training Act by 39 percent, to $4.2 billion, eliminating 307,000 public service jobs. A 3-percent cut to $757 million has closed dozens of state employment offices, including twenty-four in Michigan alone. Food stamp funding has been trimmed by 2 percent to $11.1 billion a year. Other programs that trained 1.2 million young workers a year have been cut by $600 million, or 20 percent. Funding for the 450 Private Industry Councils (PICs), which find jobs in private industry for disadvantaged workers, has been cut 7 percent to $246 million. And a 2 percent cut to $7 billion in Aid to Families with Dependent Children (AFDC), plus new eligibility rules, has reduced or eliminated benefits for 670,000 of 4 million AFDC recipients.[24]

These rules may well provide more disincentives for work than exist now, making it more profitable to stay on welfare. Plans for "workfare" would require able-bodied AFDC recipients to do enough public service work, calculated at the minimum wage, to earn their subsidy payments. This, however, ignores a whole lot of problems like the poor educational level of recipients, a shortage of child day-care centers, and motivation problems. Day-care centers have always attracted conservative budgetary axes on philosophical as well as financial grounds. Furthermore, at a time of cutbacks in local government, there is a serious problem in equity as well as skills in replacing out-of-work public employees by forced labor of this kind.

The cuts may also affect social behavior as unemployment rises. Studies by Professor M. Harvey Brenner, of the Johns Hopkins School of Hygiene and Public Health, show that when unemployment rises by 1 percent, state prison populations rise by 4 percent, murders increase by 5.7 percent, mental hospital admissions rise by 2 percent to 4 percent, and suicides increase by 4 percent. The Justice Department said on February 21, 1982, that in the first nine months of 1981 state and federal prison populations rose by more than 10 percent, exceeding the record increase of 1975, also a poor year.[25]

Conclusion

Approximately 50 million people still live in the deteriorated and socially dysfunctional areas called slums. This is in spite of the development of numerous federal, state, and local programs, and the annual expenditures of billions of dollars in attempting to solve their problems. The slum residents themselves are of course a limited source of tax funds, but, additionally, it has been shown in recent years that despite various legal provisions that were designed to make voting easier for those in all walks of life and of all racial and economic backgrounds, political participation has steadily declined until it was not much of an exaggeration in the 1982 elections to say that the poor were not a force that politicians normally have to reckon with.

As a result the social costs of poverty are likely to grow in the sense that the extra costs referred to before will have to be borne by the public at large, for at least as long as outright starvation of large (as distinct from small) portions of the population will not be countenanced in the United States. It is unfortunately not inappropriate to put it as crassly as this; the battles of the budget that shape up for 1983 promise to be a multiple tug of war, involving programs that have traditionally benefited the poor and related social purposes, the huge and swelling military budget, the tax cuts that were promised and enacted in 1981 and may be rescinded as they were in part by the 1982 tax increases, and the prospect of huge, economically destabilizing budget deficits. Whatever the outcome in detail, it cannot fail to lead to further erosion of past commitments and, therefore, inevitably to the penalties that society as a whole will have to pay for not making the poorest part of the population into productive citizens.

It would go beyond the scope of this chapter to deal in detail with some of the proposals, such as a negative income tax, that surfaced briefly around 1970 and were then scuttled. But the most important way would be the development of jobs. This then raises the whole issue of economic development in the wake of a restructuring of national priorities, a problem that will be addressed in more detail in chapter 15.

Notes

1. Department of Housing and Urban Development, *The Future of Local Urban Redevelopment: A Guide for Community Policy Makers* (Washington, D.C.: HUD, February, 1975), p. 18.

2. J. B. Conant, *Slums and Suburbs* (New York: McGraw-Hill Book Co., 1961), p. 7.

3. J. Riis, *How the Other Half Lives* (New York: Sagamore Press, 1957), p. 2.

4. D. Seligman, "The Enduring Slums," in *The Expanding Metropolis* (New York: Doubleday Anchor Books, 1958), p. 96.

5. G. Leinwand, *The Slums* (New York: Washington Square Press, 1970), p. 21.

6. K. Clark, *Dark Ghetto* (New York: Harper & Row, 1965), p. 66.

7. R. Vernon, *The Myth and Reality of Our Urban Problems* (Cambridge, Mass.: Harvard University Press, 1966), pp. 68-70.

8. Ibid., p. 70.

9. O. H. Steiner, *Downtown, U.S.A.* (Dobbs Ferry, N.Y.: Oceana Publications, 1964), p. 4.

10. Ibid.

11. D. R. Hunter, *The Slums: Challenge and Response* (New York: Free Press of Glencoe, 1964), p. 15.

12. Office of Economic Opportunity, "Community Action and Urban Housing," *Community Action*, November 1967, p. 10.

13. O. H. Steiner, *Our Housing Jungle—and Your Pocketbook* (New York: University Publishers, 1960), p. 44.

14. E. Mishan, *Costs of Economic Growth* (New York: Praeger, 1967), p. 146.

15. G. Becker, *Human Capital* (New York: National Bureau of Economic Research, 1964).

16. B. Weisbrod, "Income Redistribution Effects and Benefits—Cost Analysis," in *Problems in Public Expenditure Analysis*, ed. S. B. Chase, Jr. (Washington, D.C.: Brookings Institution, 1968) pp., 177-222.

17. H. Hill, "Planning to End the American Ghetto: A Program of Economic Development for Equal Rights," prepared for the White House Conference, "To Fulfill These Rights," Washington, D.C., June 2-3, 1966.

18. J. Rumney, "The Social Costs of Slums," *Journal of Social Issues* 7, nos. 1-2 (1959), pp. 69-85.

19. D. M. Wilner et al., *The Housing Environment and Family Life: A Longitudinal Study of the Effects of Housing on Morbidity and Mental Health* (Baltimore: Johns Hopkins Press, 1967).

20. S. Chapin, *Experimental Designs in Sociological Research* (New York: Harper, 1947).

21. C. S. Benson and P. B. Lund, *Neighborhood Distribution of Local Public Services* (Berkeley: University of California, Institute of Government Studies, 1969).

22. M. Berkowitz, *The Social Costs of Human Underdevelopment* (New York: Praeger Publishers, 1974), pp. 234-37.

23. E. W. Mills, "Taxation and the Financing of Suburbia," in *The Suburban Economic Network*, ed. J. E. Ullmann, (New York: Praeger, 1976), p. 48.

24. "Why Welfare Rolls May Grow," *Business Week*, March 29, 1982, p. 165-66.

25. Ibid.

10
Duplication of Capital Facilities

JOSEPH C. DiPASQUALE

O Imitators, servile herd! How often
have you raised my anger with all your
mad confusion!

Horace, *Epistles*

Introduction

Duplication of capital facilities is a major contributor to social costs. As Kapp puts it,

> . . . the avoidance of excess capacity and of the uncoordinated proliferation of capital facilities is a prerequisite for the maintenance of a high level of socio-economic efficiency in the utilization of scarce resources under any form of socio-economic organization. Falling short of this, society and the consumer will bear the social costs connected with duplication and excess capacity in the form of unnecessarily high prices and general instability.[1]

Excess capacity and the duplication of capital facilities are brought about, in part, by the inherent character of the free enterprise system. A business opportunity attracts a succession of enterprises until the opportunity is overexploited and troubles mount for most or all participants. Only from this perspective does it make sense to speak of duplication, excess capacity, and lack of coordination of existing capital facilities. This chapter focuses on transportation and real estate in the United States because they are two areas in which these problems are most conspicuously present.

Transportation

As Kapp has pointed out, there are three major reasons why the development and operation of a system of transportation along competitive lines leads to duplication and relatively low operational efficiency.[2] First, modern transportation facilities generally require a great initial capital investment and therefore are burdened with operating their physical plant with a comparatively high percentage of fixed costs. Track, terminals, aircraft, barges, rolling stock, and truck fleets all have high fixed investments, even though some make use of publicly owned facilities like highways and airports.

Second, operational efficiency of any single means of transportation depends also upon the extent of its integration with all other transport facilities. "Every road has to be properly connected with other roads, every railroad, every canal has to be conceived and planned as a part of the total transportation net, and railroads, inland waterways and highways must be systematically coordinated if they are to yield the highest possible utility."[3] The same applies to airlines or bus systems. This chapter deals with social costs mainly in the United States in which such an overall planning concept was not generally applied. The prevalence of private enterprises actually fostered duplication of facilities through its encouragement of competition. It is true that some regulatory measures were taken by the government to help reduce this problem, as in the utility industry, but in general it was assumed that through market competition, the consuming public will ultimately benefit by getting the best possible product or service at the most reasonable price. As will be shown, this does not always hold true so that social costs, not always easily identifiable, are borne either directly or indirectly by the public.

Third, transportation is placed in a special category due to the social character of many of the benefits provided by the system. For example, as noted by Kapp, "a railroad, by facilitating the production and exchange of commodities, enlarges the extent of the market of manufacturers, determines the location of industries, influences land values, and serves important military and cultural purposes."[4] There is no argument that this is true; however, much duplication in transportation links occurred because they were built in anticipation of economic development that never came. As matters stand, additional social costs may be incurred when some of the duplication is eliminated.

Railroads

The railroad system of the United States was created almost entirely by private enterprise under conditions of regulation that offered very little control over the proliferation of track. The construction did require eminent domain, but this was readily secured. As a result, the system grew very rapidly. By 1898 it had reached 184,648 route-miles, going on to a maximum of 254,251 in 1915. By 1975, abandonments had reduced it to 200,000 and to 184,500 miles by 1982, that is, back to the total at the beginning of the century. Neither the construction nor the current disinvestment show evidence of careful planning.

Much of the original construction was put in place at very low cost in the belief that if a certain area could sustain one railroad, it could probably sustain several. Certain major areas, therefore, had very large mileages, quite often with competing lines running within sight of each other. Examples are the Pacific Coast extension of the Milwaukee Road (of which more later) and the Northern Pacific, now part of the Burlington Northern, which occupied the same valley over several hundred miles in Montana and further west. Another case is that of the Nickel Plate, now part of the Norfolk & Western, running a few blocks from the New York Central, now Conrail, between Buffalo and Toledo. At one time, one could travel from New York to Scranton, Pennsylvania, directly by five railroads and somewhat circuitously by at least two more. The idea was to exploit the coal fields, particularly the then widely used anthracite. But even in the nineteenth century, this proved too much. The New York, Susquehanna & Western only lasted a short while, and the New York, Ontario & Western was a chronic money loser until the early 1950s. It then became the largest single abandonment in the history of New York State.

New York State, in fact, provides a typical illustration of the problem although it is not often cited in discussions of this problem. *Trains* has presented some maps which indicate that in the upstate area between Rochester and Buffalo and further south, a dense network of lines existed, but that abandonments had since reduced it by one-half to about where it was in 1870. Many of the lines survived until Conrail was formed in the spring of 1976 out of the wreckage of the Erie Lackawanna and the Penn Central.[5] The trail of mismanagement that led to the formation and demise of the latter has been well documented.[6]

Turning now to another major example—that of the Milwaukee Road—it was one of the so-called Granger lines, serving the grain-growing Middle West with the original objective that nowhere would it take a farmer more than a day's journey by farm cart to reach a railhead. That area was also one of the first where duplication became evident with the result that an attempt was made as early as 1870 to pool traffic and save money. The Chicago Northwestern, the Rock Island, and the Chicago, Burlington and Quincy Railroads pooled and divided the traffic between Council Bluffs-Omaha and Chicago among themselves. This, however, left two other carriers, the Milwaukee and the Chicago Great Western, out in the cold. Other pooling arrangements gradually had the appearance of trusts, and it was in response to these budding monopolies that the Interstate Commerce Act was passed in 1887, which made pooling illegal. This left matters in a somewhat chaotic state for a while although there was then plenty of traffic for the majority of lines; some, however, were weak from the start.

The Milwaukee then decided in 1905 to build an extension to Seattle. This helped make it into a transcontinental system that even in 1946 still had over 10,000 route miles.[7] Successive abandonments and consolidations, accomplished or in prospect, are likely to reduce the system to 2,900 route-miles. Among the lines dismantled was the one to Council Bluffs—Omaha which for a time carried the transcontinental passenger trains that continued west on the Union Pacific. Another casualty was the Pacific Coast extension which had been noted in its heyday for being partly electrified, using hydroelectric power. It was the only such line in the United States, although this method of working is by now general throughout Europe, the Soviet Union, Japan, and elsewhere. The Rock Island also became a casualty and much of it was closed. Its erstwhile main line to the Southwest, interchanging with the Southern Pacific at Tucumcari, New Mexico, was, however, upgraded and serves as a major traffic link.

The most acute current problem is that posed by abandonments. This problem also has been extensively studied. Allen[8] states that there is first a major increase in transportation costs by shippers and receivers dealing in large bulk items, including crops, coal, and so on. If another railroad still serves the community and connections can be established (not always easy or economic), these problems can of course be avoided.

Second, users generally must invest in other means of transportation like trucks, terminals, and so on. Third, it may cause companies to move away from a community that can no longer offer them rail service. However, that effect was somewhat obscured by a general trend toward national economic growth at the time of Allen's study. At any rate, the burden did not turn out to be statistically significant. One final point, however, is that abandoned railroad land, taken off the tax rolls, causes a tax loss that must be made up by other taxpayers, and in some areas this has been shown to be quite substantial (see chapter 2). On the other hand, however, a bankrupt business, such as many of the railroads would have become, does not pay taxes either. Due[9] proposes certain criteria for abandonments, based on traffic density, and finds that in actual practice not all abandonments have followed consistent criteria; that is, sometimes busy lines were abandoned and less busy ones kept.

It may at first appear that pruning back the network would be a way towards solvency. It is to some extent, but there are certain problems with this approach that may create social costs of their own in addition to the effects on the communities discussed above. One major problem concerns the emergence of two kinds of railroad operations that seem to be becoming increasingly incompatible with each other. On the one hand, without faster service the railroads will not be able to compete in certain parts of the freight business and in any passenger service, and on the other, there still is the practice of railroads gathering together enormously long trains which are then run at very slow speeds. Track, even where it is in good shape, is now constructed predominantly to accommodate such traffic. Furthermore, at a time when capital investments in railroads are totally inadequate, substantial sums are still spent on railyards for the obvious reason that long trains have to be shuffled and reshuffled many times before the different cars reach their destinations.

On the other hand, there have to be fast and frequent trains both for passengers and the kinds of freight traffic for which trucks are now practically the only way, and this means short trains with minimal switching.

But slow freight traffic is incompatible with fast service. In several of the speedways now being constructed in Europe and elsewhere (except, of course, in the United States) freight is handled by older lines that run parallel to the new ones, as in the TGV line from Paris to Lyon, the new line from Rome to Florence, and, of course, the Shinkansen in Japan. Yes, there is the Northeast corridor, but that is hardly in the same league. Some awareness of this incompatibility is brought out by L. Stanley Crane, president of Conrail,[10] who wishes a complete divorce from the passenger-carrying Northeast corridor (that is, the old Pennsylvania-New Haven line from Washington to Boston).

At the same time, however, Mr. Crane talks about cutting back part of the duplications of track. But here he is not alone. Portions of the main lines of the Gulf, Mobile & Ohio,[11] Chicago Northwestern, Illinois Central,[12] Illinois Terminal, Lehigh Valley, and Western Maryland, to name a few, are gone, with traffic going over the lines of erstwhile merger partners.

There are now two choices: one is to operate the whole system fast, with frequent trains and high density on roadbeds designed accordingly and electrified for preference. That would be the best way. Alternatively, one could recognize that fast passenger service and slow freight cannot easily use the same trackage, and make sustained use of the alternate routings that now still exist in many parts of the country. But this means preservation of all that trackage and not the new crop of abandonments.

The construction of rail speedways on the European or Japanese model appears out of the question at this time in the United States, but history suggests that one would be foolhardy indeed to dispose of rights of way that might someday be suitable for it. One particular reason for going slowly on abandonments, especially of the above kind, is the possibility of some day

constructing a basic electrified network that would save enormous energy if
the electricity it required were obtained from such now wasted resources as
cogeneration and if public policy were formulated so as to divert substantial
truck freight to the roads.[13] It can be shown that such a system could eliminate most oil imports, at least all those now derived from middle eastern
sources. Given the antirailroad orientation and middle eastern policies of the
Reagan administration, this does not appear very likely, but circumstances
may change. Late in 1980, two similar plans to the one proposed above by the
editor of this volume were put forth by the Department of Energy and the
Federal Railroad Administration but were quickly shelved at the end of the
Carter administration.

Coal Transportation

Some issues associated in part with railroads have surfaced in connection
with the greatly increased exploitation of coal. They raise issues of duplication
of capital facilities in rather clear form. First, western coal, notably in
Wyoming, is generally expected to create a boom, and this has already led to
the construction of several quite long (up to 400 miles) new lines. It has led to
proposals for the electrification of parts of the Burlington Northern Railroad
whose right-of-way runs, as noted before, next to the late electrified parts of
the Milwaukee. Conditions of lease of public lands would require an actual
mining start within ten years.[14] This would lead to precisely the kind of premature exploitation of resources with all their inefficiencies that Kapp mentioned as one of the consequences of certain mining techniques and which was
reviewed in chapter 4. As for transportation itself, the proposal has been made
to use coal slurry pipelines in which granulated coal would be transported in
water. However, the railroads will not grant rights of way to the pipelines
because they would be competitive and would also, surely, be yet another
case of duplication, given that the railroads now have ample capacity. The
environmental impact of using large quantities of water in the arid West also
has come in for criticism. A bill to grant federal eminent domain for the slurry
pipelines has been repeatedly introduced in Congress but has been blocked.

Finally, the shipment of coal, especially overseas, has brought about a boom
in coal shipping facilities. As White reports, total investment in new coal
terminals could reach $4 billion; forty-five new terminals are being built or
planned at twenty-nine harbors on the Atlantic, Pacific, and Gulf coasts. If
they are all completed, coal loading capacity will be more than 625 million
tons per year. This is much more even than an estimate of 250 million tons
shipped in the year 2000, an estimate by the Department of Energy that is

generally considered overoptimistic. Even that would require an export increased to 3.4 times the current level.[15] It is generally assumed that not all of these terminals will be built, but in the meantime the situation is reminiscent of the railroad mania of old.

Airlines

Airlines have experienced quite similar situations in which there was not merely a sustained proliferation of airlines serving similar areas, but in which the medium, with its publicly sponsored airports and traffic control systems, was particularly suitable. After years of regulated routes and fares, the Airline Deregulation Act of 1978 made it easy for airlines to fly between any destinations they chose. The result was somewhat predictable. Many new airlines sprung up, like People Express and Air Florida; others, like World Airways and Capitol, went from being charter operators to scheduled airlines, and yet a third group consisted of regional, intrastate airlines that went national or in some cases international.

While airlines have a lower fixed-cost ratio than railroads do, their fixed costs are still considerable. There still remains a large investment in aircraft and in their maintenance facilities even though there has always been some sharing. In one airport, New York's Kennedy, the airlines actually repeated the inconvenient practice of railroads in the old days of each having their own terminal, which, for example, had left Chicago with six mainline railroad stations and three suburban ones. Over the years, the owners of the large New York air terminals had to take in boarders so that clusters of them now inhabit each one. However, it makes it difficult for travelers who have to change between one terminal and another. A single building, preferably with a passenger transportation system, would have made matters much more convenient.

Competition, especially with respect to loss-leader fares to certain popular destinations, has since then made life difficult for the airlines, leading to cutbacks, sales of equipment, and outright liquidation as with Braniff Airlines. Essentially, they now operate on a two-tier system. The large ones are able to spread their costs over more aircraft. The smaller ones compensate for their inherent diseconomy of scale by having nonunion employees and paying them about half of what the majors pay. Even that apparently has led to widespread losses and to at least one demand from one of the successful newcomers for amendment of the Deregulation Act and restoration of price setting.[16] This, however, would have to include the removal of some of the newcomers from some of their markets, in order to be meaningful. Meanwhile, confusion with respect to fares is general. The famous travel agency of Thos. Cook & Son notes in its advertising that, better than anyone else, it can help its customers sort out the current confusion in fares.

Real Estate

Duplication in real estate and related infrastructure presents the same kinds of social inefficiencies discussed above. There are three major areas of interest; the first is the migration from the cities, which has brought about suburbanization and rural development in the older metropolitan areas but particularly in the sunbelt, that is, essentially the states along the southern border of the United States. As more economic activity and residents left the city, the city found itself in increasing economic and social difficulties. The social costs of slums are discussed in chapter 9. As far as duplication of capital facilities is concerned, the issue is not, in any event, merely the housing stock or the state of industrial property. Rather, such existing infrastructures as roads, sewers, water, and other utilities were often put in place at low cost long ago, but if they are now duplicated at new locations, they are enormously more costly. While in many places extensive renovation is often required in both real property and services, these can almost always be provided at very much lower cost than starting completely anew.[17] Moreover, the maintenance of an overexpanded infrastructure soon comes to exceed the resources of society. The generally observable deterioration of roads, bridges, transportation facilities, sanitary, and water supply systems makes that point with rather unpleasant clarity.

Studies of social costs and other effects of real estate developers naturally enough reflect the viewpoint of those who made them. A business executive may have one purpose, a governmental official another, an individual home buyer still another. The social costs brought about through duplication of capital facilities come from the deterioration of apartment buildings, homes, factories, and community facilities in the city which then become prime examples of unused capital assets. The people and businesses that once occupied these buildings are now located somewhere else, thus duplicating business and residential dwellings. Also included in this duplication are buildings that may not have deteriorated at all. For example, factories that have moved from the cities may be considered part of the duplication if the original factory has not been rerented or put to some other use. Many corporations have moved their corporate headquarters out of central cities into the suburbs and more recently to the sunbelt. Cities are building up an excess of unrented and deteriorating buildings, factories, and other facilities that are being duplicated in outlying regions with newer facilities. Cities such as New

York are losing companies to surrounding states and the sunbelt (see below), and the ultimate results of this are social costs. Loss of business means a loss of revenues to the city in the form of business and real estate taxes. The city must either increase the tax rate of the public and business or reduce services. Either alternative can be translated into social costs to be absorbed by the public.

Most executives say that the reason for the move out of the city is in large part due to the company's desire to locate in an area that is less stressful. One reason for the stress in the old atmosphere was that the neighborhoods were becoming an unpleasant part of town. Decline of the city is by far the most important reason so many corporations have moved their headquarters since the early 1960s. It appears that this trend of movement out of the city is continuing and if cities cannot attract new companies, the results will be more and more of a burden being placed on their citizens and eventually on everyone.

Turning now to the sunbelt migration, it became clear very early that this too would result in extensive duplication of facilities. Moreover, particularly due to pervasive shortages of water, the move also is likely to have extremely deleterious environmental results.[18] These are points that have been made extensively before, but what has escaped attention somewhat is that some portions of the sunbelt have already been overbuilt and that the results again were widespread losses and the inefficient use of capital that might have been more fruitfully employed in other ways.

One of the prime examples of overbuilding in the sunbelt states involves Atlanta, Georgia, Late in 1976 the real estate market in Atlanta was one of the worst in the United States, after more than a decade of stunning growth. The recession of 1974 cut deeper into Atlanta than into many other cities and Atlanta has never recovered.[19]

Throughout the 1960s, business surged into metropolitan Atlanta, as it did to the rest of the Southeast, sparking a boom that transformed the city's downtown skyline (thirty-six new buildings between 1960 and 1970), spawned condominiums everywhere, and filled up the suburbs with large and small office parks (at least eighty), shopping centers, and housing developments. It also provided a rich investment field for the money-center banks, insurance companies, and real estate investment trusts and resulted in an over-eagerness to produce. Developers came in and built without having tenants and no marketing studies were made. "Atlanta is booming, Atlanta is booming, Atlanta is booming." That, according to Ralph O. Hutchinson, a real estate specialist and president of Stonehenge Cos., was often the extent of marketing research by money-center financial institutions before they poured hundreds of millions of dollars into Atlanta's phenomenal building boom in the early 1970s. Atlanta never anticipated decline, but rather continued to erect buildings and assume the demand would always be there.

The influx of companies from outside the area created an Atlanta economy dependent on real estate development, housing, and other construction. When this business flood dwindled to a trickle several years ago, the local economy went into a tailspin. The real estate market collapsed, and, as one banker said, "For the first time in over a decade, we had people leaving Atlanta to find jobs."[20]

Thus, Atlanta is faced with the problems brought about by overbuilding which has resulted in duplication of capital facilities in the form of vacant office buildings, shopping centers, and houses. It was estimated that 20 percent of downtown office space and 30 percent of suburban office space remained unrented through 1976 and these statistics have not fluctuated significantly since then. One strategy being used by real estate agents is to try to lease short-term space under the best terms available and then renegotiate the lease in a few years assuming that the economy of Atlanta would improve.

A similar situation occurred in a state long notorious for its boom and bust cycles in real estate. It was overcommitment in the metropolitan areas of Florida that led to a particularly heavy impact there during the 1975-1976 recession. The Florida peninsula was growing rapidly but too many investors oversaturated the market. The result was considerable economic waste.

One method of financing much of the new expansion consisted of real estate investment trusts (REITs). They flourished in the early 1970s and became a crucial source of easy, albeit expensive, money for real estate developments. Many of them eventually collapsed and thus gave confirmation of the kind of instability to which duplication may lead. They were essentially closed-end investment trusts with major investments in real estate and mortgages. Critical examination of their portfolios disclosed that a good many of them were again betting on very intensive development of areas that had not so far experienced it. In other words, they much resembled the early railroad promotions. By 1976, the leverage which was to be their great advantage had turned against them, as interest rates rose and the doubtful nature of the portfolio items made itself forcefully clear. By 1977, except for a few trusts concentrating on good equities and long-term mortgages, they were engaged in a day-to-day struggle to avoid bankruptcy.

While this method of financing has not had a resurgence in the last few years, overbuilding in many areas continues, again notably in such sunbelt cities as Los Angeles, Dallas, and Houston, but also in New York and Chicago. In New York leasing commitments in the new buildings appear to be somewhat more readily marketable than in some of the others, but some real estate industry executives are worried that "a financial blood bath may be in the making that would overshadow the bankruptcies that ended the last boom in the mid-70s."[21] What has alarmed planners and critics about the latest real estate boom in New York is that it has taken place in the exact same overbuilt areas as the previous ones. For a time, it was more or less axiomatic that any further development in Manhattan should move toward the so-called Valley, the area between the midtown and downtown aggregations of skyscrapers, that is, 30th and Canal streets. This did not happen, however. Crowding even on sidewalks, congestion, noise, and pollution have reached levels that stretch to the utmost the vaunted ability of New Yorkers to put up with urban discomfort.[22]

Finally, there is the matter of shopping centers. These too have proliferated enormously. There are about 23,300 shopping centers of 10,000 feet or more in practically all urban and suburban areas of the United States and Canada.[23] However, here too overbuilding has given the situation in some areas an almost kaleidoscopic quality, as the various centers rise and fall, often in line with the fortunes of their principal tenants, or perhaps a game of musical chairs as property changes hands among tenants. Long Island provides a particularly good example of that kind of change. The bankruptcy of several retail chains like Korvette's, Mays Department Stores, Klein's, Great Eastern, Two Guys, and, in 1983, the closing of Woolco, led to major difficulties as all kinds of surplus commercial real estate constantly came on the market. In a manifestation of corporate *hubris*, tenants would then take over the vacated property in the belief that they could succeed where others had failed, at the same location and with the same kind of merchandise. Not surprisingly, it proved impossible to absorb this kind of business strategy, if one can call it that, and so a number of shopping centers have remained virtually derelict. In at least one case (Levittown), the affected area was to be the principal retailing hub of the community as originally planned. However, other areas rivaled it and eventually displaced it as a viable facility.

The last word on suburban and regional shopping centers and similar facilities should perhaps belong to the architect Victor Gruen who is generally credited with originating the idea. His proposal, however, was for nodes of shops, offices, and cultural activities, all located near housing rather than the often remote "merchandising machines" which shopping centers, especially the regional ones, have become. "I refuse to pay alimony for those bastard developments," Gruen was quoted as saying.[24] Even when other community facilities were built, he says, they were separated by roads and huge asphalt parking lots creating a nonwalkable, inhumane environment.

Most recently shopping centers and similar developments have encountered increasing opposition at the local zoning level, and some projects have been derailed as a result. However, a great deal of wasteful practice still continues.

Conclusion

In many of the examples cited in this chapter what is actually being described is the failure of what was made as a commercial investment. One could perhaps take the view that everyone has the right to go broke in his or her own way. However, the misuse of national resources, particularly of capital at a time when it has been generally in short supply and very costly, presents a problem of social efficiency that transcends that kind of toleration. Unfortunately, once elaborately duplicated facilities have been built, it is not easy to reverse the situation. In particular, even disinvestment of one sort or another carries costs, and may foreclose possible other social advantages, as indicated particularly by the example of the railroads. In other cases, as with cities, an existing infrastructure could be rehabilitated and used profitably at a fraction of the cost that duplication now engenders.

In the last analysis, all excess capacity puts a social cost on the public. Some of it is certainly unavoidable, given the generally poor record of human clairvoyance and the inevitably fluctuating or cyclical demand for many goods and services. That kind of misjudgment is endemic to most of human activity. However, the examples chosen here—transportation systems and real estate—should by nature lend themselves to far better planning than they have by and large received in the past. The preemption of scarce capital resources and a variety of other social dislocations have been the result. Social costs were an important addition to the losses suffered by the misguided investors.

Notes

1. K. W. Kapp, *Social Costs of Business Enterprise* (Nottingham, England: Spokesman-B. Russell Foundation, 1978), p. 218.

2. Ibid., pp. 205-7.

3. E. Sax, *Die Verkehrsmittel in Volks und Staatswirtschaft*, vol. I (Berlin: Springer, 1922), p. 139. Translated in Kapp, *Social Costs*.

4. *Social Costs*, p. 209.

5. R. B. Shaw, "A Case of Railway Mania," *Trains*, May 1978, pp. 22-27; for the total mileage, see D. P. Morgan, "How Many Class I's?" *Trains*, February 1982, p. 3.

6. For example, J. R. Daughen and P. Binzen, *The Wreck of the Penn Central* (New York: Mentor, 1971); R. Sobel, *The Fallen Colossus* (New York: Weybright & Talley, 1977).

7. J. D. Ingles, "Where Did the Milwaukee Go?" *Trains*, February 1982, pp. 49-51.

8. B. J. Allen, "The Economic Effects of Rail Abandonments on Communities: A Case Study," *Transportation Journal*, Fall 1975, pp. 52-61.

9. J. F. Due, "Factors Affecting the Abandonment and Survival of Class II Railroads," *Transportation Journal*, Spring 1977, pp. 19-36; Due is also coauthor of the authoritative study of interurban railroads, a network of electric lines with some 50,000 route-miles at their peak, that disappeared entirely. See G. W. Hilton and J. F. Due, *The Electric Interurban Railroads in America* (Stanford, Calif.: Stanford University Press, 1960).

10. News item, *Trains*, July 1981, p. 10.

11. News item, *Trains*, September 1981, pp. 12, 40.

12. News item, *Trains*, May 1981, p. 13.

13. J. E. Ullmann, "The I.D.E.R.," *Trains*, April 1980, p. 66.

14. "A Coal-Lease Auction Has Industry Fired Up," *Business Week*, March 22, 1982, p. 26.

15. D. W. White, "The Coal-Export Gamble," *Fortune*, December 14, 1981, p. 122.

16. E. Holsendolph, "Low-Cost Airline Now Seeks Fare Curbs It Once Opposed," *New York Times*, March 10, 1982; "Airline Woes Catch Up with Delta," *Business Week*, November 8, 1982, p. 131; "Six Airlines: Gaining a Bit of Altitude," *Business Week*, November 15, 1982, p. 68.

17. J. E. Ullmann, ed., *The Suburban Economic Network* (New York: Praeger, 1977). See especially chs. 1, 8, and 13.

18. Ibid.

19. "Atlanta's Building Boom Overshoots Its Mark," *Business Week*, December 13, 1976, p. 92.

20. "Atlanta's Worst Flop in Real Estate Yet," *Business Week*, February 27, 1978, p. 33.

21. "An Office-Space Boom Screeches to a Halt," *Business Week*, March 22, 1982, p. 25.

22. P. Goldberger, "The Limits of Urban Growth," *New York Times Magazine*," November 14, 1982, p. 46.

23. Unpublished survey by *Shopping Center World*, December 1982.

24. Quoted in N. Pierce, "Where Did the Shopping Mall Go Wrong?" *Newsday*, December 5, 1978.

11
The Social Costs of Drugs

DOUGLAS E. CASTLE

Oh God! That men should put an enemy
in their mouths to steal their brains!

Shakespeare, *Othello*

Introduction

Drug abuse is most obviously associated with narcotics and related substances,
the use of which is illegal altogether or sharply restricted. However, all prescription drugs and indeed every substance that claims some benefit to health
is subject to a very extensive system of control which in turn is part of public
expenditures and thus a social cost. Narcotics and related substances have
become so prevalent and are so enormous a problem that the work load of
sizable government departments primarily concentrates on their management.
The illegal trade in drugs does not, of course, meet any significant portion of
these costs, other than by what is seized in raids or paid in fines. The net costs
to society, as will be seen, are therefore most substantial.

One difficulty lies in the fact that some forms of addiction, whether physio-
logical or psychological, involve chemicals not otherwise readily identified as
"drugs" in the popular sense, such as airplane glue. Such versatility increases
both the social costs and the control problem.[1] Also, some drug combinations
have effects that may be described as greater than the sum of their parts and
this may present yet more public health and control problems.

This chapter defines the diverse ramifications of drug control, which stretch
from the local police to a large licensing bureaucracy to international negotia-
tions and diplomacy at the highest level. There is a long history of such control efforts[2] and, by and large, their costs have grown very much faster than
their effectiveness. The costs will be held to the fore in what follows. The

structure of control, however, is quite complex and part of the cost problem in itself involves understanding of the complex intragovernmental transfer of the tax dollars.[3] The particular problems of alcohol and tobacco are considered in relation to agricultural products in chapter 13.

Government expenditures on the drug problem are drawn from tax funds that are collected at the federal, state, and local levels. Actually, most drug-related projects are paid for by direct outlays from the federal government, but they are occasionally supplemented by funds from local sources. Thus, a potential double-counting of funds exists.[4]

A Classification of Social Costs

The social costs of drugs are the costs borne by each member of society without regard to the individual's associated benefits from the use of drugs or governmental regulation. What should be the costs of drug producers and users have become costs of all society. One example is the cost to the taxpaying population of maintaining half-way houses, hospitals, and antiaddiction centers, enforcement, and education, programs for the benefit of a disproportionately small number of narcotics addicts and potential abusers of illegal drugs. Another example is the costliness of various drug testing and certifying programs by the Food and Drug Administration so that harmful or ineffective drugs are kept off the market.[5] A further element is the opportunity cost in economic contributions by those members of society whose performance is inhibited or destroyed by their addictions. This set of costs resembles the social costs of unemployment (chapter 7), and the problems of measuring them are quite complex.

In situations similar to this one there is an element of choice; either society must pay the necessary cost for drug regulation and enforcement or it must be prepared to face the potentially greater costs associated with letting dangerous drugs circulate unchecked. Since no control can be absolute, the choice is resolved in the form of partial control, with a considerable added burden of social costs from the drugs that do circulate.

The costs of regulation and enforcement are difficult to measure, while the costs of ignoring the issue are only tenuously defined, far reaching, and virtually immeasurable in terms of dollars and cents. A more detailed summary appears below.

1. Cost components of drug-related problems:

   a. Medical costs to treat victims of improperly prepared, inspected, or tested drugs; foregone services of victims; foregone wages of victims; higher risks and, consequently, higher medical and casualty insurance rates for all individuals to reflect this increased risk; indeterminate risks to future generations. These costs are borne by users and, ultimately, by society.

b. The health-related costs of overusing certain drugs, mixing systemically incompatible drugs; purchasing or relying upon useless or unnecessary prescription drugs. There are also health-related costs from using dispensed drugs after their expiration dates as well as prescriptions which have been improperly stored. The costs are borne by users and, ultimately, by society.

c. The increased cost of health insurance for all insured individuals. This cost increase is geared to increases in the price of drugs as well as to the steady increase in the use of drugs by many individuals, insured as well as uninsured.

d. The increased cost of institutional medical care through cost-push inflation and through shifting of drug costs incurred by medical facilities to patients or insurance companies.

e. The costs of unintended addiction (physical or psychological) to tranquilizers like Valium, stimulants, amphetamines, or other drugs with ostensible therapeutic benefits. All such costs are hazardous side effects of prescription medications.

f. The additional shifting (from drug manufacturer to consumer) of liability insurance costs through higher pharmaceutical prices and, ultimately, more expensive health care insurance.

2. Costs associated with abuses of controlled substances and narcotics:

a. Loss of productive contribution to society in general by users of these drugs.

b. Costs to society generated by "negative output" of addicts, that is, crimes of violence and vagrancy, thefts, and so forth.

c. Inestimable costs to the population at large affecting the quality of life of every individual in the society.

This listing of costs is by no means complete. However, the difficulty encountered in assessing these costs qualitatively is small compared with the problems encountered in actually tabulating these costs.[6]

Some of the above costs can be reasonably estimated, some cannot be estimated at all, and still others are inextricably interwoven with other social costs. Rather than attempting to quantify all of them, it is somewhat more practical to quantify the costs actually incurred for the intended purpose of curbing the drug problem. From the standpoint of classical economics this makes sense. Society will pay for regulatory and preventive services to the extent that the marginal costs of regulation and prevention are equal to the marginal cost of the disease, where the "disease" in this case refers to any and all drug-induced threats to the welfare of society.[7] The cost of prevention, a public service, would then be roughly equivalent to the sum total of all federal government expenditures on drug-related problems.[8] These expenditures represent a reallocation of individual income to be applied in the best interests of the public at large. Every dollar of tax liability incurred by an individual can be said to represent foregone personal expenditures on consumption, savings, or investment. Clearly, the tax-paying public comprises individuals who are willing to forego certain personal expenditures to avoid some of the costs of drug-related problems.

Alternatively, the level of expenditures may be simply viewed as the maximum that is currently feasible politically. This obviates the rather dubious necessity of imputing public rationality in carefully examining marginal costs and benefits, as would be required by the classical model.

Federal Administrative Structure and Function

The federal government spends funds either directly or indirectly through different programs and departments. What follows is a brief outline of each of the relevant agencies, departments, or their subdivisions and their respective functions. Drug problems are, of course, a major part of the federal law enforcement function, that is, the FBI, Secret Service, and so on, as discussed later. Other special agencies are:

> *The Office of Drug Abuse Policy*—This office was established in 1976. It serves to advise the president with respect to federal drug abuse programs; it serves as a coordinating nucleus for all of the federal drug programs. Funding and supervision of this office occur directly under the auspices of the Executive Office of the President.
>
> *The Alcohol, Drug Abuse, and Mental Health Administration* (ADAMHA) is part of the Department of Health and Human Services (DHHS). Though the National Institute on Drug Abuse (a subdivision of the ADAMHA) is charged with determining and instituting national policy as well as establishing funding and distribution of resources to drug-abuse prevention and treatment programs at all government levels, other subdivisions within the ADAMHA also get involved in cosponsoring programs. In making a cost tabulation, this would present potential allocation problems in instances where one

division's expenditures represent, in part, transfers of funds to another division.

The Food and Drug Administration (FDA) is a part of DHHS. Within the FDA are the *Bureau of Drugs*, the *Bureau of Biologics*, and the *National Center for Toxicological Research*. The Bureau of Drugs, while not directly involved in controlling drug abuse, is the FDA policymaking body with regard to the safety, effectiveness, and labeling of all drugs for human use. It evaluates new drug applications, conducts tests for over-the-counter drugs, and monitors licensing and compliance of drug-manufacturing firms and practices in conformity with FDA standards. The Bureau of Biologics and the Center for Toxicological Research play similar and complementary roles, each in its respective specialty, and there is a large area of overlap between these three entities.

The *Drug Enforcement Agency* acts in the coordination of legislation, enforcement, and trial of individuals and organizations who are in violation of the drug laws or who represent a material danger to the public safety.[9]

A list of the other governmental agencies that in some way are or have been employed in the treatment of drug problems and the prevention of further drug problems is presented here:[10]

Bureau of Customs
Internal Revenue Service
Department of State
National Institute of Mental Health
Office of Economic Opportunity
Social and Rehabilitation Service
Department of Defense
Veterans Administration
Bureau of Prisons
Department of Labor
Department of Housing and Urban Development
Office of Education
Law Enforcement Assistance Administration
Department of Agriculture
Department of Transportation
National Commission on Marihuana and Drug Abuse
Special Action Office

Of the government organizations listed above, most have transient roles in overall drug policy and problems, while the others work in conjunction, through common funding, with larger or more completely involved agencies of the government.[11] Only the more readily traceable agencies and their corresponding expenditures will enter into the annual tabulation figures presented below.

Any government expenditures that are paid for directly by manufacturers of pharmaceutical products in lieu of payment through public tax receipts are eliminated from the tabulation; for example, the FDA certifies batches of certain drugs, such as insulin, prior to their release for sale. This service, as well as certain licensing services, are paid for directly by the manufacturer of the product.[12]

All this does not take into account the costs of law enforcement at state local levels and the upkeep of addicts and pushers in prisons. Some of law enforcement involves an extensive administrative burden that goes much beyond conventional police work. For instance, there is the matter of diversion of controlled, addictive substances as the result of falsified business records in hospitals and pharmaceutical firms which is often done illegally by individuals or groups of employees without knowledge of management. Perhaps of even more importance is the "overwriting" of prescriptions by doctors; "writing scrip" by cooperative doctors has long been a source of drugs that also fulfill pharmaceutical functions. Morphium addiction, which was once important but is now somewhat out of fashion, traditionally relied on that source. Amphetamines, sleeping pills, quaaludes, "uppers," and "downers" of all kinds are current favorites.

In New York State, each prescription is supposed to be in triplicate, one each for the doctor and pharmacist, and the third to a computer in the Division of Food and Drug Protection of the State Department of Health. The volume handled is very large and, except for really gross cases, it has not proved possible to discipline too many doctors; even cases of administrative prosecution may last for years. The legal provision that doctors may write only one refillable prescription per person per month for each controlled drug is circumvented by using false names.[13]

In their 1971 study, DeLong and Goldberg estimated a surcharge of 15 to 20 percent applied to federal expenditure statistics to account for these additional social costs.[14] However, this may now be a considerable underestimate; 25 percent may be more accurate.

Table 11.1 presents annual drug-related budgeted expenditures by the federal government from 1964 to 1983. Expenditure figures are based upon congressional appropriations for various agency functions whether or not the funds were actually expended in the year of appropriation. Annual figures for

Table 11.1
U.S. Government Expenditures: Drug-Related

Agency	1964	1965	1966	1967
		$ Million		
HEW: FDA				
1. Medical evaluation	3.2	4.4	6.5	9.8
2. Research	4.8	5.3	—	—
3. Research and evaluation	—	—	8.7	11.4
4. Scientific evaluation	2.0	2.5	—	—
5. Education and voluntary compliance	1.1	1.1	0.9	1.3
6. Executive direction and technical support	3.2	3.8	3.9	6.2
7. Regulatory compliance	20.0	23.1	24.5	26.7
8. Drug abuse control	—	—	1.0	5.2
Budget Grand Totals	34.3	40.2	45.5	60.6

	1968	1969	1970	1971
		$ Million		
HEW: FDA				
1. Medical evaluation				
a. Grants	0.9	—	—	—
b. Direct operations	18.6	—	—	—
2. Scientific research and evaluation	15.3	—	—	—
3. Education and voluntary compliance	1.4	—	—	—
4. Regulatory compliance	28.2	—	—	—
5. Program administration	4.9	6.6	5.0	6.9
6. Drugs and devices	—	29.3	30.5	36.2
7. Product safety	—	1.8	3.8	5.9
Total budget	69.3	37.7	39.3	49.0
Department of Justice:				
Bureau of Narcotics and Dangerous Drugs				
1. Law enforcement	11.9	14.8	22.0	33.9
2. State and local assistance	—	0.2	0.9	2.1
3. Drug abuse prevention	0.6	1.2	1.2	—
4. General administration	1.3	2.0	3.4	6.6
Total budget	13.8	18.2	27.5	42.6

Table 11.1 (*continued*)

	1968	1969	1970	1971
		$ Million		

National Commission on Marihuana and Drug Abuse:

	1968	1969	1970	1971
1. Study of marihuana and causes of drug abuse	—	—	—	0.1
Budget Grand Totals	83.1	55.9	66.8	91.7

	1972	1973	1974	1975
		$ Million		

HEW: FDA

	1972	1973	1974	1975
1. Drugs and devices	39.9	59.1	62.5	77.8
2. Product safety	6.0	—	—	—
3. Management and administration	6.9	10.7	11.5	24.2
Total Budget	52.8	69.8	74.0	102.0

Health Services and Mental Health Administration

	1972	1973	1974	1975
1. Drug abuse	101.0	147.8	190.1	268.0
2. Program direction	7.9	9.1	13.2	15.4
Total Budget	108.9	156.9	203.3	283.4

Department of Justice: Bureau of Narcotics and Dangerous Drugs

	1972	1973	1974	1975
1. Law enforcement	51.5	—	—	—
2. State and local assistance	2.4	—	—	—
3. General administration	9.6	—	—	—
Total Budget	63.5			

Executive Office of the President: Special Action Office for Drug Abuse Prevention

	1972	1973	1974	1975
1. Administration and coordination	1.3	4.5	27.3	12.5

Table 11.1 (*continued*)

	1972	1973	1974	1975
		$ Million		
National Commission on Marihuana and Drug Abuse				
1. Study of marihuana and the causes of drug abuse	1.3	—	—	—
ADAMHA: Lexington Clinical Research Center, Kentucky				
1. Operating fund	—	0.4	0.3	0.3
Department of Justice: Drug Enforcement Administration (DEA)				
1. Law enforcement	—	72.0	99.8	136.7
2. Research and development	—	1.7	2.4	3.4
3. Program administration	—	0.2	0.3	0.4
Total Budget	—	73.9	102.5	140.5
Budget Grand Totals	227.8	305.4	407.4	538.8

	1976	1977	1978	1979
		$ Million		
HEW: FDA				
1. Drugs and devices	83.3	108.5	119.4	140.1
2. Program direction	29.4	30.3	36.0	39.9
Total Budget	112.7	138.8	155.4	180.0
ADAMHA				
1. Drug abuse	222.4	244.0	250.1	272.0
2. General funds	1.2	1.2	0.3	—
3. Lexington Addiction Center	0.4	0.4	0.4	—
4. Management and direction	14.8	15.5	—	—
Total Budget	238.8	261.1	250.8	272.0

Table 11.1 *(continued)*

| | 1976 | 1977 | 1978 | 1979 |
			$ Million	
Department of Justice: DEA				
1. Law enforcement	135.2	161.5	179.9	197.2
2. Research and development	0.3	6.6	3.3	—
3. Executive direction	0.4	0.4	0.4	—
Total Budget	135.9	168.5	183.6	197.2
Budget Grand Totals	487.4	568.4	589.8	649.2

| | 1980 | 1981 | 1982 | 1983 |
			$ Million	
FDA				
1. Drugs and development	146.2	153.9	147.7	160.9
2. Program management	41.9	46.3	44.8	46.3
Total Budget	188.1	200.2	192.5	207.2
ADAMHA				
1. Drug abuse	238.6	297.3	57.8	60.3
Department of Justice: DEA				
1. Law enforcement (direct program)	195.1	214.6	232.4	246.9
2. Drug grants	—	6.3	5.7	—
Total Budget	195.1	220.9	238.1	246.9
Budget Grant Totals	621.8	718.4	488.4	514.4

Source: Office of Management and Budget, *Budget of the United States Government* (Washington, D.C.: Government Printing Office, 1966–1983), appendix.

1982 and 1983 are not actual budgetary amounts, but are based on appropriations and expected appropriations.

Budgeted appropriations for the years 1964–1967 were relatively low and were exclusively channeled through the FDA. For years beyond 1964, appropriations increased annually and grew in terms of complexity of distribution. Comparative statistics reflect increased budgetary activity in the federal government's drug-related accounts. Unfortunately, certain items are not available on a consistent year-to-year basis, so that overall trends cannot be determined in detail.

Nevertheless, government expenditures in drug-related areas have increased dramatically. Drug-related expenditures in 1978 are estimated to be 16.1 times as great as in fiscal 1964 and have increased in every intervening year. This increase, of course, greatly outran inflation in those years and thus represents a large increase in physical effort as well. There is, of course, the usual effect of budgetary inertia, but this is hardly unique to this field.[15] If, as proposed above, a 15-percent surcharge for added state and local expenditures is included at the beginning of the period, rising to 25 percent at the end, the increase factor rises from 16.1 to 17.5 times.

The last portion of the table, covering fiscal year 1980 and concluding with the budget estimate for 1983 shows that even drug-related programs have not escaped the decimation of social expenditures under the Reagan administration The expenses budgeted for 1983 are only 71.6 percent of the actual ones in 1981. The major drop comes in ADAMHA programs. Presumably, funds for such purposes may be expected to come from increases in block grants to states and localities, but those two are also expected to diminish. Unless, therefore, a substantial extra tax burden is added at the state and local level, the governmental activities in drug control will be sharply curtailed. What the consequences will be cannot be predicted. As in so many other instances in this volume, the treatment of a problem costs money and in this case is a social cost, but the really large social costs arise from the portion of the drug problem that goes untreated.

Finally, there are costs associated with expansion and simultaneous diversification of drug-abuse prevention. As funding increases, a larger proportion of funds must be channeled into program administration. Complex financial transactions require greater investments in accounting and auditing controls. With ever more agencies joining the fight, interdepartmental activity and its associated administrative costs increase significantly. Over the fifteen years surveyed, there was a marked increase in the enforcement function of government, as opposed to research and education. From 1968 to 1978, for which the data permit a direct comparison, law enforcement increased from 16.6 to 30.9 percent of total budget.

The political process evidently assigns greater priority to direct containment of violent behavior caused by drug use and drug trade; research and licensing of drugs are apparently not seen as the best answers to the drug dilemma.[16]

Conclusion

This chapter has summarized drug-related government efforts. It has focused on direct expenditures and thus necessarily has the limitation that expenditures only reflect society's judgment of what it proposes to contribute, rather than a true evaluation of a cost. Clearly, the damage done to society over and above what it spends directly on the drug problem transcends by a large margin even the considerable costs specified here. As noted in the definition of the components, drug effects permeate most social dysfunctions, from crime to the deterioration of communities to international relations, especially with such source areas of drugs as South Asia, parts of the Middle East, and much of Latin America. As in other problem areas discussed in this volume, the readily identifiable costs are only a tip of the iceberg.

Notes

1. J. H. Robertson and N. E. Zinberg, *Drugs and the Public* (New York: Simon and Schuster, 1972), p. 123.

2. P. Lee and M. Silverman, *Pills, Profits and Politics* (Berkeley: University of California Press, 1974), pp. 217-18. See also D. Musto, *The American Disease: The Origins of Narcotic Control* (New Haven: Yale University Press, 1973).

3. J. DeLong and P. Goldberg, "Federal Expenditures on Drug Control," excerpted from the Ford Foundation's *Dealing with Drug Abuse* (New York: Praeger Publishers, 1972), p. 302.

4. T. M. Eggert, *Economics and Externalities* (New York: Twayne Publishers, Inc., 1977), pp. 305-6.

5. General Services Administration, *United States Government Manual 1977/1978* (Washington, D.C.: U.S. Government Printing Office, 1977), pp. 261-63.

6. N. Strauss, *Addicts and Drug Abuse: Current Approaches to the Problem* (New York: Twayne Publishers, Inc., 1971), p. 69.

7. Ibid., p. 81.

8. M. Mintz, *The Therapeutic Nightmare* (Boston: Houghton Mifflin, 1965), p. 110.

9. General Services Administration, *U.S. Government Manual*, p. 261.

10. Ibid., p. 302.

11. Office of Management and Budget, *Budget of the U.S. Government for Fiscal Years 1966-1978* (Washington, D.C.: U.S. Government Printing Office, 1978), p. 638.

12. Lee and Silverman, *Pills, Profits and Politics*, pp. 137-39.

13. L. Jaffee, "Prescription Abuse Stirs Concern," *New York Times*, March 7, 1982.

14. DeLong and Goldberg, "Federal Expenditures."

15. V. H. Vroom and P. Yetton, *Leadership and Decision Making* (Pittsburgh: University of Pittsburgh Press, 1974), p. 143.

16. Strauss, *Addicts and Drug Abuse*, p. 148.

12

Transportation

WAYNE RICH

"Oh, Murder! What was that Papa!"
"My child, it was a Motor-Car,
A Most Ingenious Toy!"

Hilaire Belloc, "Hildebrand"

Introduction

Millions of Americans are dependent on the automobile. They use their cars in commuting to work, in shopping, and for their leisure. The automobile, however, also exacts substantial social costs. These costs not only affect the individual motorist but all drivers in general, as well as nonmotorists. The social costs of the automobile manifest themselves in automobile accidents and in the use of resources that could be conserved if other modes of transportation were adopted. This chapter will attempt to identify the various components of the social costs of transportation and quantify them.

Social costs are grouped into four main categories: automobile accidents, alternate modes of transit, federal subsidies for transportation, and road construction and maintenance costs. Finally, there is a discussion of current trends in automobile safety and pollution and of the import problem which likewise has its social cost aspects. To be sure, much of the total cost of the automobile is borne by its users and could thus in theory be avoided by not using one. However, in American society, the automobile is so pervasive and so indispensable a method of communication and contact, that not using one is not a viable option. Its social costs are thus externalities affecting practically everyone, and comprise opportunity costs and the cost consequences of social inefficiencies.

Automobile Accidents

Automobile accidents result in significant costs to individuals and society as a whole. Cost components are identified when measurable to provide some indication of the scope of the problem. However, the total of individual cost estimates of accidents should not be interpreted as the value placed on a human life or as the total cost of a fatality or injury to society. Nor is it the total amount that society is willing to spend to save a life or prevent an injury. The cost components merely serve as indicators of the significance of the automobile accident problem. As noted in chapter 5, for industrial pollution, the costs are greater than what is spent on abatement. Societal loss reflects a decrease in individual and group welfare. Societal welfare is, in general terms, the sum total of individual well-being. Specifically, social welfare includes levels of health, production of goods and services, personal satisfaction and happiness, and physical comfort.

Cost estimates have been derived that reflect certain societal losses. The two basic criteria for identifying loss components are (1) resources consumed in the repair of damage to people and vehicles that could be shifted in the long run to welfare-producing activities and (2) the consumption losses of individuals and society at large caused by losses in production and the ability to produce.[1] Costs of medical care, repair costs of automobile damage, legal and court costs, accident investigation costs, and insurance administration costs relate to the first concept of loss. The resources consumed could better be used to raise the economic and social welfare of society were they not consumed due to automobile accidents. The second concept, losses in production, relates to the accident victim's inability to produce in the market, in home and family activities, and in community services. Losses in production are also related to the time spent by others in response to accident ramifications and in traffic delays to others on the road.

Costs were estimated for fatalities, injuries, and property damage and are shown in tables 12.1 and 12.2. The Abbreviated Injury Scale (AIS) is used throughout much of this discussion. The Abbreviated Injury Scale was first published in 1971 by a joint committee of the American Medical Association (AMA), the Society of Automotive Engineers (SAE), and the American Association of Automotive Medicine (AAAM). The scale was designed to provide a consistent scale for collecting and analyzing injury severity data. The scale is as follows:

AIS Code	Category
1	Minor
2	Moderate
3	Severe (not life threatening)

AIS Code	Category
4	Severe (life threatening, survival probable)
5	Critical (survival uncertain)
6	Maximum severity (currently untreatable)

The great majority of auto accidents involve property damage only (PDO) with no resulting injuries. Costs have been estimated for these accidents also. A report by the U.S. Department of Transportation (DOT)[2] sought to identify and estimate cost components of motor vehicle accidents. This was no easy task since there is a lack of coverage for all types of accidents and all levels of severity. Further, there exists no cost data system that reports basic fatality, injury, and property damage costs. Also, most of the studies pertaining to cost data have not covered the complete range of fatality, injury, and property-damage-only accidents.

Losses in present and future production due to auto accident casualties represent significant social costs. The concept of production loss relates to decreases in both individual and group welfare. Whether the loss is largely to the individual or to the rest of society does not really matter, since the well-being of each individual in society is part of total societal welfare. Assigned compensation to the individual is one means to determine valuation of production. The quantity to be measured is average compensation in the marketplace. Lost production is made up of two components: the market portion and the home and community portion. The first measures production losses of the eight-hour day or forty-hour week. The second measures those losses in the home and community outside the eight-hour work day.

Measuring individual productivity is not easy. It has been difficult to find a common denominator for different industries and economic sectors. Thus, the basic standard for measuring market production has been market compensation. There are two indirect methods of measuring nonmarket production: market costs and opportunity costs. In using market costs, nonmarket production, such as the chores of a housewife, is estimated by identifying equivalent market occupations and associated hourly market wages. Opportunity costs are the average compensations foregone in the marketplace. This approach suits this study better than the market cost approach since distinctions of occupation are rarely made in accident data files. Average compensation in the marketplace is used to represent opportunity cost. Mean income was chosen to measure mean compensation. (For another approach to the valuation of human life and health, see chapter 3.)

The DOT study calculated future loss production for fatalities based upon age distribution and sex. The following criteria were used for production loss analysis:[3]

Table 12.1
Social Costs of Automobile Accidents: Summary, 1975 (Dollars per Case)

Cost Component	Injury Severity (AIS)						
	6	5	4	3	2	1	PDO**
Production/consumption:							
Market	211,820*	126,650*	55,550*	1,645	865	65	—
Home, family, and community	63,545*	37,995*	16,660*	425	310	20	—
Medical:							
Hospital	275	5,750	2,250	1,095	450	45	—
Physician and other	160	5,520	2,160	525	165	55	—
Coroner-medical examiner	130	—	—	—	—	—	—
Rehabilitation	—	6,075	3,040	—	—	—	—
Funeral	925*	—	—	—	—	—	—
Legal and court	2,190	1,645	1,090	770	150	140	7
Insurance administration	295	295	285	240	220	52	30
Accident investigation	80	80	70	45	35	28	6
Losses to others	3,685	4,180	1,830	260	130	32	—
Vehicle damage	3,990	3,990	3,960	2,920	1,865	1,595	315
Traffic delay	80	60	60	160	160	160	160
Total	287,175	192,160	86,955	8,085	4,350	2,192	518

* Seven-percent discount rate.   ** Property damage only.

Source: U.S. Department of Transportation, *Societal Costs of Motor Vehicle Accidents—1975*, p. 2.

Table 12.2
Average and Total Costs, 1975

	Fatality	Nonfatal Injury (AIS)					Average Injury	PDO Involvement
		5	4	3	2	1		
Average cost excluding vehicle damage and traffic delay, in dollars	283,105	188,190	82,935	5,005	2,325	435	1,360	45
Total	287,175	192,240	86,955	8,085	4,350	2,190	3,185	520
Number of occurrences in thousands	46.8	4	20	80	492	3,400	4,000	21,900
Total cost, billions	13.44	0.77	1.74	0.65	2.14	7.45	12.75	11.40

Source: U.S. Department of Transportation, *Societal Costs of Motor Vehicle Accidents—1975*, p. 2.

Begin production analysis at age twenty; end at age sixty-five

Make distinction based on sex for each age group

Increase 3 percent per year for productivity; discount at
7 percent

Calculate mean full-time income (opportunity cost)

Calculate for median age in age group

From these calculations, future income for each age group was derived as shown in table 12.3. The overall average figure for 1973 was $184,110 in future loss production per fatality. This figure was updated to $211,820 for 1975.

Table 12.3
Direct Future Productivity Loss for 1973, Fatalities (Market)

Age Group	Number of Fatalities	Average Direct Productivity Loss, in Dollars, per Fatality in Age Group*
0–4	2,000	103,935
5–9	2,005	127,100
10–14	2,120	175,320
15–19	9,310	201,965
20–24	8,725	237,960
25–29	5,115	244,155
30–34	3,505	229,805
35–39	2,740	213,245
40–44	2,655	172,020
45–49	2,740	156,720
50–54	2,705	120,720
55–59	2,435	79,365
60–64	2,340	31,700
Overall average direct productivity loss per fatality		184,110

* Seven-percent discount rates applied.

Source: U.S. Department of Transportation, *Societal Costs of Motor Vehicle Accidents—1975*, p. 5.

The value placed on lost production for nonfatal injuries is dependent upon the disability for each injury level. From the various data available, production losses were calculated for each AIS level. The average value of lost production for an AIS-1 injury in 1975 was $65. The loss for an AIS-2 injury was estimated at $865, while an AIS-3 injury was estimated to be worth $1,645 in lost production.[4]

Estimates of production losses for AIS 4 and 5 were based upon various studies by the federal government on serious motor vehicle injuries that showed the incidence of spinal cord injuries and the incidence of victims who are receiving federal disability payments. The study used data collected in another study, *Incidence of Traumatic Spinal Cord Lesions*.[5] These injuries were categorized as quadriplegia-paresis, paraplegia-paresis, other paralysis, or no paralysis-other impairment, and were distributed among the AIS 4 and 5 levels. Calculations estimated the average market production losses for AIS 4 to be $48,280 in 1973 and $55,550 in 1975. Production losses for AIS 5 in 1973 and 1975 were estimated to be $110,080 and $126,650, respectively.[6]

Production losses related to activities outside the forty-hour week were measured using opportunity costs in order to be consistent with the market production analysis. Replacement cost is not applicable because many home or volunteer services, if lost, might not be replaced. The average production loss in home, family, and community services was estimated for fatalities and injuries on the basis of the time allocated to the activities. The time was taken as a percentage of the forty-hour week and this percentage was applied to the average market production loss for each AIS level. The average production time for home and family was determined to be ten hours per week and volunteer or community service was found to be two hours per week. Thus, the combined twelve hours represented 30 percent of the forty-hour week. This percentage was applied to each AIS level.[7] The results are seen in table 12.1

Billions of dollars are spent each year on medical care costs. Of the total $96.8 billion spent on medical care in 1974, approximately $37.2 billion, or 38 percent, was paid out of public funds.[8] Just how much of these public payments has been related to motor vehicle accidents is difficult to pinpoint. There has not been much attempt to identify the source of payment.

Medical costs related to automobile injuries and fatalities are a social cost in that they use medical resources that could be better put to use in the prevention and treatment of diseases. The following components of total medical costs can be identified: medical treatment at the scene, transportation and treatment en route to medical facility, emergency room treatment, hospitalization, rehabilitation, long-term medical care at home or in extended-care facilities.[9] The emerging specialty of trauma medicine to a large extent deals with the consequences of auto accidents. The nature of the injury determines the consumption of medical resources required. Long-range effects of serious injuries are difficult to determine since they require long-range studies which have not been undertaken.

In estimating the medical costs for nonfatal injuries caused by auto accidents, it has been necessary to base these estimates on the few available sources that exist. Two such sources are the Restraint System Evaluation Program (RSEP) and the Department of Health, Education, and Welfare (HEW). The RSEP collected data on 16,000 auto occupants in 1973-1975 model vehicles according to different factors. However, when the RSEP study was done, it covered only late-model vehicles in tow-away accidents. The HEW survey, on the other hand, collected data on all moving vehicle injuries. It showed that out of approximately 3.9 million motor vehicle injuries, 88.3 percent were seen by a physician and 14.3 percent required a hospital stay. Since there was more specific data in the RSEP file, that study was emphasized. According to the RSEP study, of the total number of occupants involved in auto accidents, 48.2 percent were not injured. The percentage of occupants fatally injured was 0.5 percent.[10] The data on the remaining percentage of occupants in the nonfatal injuries group was distributed by AIS level and type of treatment as shown in table 12.4. A survey done in conjunction with *The Statewide Highway Safety Program Assessment*,[11] and a study of Blue Cross records done in conjunction with the RSEP were used to estimate the average transportation and emergency room care costs as follows:

AIS	Transportation	Emergency Room Care
1	$15	$ 20
2	35	55
3	35	70
4	40	145
5	40	190

The Commission on Professional and Hospital Activity (CPHA) keeps records on 16 million patients in 2,000 short-term general hospitals. Short-term is generally accepted as less than 30 days. A study collected data for 1973 using the CPHA seventh patient sample. Of the 23,168 patients studied, 93.6 percent were discharged, 4.2 percent were transferred, and 2.2 percent died. The average stay of the total number of patients was ten days. The average daily charge in 1973 was $109. The first two days of a hospital stay are the most expensive because intensive treatment, tests, operations, and x-rays take

Table 12.4
Percent Distribution by Type of Treatment for Nonfatal Injuries

Treatment Categories (Mutually Exclusive)	AIS Level				
	1	2	3	4	5
Received no treatment	26.8	1.7	0.6	—	—
Received first aid at scene	3.1	0.2	—	—	—
Directed to consult doctor	7.1	0.6	—	—	—
Consulted doctor only	19.0	7.1	3.6	—	—
Received emergency room treatment and released	40.8	62.5	23.7	—	—
Admitted to hospital	3.2	27.9	72.1	100.0	100.0
Total	100.0	100.0	100.0	100.0	100.0

Source: U.S. Department of Transportation, *Societal Costs of Motor Vehicle Accidents*, p. 14.

place then. During the following days, maintenance costs make up a larger portion of total hospital costs. Certain serious injuries result in longer hospital stays or confinement in nursing homes. Data from the American Hospital Association and the 1973-1974 National Home Survey were used to estimate long-term care costs. The hospital costs listed in table 12.1 represent an average of the total short-term and long-term hospital stays for each AIS level.

For some injuries, patients received treatment by a physician outside a hospital, while other injuries required treatment by a physician while under hospitalization. The average physician cost per injury depended upon the incidence of treatment. The average physician costs based on combined data for the two sets of circumstances were presented in table 12.1.

Rehabilitation costs are a social cost since the resources used in rehabilitating serious motor vehicle injuries could be used for treating physical problems from disease or for general health care. Rehabilitation costs are usually required only for serious injuries at AIS levels 4 and 5. These rehabilitation costs were shown in table 12.1.

Medical costs have been discussed for nonfatalities. However, there are medical costs incurred by accident fatalities too. The resources devoted to fatalities are related to the time and place of the accident. Emergency transportation costs apply to all fatalities, whether they are taken to a hospital or to a mortuary. Only a portion of fatalities live long enough to require emergency room and hospital care costs.

The measurement of funeral costs is the difference between the present value of average funeral costs that would occur in a future year and the

average funeral cost in the current year. Even though funeral costs are experienced ultimately, funeral costs experienced currently are higher because
future money is worth less than present money. Funeral costs were estimated
as follows: The average funeral cost in 1973, $990,[12] was updated to $1,125
for 1975 based on the consumer price index.[13] The median age of fatality
among males in accidents is twenty-six years and among females, thirty-two
years.[14] The remaining years of life expectancy was estimated to be forty-four
and one-half years for males and forty-five and one-half years for females.[15] Of
the total motor vehicle fatalities, 73.5 percent were male and 26.5 percent
were female.[16]

Weighted average remaining years: 44.5(0.735) + 45.5(0.265) = 45
Productivity price increase, 3 percent per year: $1,125(3.7816) = $4,255
Discounted (7 percent present worth factor): $4,255(0.0476) = $200
Net difference 1975, future cost: $1,125 − 200 = $925[17]

Thus, the average funeral cost due to auto accidents can be estimated as
$925.

Another component of social costs due to automobile accidents is losses to
others. This could include employer losses due to temporary or permanent
replacement costs, time spent visiting patients, transportation for medical
attention, home care, and time spent in vehicle repair and replacement. These
losses are measured based on the opportunity cost of time spent in these
activities. The cost of losses to others per injury was presented in table 12.1.

Another component of the cost of accidents is legal and court costs.
Resources used for automobile accidents are legal and judicial. These legal and
court costs are divided into tort actions and accident citation costs. Each of
those is composed of private and public costs. Like other losses, legal and
court costs are not applicable to all fatalities and injuries. Therefore, the costs
are higher for each individual case than they are averaged over all injuries at a
given injury level. The average court costs in tort actions were $4,675 per case
in 1968.[18] This was updated to $7,370 for 1975 based on the government
wage index from 1968 to 1975 of 57.7 percent.[19] In 1968 the defendant's
cost was $820 per case plus $250 in expenses.[20] The consumer price increase
in legal services from 1968 to 1975 was 71 percent. Thus, for 1975, costs
were $1,400 per case plus $430 in expenses. The other component of legal
and court costs are the costs associated with traffic citations issued in accidents. Of the total number of accidents in 1973, 29.5 percent involved citations. These citation costs comprise court and prosecution costs. The average
legal and court costs were combined for tort actions and citations and appeared
in table 12.1.

The cost of insurance overhead represents resources devoted to accidents that could be saved with a reduction in auto accidents. Estimates of insurance overhead costs were based on a study of indirect costs of auto accidents conducted by the Center for the Environment and Man (CEM).[21] Insurance administration costs for 1975 were estimated in table 12.1.

Accident investigation costs apply to all injuries, accidents, and a significant portion of those accidents involving property damage only. The amount of resources used in the investigation is dependent upon the severity of the accident. The average costs related to accident investigations according to severity were estimated in table 12.1.

Although automobile insurance overhead costs have already been mentioned, the social cost of auto insurance as it relates to vehicle damage needs to be discussed further. Vehicle damage is a significant component of the social cost of the automobile. It is related to the rising cost of auto repair and is a large factor in the escalating rates of automobile insurance. Automobile insurance can be classified as a social cost in that everyone who owns a car must pay auto insurance premiums to subsidize those drivers who are involved in auto accidents. The high cost of insurance is thus a pervasive charge upon the economy in general.

Auto claims consist of various components such as auto repair, medical care, physicians' fees, and hospital room charges. As of August 1982, auto insurance premiums rose to an index level of 275.8 (1967 = 100), which is substantial, though less than other auto claims-related items. Auto repairs and maintenance reached 319.2, medical care costs went to 333.3, and physicians' fees rose to 330.4. Hospital room charges reached a level of 565.5.[22]

The cost of repairing automobile damage represents a large portion of the total costs involved in accidents of low severity. The resources consumed in repairing cars could be shifted in the long run to raising the current levels of safety and maintenance in cars on the road. The social cost of automobile damage can be measured by claim costs, that is, the cost to repair the auto, minus the amount deductible by the insurance company. The deductible is an out-of-pocket expense paid by the individual car owner. Attempts to pinpoint average auto damage costs are not easy due to the absence of a comprehensive data collection system on vehicle damage. Most data systems cover a limited segment of accidents. One system run by the Highway Loss Data Institute (HLDI) has data from seven of the largest auto insurance companies on policy coverage and accidents. Although the system has some good points, the HLDI file contains collision claims only and does not identify injury and severity. Another data source is the State Farm Insurance Company's *Current Model Year Study*. Although it contains repair cost estimates for both collision and property damage claims, it is somewhat biased in estimating costs at the lower end of the spectrum due to the fact that the study only includes cars that come to drive-in claim centers, thereby eliminating disabled cars from the study. Also, like the HLDI files, this study does not identify injury severity. A computer run done by State Farm on their general claim file for all claim activity during November and December 1974 came up with the following average claim costs: collision coverage, $474 (all claims) and $491 (all nonzero claims); property damage liability coverage, $350 (all claims) and $353 (all nonzero claims); and a weighted overall average of $415 (all claims) and $426 (all nonzero claims).[23]

One study conducted by the General Electric Company for the National Highway Traffic Safety Administration (NHTSA) under Title II of the Motor Vehicle Information and Cost Savings Act[24] did collect data according to injury levels. Data was collected from the files of twenty insurance companies. The average repair costs were shown in table 12.1.

The American Mutual Insurance Alliance reported in 1977 that repairing a completely demolished car can cost more than four times as much as purchasing a new car. According to the Alliance study, it would cost $21,471 to replace all the parts on a totally demolished 1977 standard automobile worth $4,681.[25] Damage to less than one-fourth of a car's parts can cost more to repair than the car is worth. If 25 percent of a car's parts had to be replaced, the cost would be 25 percent of $21,471. The repair cost would therefore be $5,368 or $687 more than the original purchase price of the car. A replacement of 1 percent of an auto's parts can come to over $200.

The cost of repairing crash damage also is pushing up the cost of collision, comprehensive, and property damage insurance. The cost for these coverages is rising faster than the cost of bodily injury insurance, despite the rising cost of hospital and medical care. Drivers of late-model, medium-priced cars are likely to spend 60 to 70 percent of their total auto insurance premiums for collision, comprehensive, and property damage coverages. Thus, the cost of auto repair is the largest contributor to the rising cost of automobile insurance.

In addition to rising repair costs, the number of claims paid out and the method by which auto insurance policyholders are assigned to risk groups are responsible for the high cost of premiums. Automobile insurance has been increasing at a rate of about 25 percent a year, which makes it possible that insurance premiums could double in four years. The cost of auto insurance is affecting the type of car that people buy and whether they can afford to buy a car at all. Meanwhile, automobile insurance companies were very profitable in 1977, as the frequency of auto claims fell 6.6 percent.[26] This was partially due to consumers increasing their deductibles by $50 on average over the previous two years in order to economize on premiums.

A final component of the social costs of automobile accidents is the loss to others in time caused by traffic delays due to accidents. There is little research in this area on which to base estimates of the costs due to traffic delays. One study measured time lost because of rush-hour accidents.[27] Estimates based on this study, however, were conservative because the figures were for a minor accident. Response time to the scene of the accident was shorter than normal due to the fact that it was a freeway accident and greater effort was made to clear the road. The average costs for traffic delays were presented in table 12.1.

Automobile Design

The foregoing statistics are considerably affected by changes in the design of automobiles and environmental regulations. Since the late 1960s, government intervention in the design and performance of automobiles has increased greatly so that the automobile eventually became the most regulated major consumer product. This intervention followed a lengthy series of exposés of which Ralph Nader's *Unsafe at Any Speed* became the major one.[28] The details of the long controversy are less important than some of the end results that have been obtained. Table 12.5 shows the changes in death rates per 100 million miles driven and 10,000 vehicles. While it is clear that there has been a long-term trend toward greater safety on the road, it is equally clear that the very small change in the fifteen years between 1952 and 1967 contrasts sharply with the 39-percent drop recorded between 1967 and 1977. It is, however, noteworthy that this record has been paralleled in most other countries, several of which have had even greater rates of improvement.

Pollution likewise came in for sharply increased controls beginning with breather valves for crankcases and proceeding to catalytic converters for exhaust gases. As a result, a general reduction in emission standards was recorded. From 1967 to 1977-1978 car emissions dropped 81 percent and, further, by 95 percent in 1981. Comparable percentages for light trucks were 63 and 68 percent. Clearly, these are substantial changes.[29] Depending upon its audience, the automobile industry has congratulated itself considerably on these attainments. However, there is a substantial record of resistance by the industry all the way to the present levels and arguments with respect to further changes are almost invariably couched in terms that enough progress has been made so that now a pause may take place and there need not be any further effort at making cars less polluting, safer, or more fuel efficient, because from now on, it would *really* be expensive.

Not surprisingly, the automobile industry has received far more sympathetic attention to its needs from the Reagan administration than it did under President Carter, when Joan Claybrook, a long-term activist in the field, was administrator of the National Highway Traffic Safety Administra-

Table 12.5
U.S. Traffic Fatalities: Average, 1923–1927 and Selected Years, 1952–1980

| | | Death Rates per | |
	Total Deaths	100 Million Miles Driven	10,000 Vehicles
1980	53,300	3.4	3.3
1979	52,800	3.3	3.3
1978	52,400	3.3	3.3
1977	49,200	3.32	3.35
1972	56,278	4.24	4.28
1967	52,924	5.50	5.35
1962	40,804	5.32	5.12
1957	38,702	5.98	5.73
1952	37,794	7.36	7.10
1923–1927 Average	21,800	18.20	11.10

Source: National Safety Council, Accident Facts, 1977.

tion. Under the director appointed by Mr. Reagan, R. A. Peck, Jr., "deregulation" has been the watchword.[30] Several examples will make this clear. Under various laws and regulations, air bags and passive seat belts that would envelop passengers automatically on entering cars, were scheduled for 1983. That regulation has been rescinded. It was intended that results of crash tests at thirty-five miles per hour should be displayed on window price stickers. Federal standards on gas mileage are scheduled to expire in 1985; further rules were planned beyond that date. New rules were to be required for minimum fields of direct view through the windshields of passenger cars and trucks, with the objective of eliminating blind spots. All these rules were likewise rescinded.

As to bumpers, the existing rules required protection from damage at speeds up to five miles an hour. Mr. Peck's NHTSA changed the safe speed to two and one-half miles per hour. The plan engendered opposition from the insurance industry which predicted $1 billion more in claims from increased collision damage. In support of the plan, General Motors Corporation claimed that the automobile industry would save $140 million from this change. It was also claimed that that there would be a significant saving in weight and thus of fuel, and that customers would have first cost savings as well. By the end of 1982, it was reported that there would be no significant savings in price ($15 was one estimate) nor in weight (15 lbs., that is, less than 0.5 percent). Furthermore, an entire complicated redesign of the frame was needed because bumper supports are a principal component of the whole system.[31] The change would thus take years to implement and would not provide the quick fix for the industry that its proponents had wanted; the damage to customer interests and the net increase in social costs were, on the other hand, all too clear. These and other problems have enveloped the NHTSA in political controversy and legal challenges that certainly preclude at this time any significant progress in reducing the social costs and dysfunctions of the automobile.

Finally, the fortunes of the automobile cannot be divorced from the troubled state of the American industry itself. Beginning with a negligible impact that was primarily concentrated in luxury cars during the 1950s, over one-quarter of all automobiles sold in the United States are now imported. This has necessarily led to very large job losses and to arrangements made between the United Automobile Workers, General Motors, Ford, Chrysler, and others to give back several of the benefits and forego wage increases to keep the industry afloat. Whether bilateral arrangements between unions and managements will be sufficient to assure a more prosperous future for the industry remains to be seen.[32] The market advantages of the small fuel-efficient foreign cars have been quite compelling, although, as gasoline prices declined somewhat in the spring of 1982, there appeared to be a tendency back toward cars slightly larger than the small models in which imports were primarily concentrated. For General Motors, for example, this meant more activity in the otherwise poorly reviewed X-series of cars rather than its newer and smaller A-series. On the other hand, car sales were so extremely poor in the aggregate that the whole issue is still very much up in the air.

Meanwhile, by dint of very severe international pressure, Japan was persuaded to establish quotas for automobiles; and the arguments presented for and against such matters have been well set forth in congressional hearings. These, incidentally, show that when the totality of social benefits in Japan is included, the margin between American and Japanese labor costs that is so often cited as Japan's principal competitive advantage is very sharply diminished.[33] Space does not permit a detailed recounting of these arguments but the social cost of a protectionist policy is clearly evident here. If quotas and tariffs increase the price of imports, this again removes a major incentive for cost-effective vehicles manufactured within the United States. To make cars cheaper, given tariff or quota protection, would be "leaving money on the table" as industry spokesmen have admitted in their less guarded moments.

Alternate Modes of Transport

The ubiquitous use of the automobile cannot be separated from the patterns of settlement that have developed in the United States over the past fifty years. Essentially, there has been a trend toward suburbanization which accelerated sharply in the years following World War II. By suburbanization is meant not merely the literal movement of people out of central cities but rather a pattern of low-density settlements in one-family houses that prevails even within most of what are still termed "central cities." It is this way of using space and designing communities that has made the automobile far and away the most convenient means of access and communication and has placed other forms of transport under considerable handicaps. It is not that they could not be used; rather that planning for these communities, insofar as the term "planning" is deserved at all, never took such alternates seriously into account, with but rare exceptions.

The development of suburbia and its social and economic implications has been extensively addressed in a study directed by the editor of this volume.[34] Suffice it to say here that a great variety of economic activities take place primarily because we have chosen to live in suburbs and that the entire economy would look very different if, for example, it had been decided instead to settle in population nodes linked by fast, efficient, and economical public transport. This form of settlement has been widely advocated in the city planning literature for much of this century, but it has not generally been translated extensively into actuality except again for a relatively few communities mostly situated in western and northern Europe. Otherwise, more or less uncontrolled urban and suburban sprawl has been the rule.

Referring to alternate means of transportation, it can in fact be shown that the majority of metropolitan areas in the United States once had very substantial rail rapid-transit networks in the form of trolley cars or interurban railroads on largely private rights-of-way that could have been turned into rapid transit systems suitable for a modern group of communities. It is unfortunate that in several cases these systems were torn out at a relatively late time, when suburbanization was well on its way and when saving them would have been far cheaper than trying to re-create a new and usually very much smaller system later on. Both the Washington Metro and San Francisco's BART essentially duplicate lines that existed earlier, especially the latter. The most notorious case is that of Los Angeles in which the Pacific Electric lines were eventually removed, thus destroying a system that at its peak was twice the combined size of New York's subway and commuter railroads; these are today the largest system operating in the United States.[35]

There is no doubt that rail systems, particularly, are expensive and require high capital investment. In some cases that has been greatly reduced by making use of existing industrial railroads; this happened, for example, in Cleveland and San Diego. But otherwise, the nature of suburbanization is frequently insufficient to sustain anything more substantial than a bus system, if that. Buses, of course, can also be highly effective in saving energy and, if service is good, remove the necessity for people to purchase more than one automobile, or perhaps enable them to do without altogether.

The social cost aspect is that with few exceptions bus or rail transportation systems have to be subsidized, as a rule both for capital and operating expenses.[36] After considerable pressure, the federal government established the Urban Mass Transportation Administration to administer federal funding. It now requires highly detailed analyses of all reasonable transit alternatives in terms of objectives and goals. This includes identifying the sources of funding for anticipated operating deficits, monitoring to prevent overdesign, and other requirements related to rail-oriented decisions because of their high cost. It is noteworthy here that highway investment is rarely, if ever, subjected to the same rigorous attempts at cost-benefit analysis.

In any event, federal support for public transportation of any description is rapidly becoming a thing of the past. Federal funding for public transportation is being rapidly phased out with respect to operating subsidies, and there is at present no way of making up the gap. Arguments that putting a public transport system together is by far the cheapest way for communities to provide internal transportation are generally roundly ignored. Again, it is an example of the generally favored treatment of highways. (Of course, the increasing incidence of potholes in cities makes claims of good treatment of *anything* relating to transportation somewhat suspect.)

In support of these policies of neglect, it has been argued that a rancher in Wyoming, say, should not have to pay for the commuter bill of a New York executive. It is also true, however, that every time said New York executive goes to a grocery, his meat price includes a not infrequently handsome contribution to the agricultural subsidies received by the very same Wyoming rancher. Put another way, it is unfortunate though not surprising that that kind of sectional infighting is a consequence of the "new federalism" espoused by the Reagan administration.

Certain broader issues of rail transportation, especially relating to freight, were addressed in chapter 10 in connection with the duplication of capital facilities. The federal government was active for a time in providing some funds for the general reconstruction of the railways, but this too is unlikely to continue.

Such plans were made under the Railroad Revitalization and Regulatory Reform (4-R) Act of 1976 and, previously, the Regional Railway Organization (3-R) Act of 1973. It became possible under certain circumstances to subsidize the continuation of rail service if that would cost less than abandonment of the service. These plans, as noted earlier, were nowhere near sufficient. For instance, a relatively small contribution of about $27 billion would provide what every significant European country as well as Japan and others already have, namely an electrified network of main lines that would shoulder the principal fast rail traffic and whose power supply, having the flexibility of electricity, would be immune to outside interference.[37]

One eventual consequence of the 3-R Act was the establishment of Conrail as a consolidated way of operating the railroads of the Northeast; most of its previously independent major systems are included in it. However, under the Northeast Rail Service Act (NERSA) of 1981, Conrail must be fully profitable in 1983. If it fails, it can be broken up with only the most profitable parts sold piecemeal and the rest simply junked. The economic problems this would pose for an already deeply troubled region can hardly be underestimated. Yet, again by dint of the national fragmentation implicit in the new federalism, it may very well come to pass. Conrail showed a small operating profit in 1981 for the first time, but as the economy moved into serious recession in 1982, it again began to lose money, and its outlook was cloudy indeed.[38] It would be a calamity of the highest order if short-run thinking of the kind described would destroy an asset of the greatest potential value, if only it were properly maintained and protected.

Road Construction and Maintenance

The costs related to road construction and maintenance have doubled since 1967.[39] Most road and bridge repairs are paid out of the federal trust fund and state gasoline taxes. However, the cost of fixing roads and bridges is soaring and the trust fund is not likely to be enough to cover costs. Some repair bills on interstate roads are likely to be greater than the original cost. An increase in the federal gasoline tax was therefore enacted at the end of 1982. The legislation, hastily enacted in the lame duck session of Congress, also provided for higher taxes on trucks, thereby turning into a business cost some of the damage they now wreak on roads. To sweeten that provision, however, trucks were now permitted to use "double bottoms," that is, truck and full trailer combinations, everywhere in the country. The situation in early 1983 was that the trucking industry, claiming hard times, was trying to get the new taxes repealed and communities, notably New York, were asserting that the new trailer combinations would not fit on their streets. Thus more conflict was clearly in the offing.

It is impossible to get a good estimate of total road-related costs across the entire country, but certain instances can be pointed out to shed light on the problem. Severe winter conditions are a major factor in the need for road repairs. After the winter of 1977, city, county, and state agencies were left with a $2.8 billion repair bill for bridges and highways. There were an estimated 18.4 million more potholes to fill than in 1976. The cost of repairs fell largely to local governments rather than the federal government. The federal trust fund was virtually exhausted by 1979 with hardly a dent made in the job required. Clearly, a great deal of money will be needed.

The Road Information Program (TRIP) revealed that heavy icing destroyed approximately 6,000 miles of road pavement and more than 1,600 bridges on noninterstate roads. Snow removal costs rose $270 million from 1976 for state and local governments.[40] According to TRIP, the winter damages were so great because more than half of the nation's 1.8 million miles of paved road and 19 percent of its bridges were badly worn or obsolete to begin with. Road repairs cause states to cancel new road construction and improvements. Three-fourths of the nation's 563,500 highway bridges were built more than forty years ago. More than 208,000 of the nation's paved roads are rated "poor" or "very poor." The states were allocated $12.4 billion in federal highway trust funds, some of which would be used for repairs.

In 1981, a study by the Council of State Planning Agencies, significantly titled "America in Ruins" discussed the severe shortfalls in road maintenance. Details are given in chapter 15, but it can be noted here that both the interstate system, other roads, and urban streets are all falling into ruin and that maintenance and repairs are nowhere near sufficient to keep up with a steady deterioration.[41]

Conclusion

In this chapter extensive documentation of the costs of automobile accidents and their many ramifications was first presented. The analysis is given in considerable detail because it encompasses not only money costs but also, as discussed earlier in chapter 3, involves the valuation of human life and suffering.

The issue of social efficiency is then addressed in an examination of the choices presented with respect to alternate means of transportation. It has long been evident, however, that relatively little can be done because the automobile industry and its related activities are very strongly entrenched and politically favored. A large reason for this is not merely the clear political strength of the road-oil-truck lobby but also the fact of suburbanization which, by making low-density one-family housing the norm throughout most of the country, has made the automobile the vehicle of choice for most people physically able to drive (and for some who, alas, do so anyway).

For a time after the oil embargo of 1973, it looked as if the old ways of automobile preeminence were going to be modified. However, as people became used to gasoline prices that but a few years ago would have been considered incredible, the erstwhile determination began to be eroded, and under the policies currently being followed, even the relatively modest subsidy program for alternate means of transportation seems certain to be severely cut or eliminated. The consequences of this are hard to predict. In the form of more accidents, generally poorer living, reduction of public welfare and, in some areas, increasing poverty, unemployment, and disuse of otherwise viable capital facilities, the consequences in terms of social costs promise to be grave indeed.

Notes

1. U.S. Department of Transportation, *Societal Costs of Motor Vehicle Accidents—1975* (Washington, D.C.: DOT, December 1976), p. 1.

2. Ibid.

3. Ibid., p. 5.

4. The data and calculations for these figures may be found in U.S. Department of Transportation, *Societal Costs*, pp. 7-8.

5. J. F. Kraus, et al., *Incidence of Traumatic Spinal Cord Lesions* (Davis: University of California, 1974).

6. U.S. Department of Transportation, *Societal Costs*, pp. 10-11.

7. Ibid., p. 11-12.

8. M. S. Mueller and R. M. Gibson, "National Health Expenditures, Calendar Year 1974," *Research and Statistics Note*, no. 5 (Washington, D.C.: Social Security Administration, April 1976).

9. U.S. Department of Transportation, *Societal Costs*, p. 13.

10. U.S. Department of Transportation, *Restraint Systems Evaluation Program* (Washington, D.C.: National Highway Traffic Safety Administration, 1976).

11. U.S. Department of Transportation, *The Statewide Highway Safety Program Assessment: A National Estimate of Performance* (Washington, D.C.: NHTSA, July 1975).

12. *Federal Trade Commission Survey of Funeral Prices in the District of Columbia* (Washington, D.C.: FTC, Bureau of Consumer Protection, Division of Special Projects, 1974).

13. "Consumer Price Index—U.S. Average," *Monthly Labor Review*, U.S. Department of Labor, Bureau of Labor Statistics, table 25.

14. "Motor Vehicle Deaths, 1973," *Vital Statistics of the U.S., 1973* (Rockville, Md.: U.S. Department of Health, Education, and Welfare, National Center for Health Statistics, 1975).

15. Social Security Administration, Office of the Actuary.

16. *Fatal Accident Reporting System* (Washington, D.C.: U.S. Department of Transportation, NHSTSA, 1976).

17. U.S. Department of Transportation, *Societal Costs*, p. 18.

18. "Automobile Accident Litigation," *Automobile Insurance and Compensation Study* (Washington, D.C.: U.S. DOT, 1968).

19. *Statistical Abstract of the U.S.* (Washington, D.C.: U.S. Department of Commerce, Bureau of the Census, annual).

20. "Automobile Accident Litigation."

21. H. Wuerdemann and H. Joksch, *National Indirect Costs of Motor Vehicle Accidents* (Hartford, Conn.: Center for the Environment and Man, June 1973).

22. U.S. Department of Labor, Bureau of Labor Statistics, *CPI Detailed Report*, August 1982, p. 24.

23. Special computer runs, State Farm Mutual Automobile Insurance Company, Bloomington, Ill., 1975.

24. "Development of Vehicle Rating for the Automobile Consumer Information Study," General Electric Company, DOT Contract no. DOT-HS-4-00903, unpublished, special computer run.

25. "Auto Repair Costs Continue Rise . . . ," *National Underwriter* (prop. ed.), May 27, 1977, p. 49.

26. "Sudden Riches for the Casualty Insurers," *Business Week*, May 1, 1978, p. 68.

27. M. A. Pittman and R. C. Loutzenheiser, *A Study of Accident Investigation Sites on the Gulf Freeway* (Texas Transportation Institute, 1972).

28. R. Nader, *Unsafe at Any Speed* (New York: Grossman, 1965); for earlier work, see Consumers Union of the U.S., *Passenger Car Design and Highway Safety*, (Mt. Vernon, NY: Consumers Union, 1962) and J. Keats, *The Insolent Chariots* (Philadelphia: J. B. Lippincott, 1958).

29. W. Niskanen, "Federal Regulations of Automotive Safety, Pollution and Energy Consumption," presentation at Hofstra Public Policy Workshop, November 16, 1978 (mimeographed), citing NHTSA standards. Dr. Niskanen was then chief economist of the Ford Motor Company. See also note 30 below.

30. U.S. Senate, Subcommittee of International Trade, *Issues Relating to the Domestic Auto Industry*, hearings, March 9, 1981; see especially the presentation by General Motors Corporation, p. 240ff.; for actions taken, see J. Holusha, "What Deregulation Means for G.M.," *New York Times*, November 1, 1981. See also "Retreat on Clean Air," *Consumer Reports*, April 1982, p. 177.

31. J. Dunne, "Bumper Backpedal," *Popular Science*, December 1982, p. 10; for the original announcement of the change, see, "A Bumper Standard That's Hitting a Wall," *Business Week*, April 5, 1982, p. 31.

32. R. L. Ruggles, Jr., and V. Kumar, "The Dark Side of Ford's Contract," *New York Times*, March 1, 1982; for a comment, see J. E. Ullmann, Letter to the Editor, *New York Times*, March 17, 1982.

33. U.S. Senate, *Domestic Auto Industry*; see especially the presentation by the American International Automobile Dealers Association, p. 90ff.

34. J. E. Ullmann, ed., *The Suburban Economic Network* (New York: Praeger, 1977).

35. Ibid., chs. 7 and 8.

36. "A Dismal Track for Rail Commuters," *Business Week*, April 5, 1982; for Amtrak, see "Bursting the Balloon," *Trains*, April 1982, p. 66.

37. J. E. Ullmann, "The I.D.E.R.," *Trains*, April 1980, p. 66.

38. "Conrail Scores a Point as It Races the Clock," *Business Week*, April 5, 1982, p. 72.

39. "Road, Bridge Repairs to Cost $2.8 Billion," *The American City & County*, May 1977, p. 18.

40. "Nation's Roads Deteriorating Rapidly," *Engineering News Record*, November 10, 1977, p. 14.

41. S. Walter and P. Choate, *America in Ruin* (Washington, D.C.: Council of State Planning Agencies, 1981).

13
Food

FREDERICK P. GERKEN

Ill fares the land,
to hastening ills a prey,
When billboards flourish
And the farms don't pay.

After Oliver Goldsmith, c. 1925

Introduction

Social costs of food in the United States are first of all the result of government subsidies to farmers. Some social programs like food stamps result ultimately in food purchases and so also contribute a share. True social costs are involved here because they are borne by all of society and not merely the consumers of specified commodities. On the other hand, the subsidies also result in higher prices to consumers; while the surcharge can be avoided by not eating the subsidized food, the program is so extensive that this is not practical.

Thus, another kind of social cost is ultimately involved there as well. It cannot, however, be accurately estimated because one cannot determine the final cost of commodities in the absence of subsidies. In such a case, would many suppliers go bankrupt, so that the supply eventually falls and prices rise again? The answer may well be yes, but the estimation of the extent would be difficult, involving as it does, not only the formulation of an economic model of which there are several plausible ones, but the prediction of political reaction of those affected.

Finally, there are issues of public health in diet and especially in the consumption of products that have agricultural origins, like alcohol and tobacco. The damage of the last two, especially, clearly imposes social costs much along the lines of drugs, as described in chapter 11.

Governmental intervention was originally the result of great and wide-spread distress in farm areas whenever prices dropped below costs of production. Farmers had the political strength to attain programs whereby they were cushioned against sharp declines of their incomes, and thus were able to acquire a safety net rather better than that for other individuals and businesses. These programs, which have existed for a long time, must, however, be viewed together with the profoundly troubled state of American farming and its declining trends after 1981. For this reason, it would be facile, but inaccurate, to present these issues as unfair political advantage. In 1924, long before the programs discussed below were in place, H. L. Mencken remarked: "One might almost argue that the chief, and perhaps even only aim of legislation in These States is to succor and secure the farmer."[1] Mencken was speaking in part about the intolerant and repressive social and political atmosphere fostered in other areas of society by farm area legislators, but it is true that agricultural lobbies, such as those for dairy products, tobacco, grains and sugar, have been highly successful in securing economic advantages for themselves. Still, agricultural health is an enormously important element in the American social fabric and profound damage and costs are incurred if severe problems arise. It is obvious that a well-organized food supply is vital to the United States in its domestic needs and, increasingly, in its international relations.

It is well to begin by placing government subsidies in perspective. Table 13.1 shows total farm income, government payments, and their relationship. It is clear that the proportion of subsidy has fallen in the period shown, although it was rising again at the end. Farmers are also aided by loan programs and surplus commodities stored by the government through the Commodity Credit Corporation (CCC). These are also shown in the table. The fluctuations of all these programs will be discussed in more detail in the next two sections.

The farm support programs are also related to what farmers are paid for their crops and what they have to pay for their supplies. A comparison of the relevant price indexes appears in table 13.2. As is clear from the last column, except for 1973-1974, the index was about 100 or slightly below; in some crops it has become substantially worse. It should also be noted, however, that many individuals in the rest of society have lagged severely in the struggle against the inflation of recent years. Even an aggregate measure like average hourly earnings shows a slight decline that has gone on since 1967 ($2.74 then and $2.71 in 1980, in constant 1967 dollars).[2] In short, farmers do not appear to be conspicuously worse off than the rest of society but such factors as high interest rates, bumper harvests, overcapacity, foreign competition and falling exports have produced a downturn that may prove quite resistant.[3]

Table 13.1
CCC Operations and Governmental Contributions to Cash Income,
1965–1979

	Farm Cash Receipts			CCC Operations	
	Total	From Government	Percent	Value of Loans Outstanding	Value of Commodities Owned
		$ Billion		$ Million	
1965	41.8	2.5	6.0	2,598	4,110
1966	46.7	3.3	7.1	2,069	2,340
1967	45.9	3.1	6.8	2,355	1,005
1968	47.6	3.5	7.4	3,605	1,064
1969	52.0	3.8	7.3	3,628	1,784
1970	54.3	3.7	6.8	2,973	1,594
1971	56.0	3.1	5.5	3,186	1,118
1972	65.2	4.0	6.1	2,438	830
1973	89.7	2.6	2.9	1,266	394
1974	93.0	0.5	0.5	681	188
1975	89.0	0.8	0.9	871	402
1976	95.5	0.7	0.7	1,786	634
1977	97.6	1.8	1.8	5,414	1,104
1978	115.6	3.0	2.6	5,655	1,186
1979	132.8	1.4	1.1	606	1,237

Source: U.S. Department of Agriculture, Agricultural Statistics, 1980 (Washington, D.C.:
U.S. Government Printing Office, 1981), pp. 460, 506, 507.

Commodity Credit Corporation

The foremost government agency providing direct farm support is the
Commodity Credit Corporation, which was chartered on June 6, 1948, for
the purpose of regulating food prices; it was capitalized at $100 million with
borrowing limits up to $14.5 billion.[4] The corporation's objective was to pro-
tect and stabilize farm income and prices. The orderly distribution of farm
commodities maintained balance and adequate supply. Later, other government controls were established. An example of this was the Agricultural and
Consumer Protection Act of 1973 which gave the corporation power to
establish target prices for selected commodities and set minimum loan rates to
farmers.[5] The rates and prices set by the corporation are the minimum that a
farmer would receive for his crops.

Table 13.2
Prices Paid and Received by Farmers, 1965–1979

	Prices Paid by Farmers*	Prices Received by Farmers	Ratio 100 Received/Paid
	1967 = 100		
1965	94	98	104
1966	99	106	107
1967	100	100	100
1968	103	102	99
1969	108	107	99
1970	112	110	98
1971	118	113	96
1972	125	125	100
1973	144	179	124
1974	164	192	117
1975	180	185	103
1976	192	186	97
1977	202	183	91
1978	219	210	96
1979	250	241	96

* Total, including taxes, interest, and wage rates.

Source: U.S. Department of Agriculture, Agricultural Statistics, 1980 (Washington, D.C.:
    U.S. Government Printing Office, 1980), p. 517.

For example, working with data for fall 1978, a farmer with 2,000 acres in wheat could take 20 percent of that acreage, or 400 acres, out of production and receive payment at the rate of $3.40 a bushel for it, when the market price was only $3.00. The $3.40 was the government guaranteed target price and was thus about 13 percent above market.[6] At an average yield of 31.5 bushels per acre,[7] this means an income of 31.5 [(1,600)(3.00) + (400)(3.40)] = $194,040, compared with 31.5 (2,000)(3.00) = $189,000 otherwise. This is only 2.7 percent more, but, as noted in the introduction, the latter figure assumes that if all the acreage turned out wheat, the price would remain at $3.00 a bushel which it very probably would not. In all, 305 million bushels of wheat were removed from production at a cost of $122 million to the taxpayer.

    The mechanics of CCC loans have not changed for three decades. According to the loan agreement, the farmer must store the grain until the loan is repaid or matures. This gives the farmer a way to raise capital in markets glutted just after harvest. The farmer can fulfill his loan obligation in two ways:

1. He can repay the loan plus interest any time up to maturity while keeping unencumbered control of the grain.

2. He can default at maturity keeping the proceeds of the loan and turning the grain over to the CCC.

The choice the farmer makes depends on the market price of grain and the loan rate. If the market price exceeds the loan rate plus interest charges, the farmer sells his crops, keeping the difference. If the market price fails to reach this price or declines, the farmer defaults. Loan defaults during the late 1950s and early 1960s led to large government stocks of grains. This occurred because market prices nearly always averaged less than the loan rates and led to predictable defaulting on CCC loans. These defaults, combined with a lack of effective production controls, led to a record accumulation in 1961 of 85 million metric tons in government-owned grain stocks.[8]

During the first half of the sixties, the policy shortcomings were corrected. Grain production was put into better balance with utilization through programs that removed considerable acreage from production. This, coupled with expansion of exports of CCC stocks and the Food for Peace program, stabilized government stocks around 16 million metric tons in the late sixties. However, shortages occurred when prices skyrocketed in 1973. This is because the CCC can sell its grain on the commercial markets once the market price exceeds 15 percent of the loan rate. Thus, in 1974, government stocks of grains were exhausted.

The producer-held domestic grain reserve program now serves as the major vehicle for accumulating buffer stocks of grain, operating as an extension of the CCC loan program. Farmers in the new program agree to keep their crops off the market for three years or until market prices exceed designated "trigger levels." As long as prices remain under trigger levels, there are several incentives to participate in the program. The farmer receives "up front" storage payment for storing the grain for the three-year period. Interest charges on the CCC loan are terminated after the grain has been stored in reserve for one year. Another incentive is a companion program for lending farmers enough money to build or repair facilities for storing two years, worth of grain production. Since these loans are fully amortized over eight years, the reserve storage payments are usually enough to meet the annual payment on the storage facility loan.

The trigger levels are implemented at two tiers; a lower tier that allows farmers to repay loans *voluntarily,* and an upper tier that *requires* farmers to repay their loans. This means the relationship between the trigger levels and grain prices determine entry into the program. Grain prices lower than the trigger levels encourage entry, while prices above trigger levels will not. If prices decline after exceeding trigger levels, storage payment would resume to the farmers still in the program. The net results of this in 1978 were about $275 million in storage payments and, at then-current loan rates, another $150 million for waived interest charges.[9]

Government Subsidies to Farmers

The federal government also gives farmers cash subsidies. As table 13.1 showed, they reached a peak in 1969. The upward trend was slowed and eventually reversed by new regulations for loans and by higher food prices. Both can be attributed to the large number of defaults that occurred during the early sixties. Under new rules established around 1965, acreage was withheld from production instead of crops being stored in CCC bins, while defaults were still occurring under the old program. Therefore, as prices increased, idle acreage was put back into production, but crops in storage were not released to the market. An examination of prices sheds some light on these trends. Referring to tables 13.1 and 13.2, in 1970-1975, both cash payments and prices received for food increased faster than the wholesale price index. Although cash payments were starting to decline after 1973, prices stabilized at the new higher levels. Once the prices had reached these levels, subsidies declined because of the higher profit received on the market.

Going back further, the record shows that between 1959 and 1970, prices fluctuated within a ten-cent range.[10] However, in a five-year period, 1970-1975, commodities demonstrated high, volatile price fluctuations that were greater than the preceding eleven-year period. During 1969 payments to farmers were at an all-time high of $3.79 billion. The price received for these farm commodities was at an all-time low. The reverse is true when we review 1974: prices of commodities had reached all-time highs; government payments to the farmer were lower than 1959. A trend therefore emerges that shows the farmer becoming less dependent on these programs in higher price periods (1973-1976) and returning to them as the prices declined. However, the programs now are burdened with higher production costs that would need higher prices to make farming profitable.

A parallel program involves control of acreage and therefore of supply. As table 13.3 shows, there has been a slow but steady decline in total farm acre-

Table 13.3
Farm Lands and Conservation, 1959–1980

Years	Total Land Millions of Acres	Average Size of Farm Acres	Conservation Subsidy $ Million
1959	1,182	288	210
1960	1,175	297	213
1961	1,167	305	238
1962	1,159	314	221
1963	1,151	322	218
1964	1,146	332	221
1965	1,139	340	231
1966	1,131	348	217
1967	1,123	355	226
1968	1,115	363	209
1969	1,107	369	193
1970	1,102	373	189
1971	1,097	377	161
1972	1,093	381	200
1973	1,089	383	220
1974	1,087	384	83
1975	1,063	427	146
1976	1,059	432	149
1977	1,055	438	194
1978	1,052	444	197
1979	1,049	450	
1980	1,048	453	

Source: U.S. Department of Agriculture, Agricultural Statistics, 1977, 1980 (Washington, D.C.: U.S. Government Printing Office, 1977, 1981), p. 528, p. 417.

age, at an annual rate of about 0.6 percent. The payments offered by government to encourage withdrawal of land for conservation purposes are also shown and reflect increases at times of low prices and decreases when prices are good. It is noteworthy, however, that in spite of falling prices, the annual amounts spent from 1977 onward were less than from 1959 to 1969 which, considering inflation in the entire period, represents a very substantial overall drop in real dollar terms.

Table 13.3 also shows a steady increase in the average size of a farm, at an annual rate of about 2.2 percent. This bears on another problem. An examination of farm productivity[11] discloses that by many measures, crop yield appears to be reaching a ceiling and that the economy of scale realizable by larger farms, larger farm machinery (which itself requires larger farms to be economical), more intensive use of agricultural chemicals, and so on is likewise approaching an economic maximum.

It is therefore clear from the foregoing description of subsidy programs, both with respect to crops and acreage, that the program is heavily used when prices fall and less so when they rise. Nevertheless, overall government policy in such matters as setting trigger prices, parity, and so on have sufficient flexibility as to result in substantial uncertainty for farmers. In the period discussed here, the government first took the road of restricting production and selling at high government-supported prices. These in turn helped fuel inflation and, added to provisions in various industries and among social security recipients and others of cost of living increases, had a significant multiplier effect throughout society. In the early 1970s, the government encouraged production to the maximum levels but in the early years of the Carter administration restrictions of acreage and output were again encouraged.[12] Later still the policy changed once again so that by 1982 the United States produced approximately 1.6 times its domestic needs. This will lead to a record $18.8 billion payment to farmers in 1983.[13] A vast surplus of stocks and capacity has been created in a time when domestic and international demand has weakened. The strength of the dollar, which is a result of high interest rates, in particular had a restricting effect on sales other than through foreign aid agencies (see next section).

The continuing high interest rates have had a devastating effect on farm costs. Futhermore, there are signs of weakening in prices and values of the farms themselves. As a result, the amount that farmers can borrow on their land has been restricted. The result is that corn is estimated to cost between $4.25 to $4.75 per bushel to produce and sells for only $2.75. This has led to a sharp upturn in farm failures. The Farmers Home Administration, an agency concerned with farm financing, recorded 871 "voluntary liquidations," meaning the farmers sold out to satisfy debts, and also foreclosed on 421 farms, all between October 1, 1981, and January 31, 1982. In the entire preceding year, the government agency had 127 voluntary liquidations and 133 foreclosures.[14]

One result of this most troublesome situation has been a demand by some farmer groups for a drastic cutback in acreage to produce no more than domestic needs plus whatever export needs are fully contracted. However, this would run into difficulties on another front; it has been pointed out that the agricultural trade surplus of about $27 billion offset almost half of the country's petroleum trade deficit.

Social Programs

Substantial food purchases are made by the government for various social programs. In part these are made from CCC stocks so that their cost, as detailed below, is double-counted with reference to the statistics shown earlier. However, much food for all these programs is also bought on the open market. Table 13.4 shows the expenditures by principal category for the fifteen years, 1965-1979. The principal categories are school feeding, food stamps, and distributions to institutions and needy persons, which is a group of programs that have largely been taken over by other parts of the welfare system. The total amounts have risen at an overall rate of about 17 percent, with the rate increasing somewhat more slowly (13 percent) from 1972 on. At the same time, the consumer price index for food increased at an annual average rate of about 10.6 percent.[15] Actually, these distributions are subjected to upward pressure by the same subsidies, cutbacks in acreage, and price guarantees as food purchases in general.

Clearly, very substantial sums are involved. Predictably, these programs have attracted severe budget cuts and general hostility on the part of the Reagan administration. As a result, school meals particularly have been cut and eligibility has been tightened. In spring 1981, the Department of Agriculture received much adverse publicity when it proposed tofu and ketchup as an acceptable substitute for meat and vegetables. The 1983 budget likewise proposes further cutbacks.

Table 13.4 also includes data on the food stamp program which has risen greatly, primarily because, under its funding rules, the federal subsidy rises as food prices increase. The food stamp program also has attracted sustained hostility on the part of the administration. Yet, it is clearly indispensable to ensuring an adequate diet for a substantial part of the population. Some preliminary indications have been reported that the cutbacks enacted in 1981 have already brought in their train a measurable decline in nutrition, with all the difficulties that entails. One of the great social benefits of all these programs is to have reduced starvation in the United States to a minimal level. It appears inescapable that this trend will now be reversed.

The principal export activity is the Food for Peace program (P.L. 480), which was started in 1955. The cost of this program from 1955 to 1975 was $24.2 billion in farm products with $10.9 billion being accounted for by wheat. For its first twelve years, this program consisted of more than a quarter of the agricultural exports of the United States by value. This share had decreased to less than 5 percent in 1973. The cost in recent years has averaged $1.2 to $1.4 billion, but the entire cost since 1954 has exceeded $31.8 billion.

Table 13.4
Food Purchases for Social Programs, 1965–1979

Fiscal Year	Cash Payments	School Feeding Commodities	Milk	Institutions and Needy Persons	Food Stamp Subsidy	Total
			$ Million			
1965	130	272	97	257	33	789
1966	141	175	97	151	65	629
1967	151	188	99	116	106	660
1968	162	276	102	147	173	860
1969	220	272	101	250	229	1,072
1970	328	266	101	312	550	1,557
1971	588	279	91	346	1,523	2,827
1972	780	315	90	338	1,797	3,320
1973	930	331	91	282	2,131	3,765
1974	1,169	319	49	230	2,718	4,485
1975	1,400	423	124	76	4,386	6,409
1976	1,633	430	144	54	5,327	7,588
1977	1,849	557	154	62	5,058	7,680
1978	2,029	624	142	93	5,165	8,053
1979	2,258	703	141	39	6,478	9,619

Source: U.S. Department of Agriculture, *Agricultural Statistics, 1980* (Washington, D.C.: U.S. Government Printing Office, 1981) pp. 556, 557.

Eleven countries accounted for 64 percent of the total cost or $15.6 billion. They are: India, $5,010 million; Pakistan, $1,833 million; South Korea, $1,678 million; Yugoslavia, $1,133 million; Indonesia, $934 million; Brazil, $859 million; Egypt, $829 million; Israel, $625 million; Turkey, $561 million; Poland, $519 million; and South Vietnam, $1,768 million.[16]

The Food for Peace program was originally promoted to Congress as a means of implementing foreign policy objectives of the United States. As an example, Yugoslavia is frequently cited; it received most of its aid during 1954-1966, while it was becoming increasingly independent of the Soviet Union. Despite all this, the United States has extended credit facilities to the Soviet Union itself in connection with the latter's increasingly large grain purchases.

Social Costs of Farm Products

In addition to the financing and management of farm crops in general, certain products raise problems of social costs in themselves. The best example is tobacco. Beginning in the 1950s, the damage caused by cigarette smoking has been elaborately documented, both by statistical analysis and by admittedly still incomplete knowledge of cancer causation. In successive reports by the surgeon general of the United States from 1964 until February 1982,[17] cigarette smoking has been linked to cancer of several organs, especially of the lungs. Pipe and cigar smoking have been linked to cancer of the mouth and bladder and all smoking is associated with emphysema, heart conditions, and other ailments. The social costs involved are those of a major public health disaster, including some 340,000 cancer deaths a year, as well as other suffering.[18]

Of this number, 111,000 deaths were from lung cancer alone. This estimate for 1982 contrasts with only 18,313 deaths in 1950. More than $13 billion a year is spent on health care related to smoking and at least another $25 billion is lost in foregone economic contributions.[19] This is partly offset by the $10 billion or so collected in taxes on tobacco products; it is a favorite argument of the tobacco industry that to the extent that tobacco products are restricted, a shortfall in taxes will have to be made up otherwise. Nevertheless, it is clear that the cost is almost four times the tax receipts, even if no allowance is made for pain and suffering. The report concludes: "Cigarette smoking is clearly identified as the chief preventable cause of death in our society and the most important public health issue of our time."

There is an even more direct social cost involved, albeit on a smaller scale. The Department of Agriculture includes tobacco among its crop support programs. In all programs, CCC, subsidies, and so forth, it has spent as much as $231 million in one year (1980). The absurdity of government on the one hand establishing the responsibility of tobacco for a variety of ills, and on the other, subsidizing it, has long been pointed out. The Department of Agriculture even maintains a research service for the tobacco industry which, according to one critic, "assigns more space to research on tobacco than on food distribution. What's more, its concern is to produce a more marketable product, not a safer product."[20]

The Department is also actively promoting tobacco exports. Since 1955, The United States has sent some 330 metric tons of tobacco abroad, paid for by the Food for Peace program. In 1977, 13.5 metric tons were shipped, with a value of $55 million.[21]

Government support for tobacco is regularly challenged in Congress at budget time, but so far has resisted all efforts to reduce it. It always has powerful champions, and the tobacco lobby and congressional tobacco block have always been able to bargain powerfully with other agrarian interests as well as the leadership of the political parties in general. It is instructive that at present, the leading champions are the two Republican senators from North Carolina, Jesse Helms and James East, who assail even such proposals as sterner warnings on cigarette packages as "prohibitionist," but are otherwise united in a whole range of restrictive measures aimed at personal freedom and civil liberties. As a result, the sterner warnings which were prompted by the latest report of the surgeon general soon wound up in legislative limbo.

Alcohol likewise poses grave social cost problems. The damage done by it is enormous. Estimates of the number of alcoholics and "problem drinkers" range from 5 to 9 million. The lost economic contribution of such a population can hardly even be guessed at. Alcoholism is a very large part of the law enforcement problem, in that many crimes are committed while the participants are under the influence, and driving while intoxicated (DWI) is a major cause of the worst automobile accidents. It is estimated that alcohol is involved in 55 percent of all arrests. In a study of homicides in Philadelphia, it was found that alcohol was *absent* from both killer and victim in only 36 percent of the cases. Child abuse, suicide, domestic violence of all kinds are all alcohol related. In spite of the publicity given to what are usually called drugs, moreover, alcohol is the "drug" most often consumed, and by a very large margin.[22]

Alcohol can be made from many agricultural crops. In the United States it is mostly grain, but also sugar beets, potatoes, and other materials. Agricultural support programs are thus involved in setting its price. The use of alcohol as a motor fuel has raised the question of whether it is ethical to burn a food as fuel. However, it is difficult to balance the merits of that argument against the alternate of using an irreplaceable natural resource derived from petroleum. It could in fact be argued that, in countries like Brazil where alcohol from sugar beets and (experimentally) cassava is used as automobile fuel, the result has been to smooth out the demand in what is otherwise an exceedingly volatile crop.

Sugar is also one of the relatively few foodstuffs that are protected from import competition by tariffs and quotas so that the price to U.S. consumers is kept high. The United States produces sugar from both cane and beets (the latter mainly when prices are high) and is a high cost producer compared with its tropical competitors, like the countries of Central America, the Philippines, and others. But even domestic sugar, protected as it is, has had to contend with attacks on its traditional markets from corn sweeteners, as well as artificial sweeteners.

Social Costs of Farms

Finally, farms themselves raise issues of social costs. First, they are substantial polluters, because the run-off from them contains large quantities of toxic sprays, nutrients from fertilizers, and animal wastes. Run-off makes its way into water courses and has contaminated an estimated two-thirds of the 246 hydrological basins in the United States. Furthermore, some 2 billion tons of topsoil are washed away every year, silting up thousands of rural creeks, disrupting natural drainage patterns, and carrying further toxic chemicals with them.[23] Farms are therefore major contributors to pollution damage, which was discussed in chapter 5 in an industrial context.

So far, water pollution laws applying to farms are vague and spottily enforced. Studies are under way to devise a a control system comparable to that of industry, but one cannot be sanguine about its prospects. Given the current political atmosphere and the still considerable power of farm lobbies, they could hardly be expected to take a more friendly view of stricter laws than their industrial counterparts.

On his appointment as secretary of agriculture in December 1980, J. R. Block declared that "food is America's greatest diplomatic weapon."[24] Yet, only shortly before this, his own department had published most alarming reports on the acceleration of soil erosion and destruction of agricultural land. As a result of pushing for ever higher food production, as noted before, even such elementary conservationist rules as contour plowing were being widely ignored.[25] The current physical state of the farm structure thus raises social cost issues encompassing social efficiency and the premature exhaustion of natural resources as well.

A virtual textbook example of the latter kind of social cost is presented by the developing policy of allowing ranchers ever greater authority over federal lands, especially grazing and water rights. Overgrazing and premature exhaustion of aquifers are, of course, the leading problems in these rather arid regions, and allowing this degree of discretion to exactly those who had wrought the existing and all too evident ecological damage is a sharp and deplorable reversal of a modest trend to conservation before the Reagan Administration.

This chapter has dealt with price setting by and on behalf of farmers but it is appropriate to conclude by noting that farm prices themselves cannot properly be given the full blame for the sustained rise in food prices. Rather, the burden rests much more on the processing and marketing cost associated with food. Farm prices are determined by demand which affects the farmer's income but have shown themselves to be a relatively small influence on food prices when compared to changes in processing and marketing costs. Since the marketing cost represents about 60 percent of the total expenditures for food, a change in this cost results in a greater increase in price. Since 1974, the farmer's share has leveled off and the recorded increase in food prices is primarily due to increases in processing and distribution costs.[26]

Conclusion

The social costs of food arise primarily from the various support programs for farmers by which acreage is taken out of production in order to support prices and minimum prices are established for a variety of farm commodities. The costs of these programs are substantial, depending upon the farm situation. Support payments are high when prices are low and vice versa, but since base prices are seldom if ever reduced, the whole process contributes to the ratchet mechanism long associated with inflation. The associated practice of restricting supply amidst widespread global starvation also exacts a social cost as well as being morally questionable.

The second major sources of government support are the direct food programs of which food stamps and school meals are the best known. Their combined cost is on the order of $10 billion.

In addition to these direct support efforts, serious social costs are also incurred as a result of the consequences of certain agricultural commodities, most notably tobacco and alcohol, which are likewise derived from a variety of agricultural raw materials. Tobacco subsidies still are paid by the government even though the disastrous impact of it on public health has long been known and is well established. Unfortunately, however, tobacco provides one of the highest yields in dollars per acre of any crop. This fact in itself is a major element in the political pressures with which the privileges of that industry are defended.

There is other evidence that the purchase and storage of surplus food has gotten grossly out of hand. At a time when the Reagan administration was cutting 900,000 households off welfare rolls and reducing benefits to 70 percent of all food stamp recipients, $2.2 billion will have been spent by the end of the 1982 fiscal year just to keep certain dairy products off the market; some 13.8 billion pounds of milk, about 10 percent of production, had to be bought by the government. Some $400 million must be spent on storage and interest on the money paid out for the 1 million tons of commodities that are involved. The give-away program of surplus cheese in 1981-1982 attracted wide attention, but it will only dispose of some 100 million out of 600 million pounds in the stockpile.[27] In part, the problem is one of changing dietary habits; consumption of dairy products and fats in most forms is down substantially. But just as in tobacco, the real issue is the political strength of the dairy lobby which again translates, at one remove, into a societal inability to find a remedy when large numbers of people are threatened with a substantial reduction in their livelihood. A $2.2 billion investment plus $400 million a year maintenance are large social costs, but others would arise if instead there were wholesale economic devastation in the dairy-producing regions. That is a pervasive issue, as will be noted again in a different context in chapter 15.

Finally, there are issues concerning the farms themselves. Farms are not necessarily good environmental neighbors, and the problems posed by them have barely begun to be systematically examined. It is clear as noted at the outset, that a secure food supply is essential to any society; however, the results presented in this chapter indicate that, as presently organized, such a desirable attribute does not come without its cost.

Notes

1. H. L. Mencken, *Prejudices: A Selection* (New York: Vintage, 1959), p. 158.

2. *Statistical Abstract of the United States, 1980*, p. 425.

3. "Why the Recovery May Skip the Farm Belt," *Business Week*, March 21, 1983, p. 106.

4. *United States Government Manual, 1977-1978* (Washington, D.C.: U.S. Government Printing Office, 1978), p. 126.

5. Ibid., p. 125.

6. "The New American Farmer," *Time*, November 6, 1978, pp. 96-97.

7. U.S. Department of Agriculture, *Crop Production*, October 11, 1978, p. A-3.

8. G. L. Benjamin, "The New Grain Reserve Programs," *Economic Perspectives*, November-December 1978, pp. 11-12.

9. Ibid., p. 13.

10. U.S. Department of Agriculture, *Agricultural Statistics, 1977* (Washington, D.C.: U.S. Government Printing Office, 1978), p. 527.

11. J. M. Svrcek, "Agriculture," *The Improvement of Productivity*, ed. J. E. Ullmann, (New York: Praeger Publishers, 1980), ch. 2.

12. "The American Farmer," p. 102.

13. "Why the Recovery May Skip the Farm Belt."

14. G. Jaynes, "U.S. Farmers Said to Face Worst Year Since 1930s," *New York Times*, March 28, 1982.

15. U.S. Department of Agriculture, *Agricultural Statistics, 1980,* (Washington, D.C.: U.S. Government Printing Office, 1981), p. 559.

16. Library of Congress, Congressional Research Service, *Use of U.S. Food Resources for Diplomatic Purposes: An Examination of the Issue* (94th Cong.: January 1977).

17. *Report of the Surgeon General on Smoking* (Washington, D.C.: U.S. Government Printing Office, 1982).

18. Ibid.; see also E. M. Brecher et al., *Licit and Illicit Drugs* (Mt. Vernon, N.Y.: Consumers Union, 1972), chs. 26 and 27, esp. p. 243.

19. *Report of the Surgeon General on Smoking.*

20. E. Eckholm, "The Unnatural History of Tobacco," *Natural History*, April 1977, pp. 21, 31.

21. M. J. Sheridan, "Filter Fun for Third Worlders," *New York Times*, April 13, 1980.

22. Brecher, *Licit and Illicit Drugs*, pp. 260-66.

23. S. S. King, "How to Keep Runoff Down on the Farm," *New York Times*, February 3, 1980; see also R. Weinstein, "The Duck Industry of Long Island," in *Waste Disposal Problems in Selected Industries*, ed. J. E. Ullmann (Hempstead, N.Y.: Hofstra Yearbooks of Business, 1969).

24. S. S. King, "Block Sees Food as U.S. Weapon in Foreign Policy," *New York Times*, December 24, 1980.

25. A. Crittenden, "Soil Erosion Threatens U.S. Farms' Output," *New York Times*, October 26, 1980.

26. A. M. Young, "Marketing Costs Boost Food Prices," *Voice of the Federal Reserve Bank of Dallas*, March 1978, p. 7.

27. A. Peracchio, "U.S. Troubled by Abundance," *Newsday*, April 6, 1982, see also "We Can't Afford the Butter Mountain" (Editorial), *New York Times*, November 15, 1982.

14
General Government

DAVID WOTMAN

> Government is emphatically a
> machine: to the discontented
> a "taxing machine," to the con-
> tented a "machine for securing
> property."
>
> Thomas Carlyle, *Signs of the Times*

Introduction

The social costs of government require some additional discussion; the salient points are briefly summarized in this chapter. Throughout this volume, it has been shown that certain costs of economic activities have been put into the public sector by being converted from a business expense to a government expense, which is borne by taxes and, as is well known, by deficits. The ability to convert them into a public responsibility reflects in large measure the political strength of those responsible for them in the first instance. Subsidies and other ways of shouldering public responsibility therefore are the primary vehicles by which government assumes social costs.

In this chapter, however, the social costs incurred by government itself are delineated. The government is involved in a number of activities that generate social costs themselves. By far the most important one is the military sector whose particular problems and ramifications are treated in chapter 15. Transfer payments to individuals, which are another important aspect of government work, were discussed in several previous chapters. Finally, chapter 13 gave details of the largest outright subsidy to an industry, that is, agriculture subsidies.

The government is, however, engaged in a variety of activities that go beyond the ones just noted, and before discussing them, it is important to deal with a definitional aspect. Kapp[1] has noted that in order to qualify as a social cost, it must be avoidable. It could be argued that since governments collect taxes, and compel their citizens to pay them, the cost is not avoidable. Therefore, the costs of government should not be considered a social cost in Kapp's terms. However, this argument fails on the grounds that government has a wide variety of policy choices and that if it is eventually considered unacceptable for government to make a certain kind of expenditure, the political process will see to it that it ceases, unless the government were of a totally despotic variety and could rule without reference to public response.

The effective working of popular feedback requires a reasonably well-functioning interaction between government and governed. Such a relationship has existed at many levels in the past, but as one indication of its recent deterioration, the United States now has a very large underground economy. It has been growing for some time but has not previously attracted the kind of attention that it has of late. It expresses itself in an economic sense in some $380 billion of concealed income, of which about $125 billion is estimated to come from illegal activities and the remainder, $255 billion, from legal activities that go unreported to the tax collector.[2]

Underground economies are a global phenomenon. It is, however, instructive to note one interpretation of some rather considerable national differences. The economist E. Feige has suggested that a general distrust of government is responsible, which, in the United States, was heightened after Vietnam and Watergate. Though realizing the problems in making international comparisons, he also notes that Sweden, with very high taxes, has a small underground economy; it is a cohesive society in which trust of government is largely the rule rather than the exception. In Italy, on the other hand, there are relatively low taxes but an underground economy that may amount to 25 percent of the recorded gross national product.[3] However, the individual is seriously alienated from government authority. The reasons are, of course, rooted in Italian history in much of which the country was parceled out among a multiplicity of states, exposed to dynastic rivalries, papal politics, outright foreign conquests, and declining local oligarchies. Mistrust is clearly well founded.

How does this relate to the United States at this point, however? One must recall that a perception of overall incompetence and alienation is largely spawned by societal conditions that clearly show a decline. Particularly at the time of writing, that is evident to most citizens other than the relatively few who have benefited from the current state of the economy.

There is a second point, however. Since at least 1968, political candidates from presidents down have run on platforms that in one way or another assailed "government." Virtually any activity of government, other than the organization of violence in the military sector, came in for criticism as being dominated by a bureaucracy that was impervious to productivity improvement and efficiency and could only obstruct. The "regulation" issue spawned by such views was discussed in some detail in chapter 1 of this volume. The stridency of this kind of a campaign became all the more bizarre in that candidates were running against the very enterprises, the management of which they were asking the public to entrust to them. To be sure, there are employers who hate their employees. But in conventional business management and personnel relations, that tends to be regarded, and very properly so, as a pathological condition.

This kind of policymaking reached a crescendo with the start of the Reagan administration and the results have been detailed in several places throughout this volume. The appointments that were subsequently made to the cabinet, subcabinet positions, and regulatory commissions were, to a large extent, of individuals who had made a career out of trying to destroy the very functions they were now being asked to manage. That kind of policy is to personnel management what asset stripping is to financial management.

Bureaucracy and the Control of Operations

The present chapter focuses primarily on fraud and mismanagement within government. It therefore concentrates on opportunity costs that are involved whenever that kind of practice occurs. It must be very clearly emphasized here that these conditions are also found in the private sector; no reliable data exist for determining whether they exist more often in the private than the public sector, although the estimated size of the underground economy discussed above is perhaps an indication. However, what has been identified as government fraud and mismanagement often has to do not so much with criminality but with sheer mismanagement, with waste motion, and with other problems of this sort.

An important aspect of the problem, however, lies in the data themselves. Government activities are scrutinized in a very different way from those in the private sector. Public funds are involved in the operation of government and there is a multitude of internal watchdogs. By contrast, in businesses, audits by public accountants seldom deal with justification of expenses rather than their bookkeeping details. Internal audit departments, such as exist in some large organizations, may ask for more detailed operational justifications, but much of public supervision of business activity is primarily concerned with making sure that the numbers are added up right. It is assumed that if the internal mismanagement were to become gross enough, the business would fail, or its profitability would be sufficiently impaired to cause an internal shakeup. To that extent, then, self-regulation is practiced. Government is, of course, circumscribed rather tightly by budgets, and these are legally binding. It is essentially the quality of expenditures that then becomes an issue.

A brief discussion of the purpose of bureaucracy is germane at this point. "Bureaucracy" in its modern (that is, post-Roman or ancient Chinese) context was established in order to make sure as far as possible that equal circumstances were treated equally by public officials and, for that matter, by private bureaucrats as well. As Blau and Meyer point out:

> Capitalism . . . promotes effective and extensive operations of the government. It also leads to bureaucratization in other spheres. The expansion of business firms and the consequent removal of most employees from activities directly governed by the profit principle make it increasingly necessary to introduce bureaucratic methods of administration for the sake of efficiency. . . . Strange as it may seem, the free-enterprise system fosters the development of bureaucracy in government, in private companies, and in unions.[4]

Whether this process has been carried to excess is another matter, but it is well to remember that bureaucratic employment carries social status and, for a long time, was regarded as the wave of the future in a so-called post-industrial society. Andrew Hacker has called attention to the rise of "conversational employment." As he puts it, "We want jobs where we will spend most of our time talking. Indeed, millions of adult Americans now receive salaries for spending most of their daylight hours in meetings, conferences and committees."[5]

In the regulatory sphere which has become so controversial, much of this activity involves hearings, litigation, and other adversary proceedings. Protocol and one-upmanship at such functions have attracted the attention of writers on management topics, both straight and deservedly satirical. There tends to be a certain symbiosis, an almost ritual atmosphere of tournament and tilt in many of these functions. Moreover, much of the workload relates to safeguards, loopholes, adversary proceedings, and other details that were put into the original laws by the very industries that are to be regulated or to stop fraudulent transfer payments or to stop internal abuses and arbitrariness.

Procedures can give a certain degree of predictability to the actions of civil servants and others, whereas societies lacking that kind of system can only be arbitrary. In feudal France, for example, the same offense could call for drastically different treatment, depending upon the whims of the local lord. Later French centralism was largely a reaction to this. That kind of system still exists in countries such as Saudi Arabia where laws tend to be a matter of ad hoc decisions.

This is not to suggest that bureaucracies do not create enormous problems in themselves. The idea that they are permanent whereas other parts of government are temporary creations of the prevailing political mood has been a pervasive source of mischief. At the least it manifests itself in a very distorted notion of "service" in which the convenience of the bureaucracy invariably takes precedence over that of the clients. It shows itself most obviously in the long waiting lines in government offices all over the world, of people who in most cases are asking for nothing more than their exact right and due. Such attitudes flourish whenever organizations are encouraged to value the time of their customers at zero; it occurs quite conspicuously in private bureaucracies as well. The right to say "no" to everything and anything is a cherished prerogative.[6]

Fraud

Fraud has often occurred in cases in which controls over funds have been slack enough to permit it. A former comptroller general of the United States, Elmer Staats, estimated that fraud in economic assistance programs ranges from 1 to 10 percent of authorized expenditures, which suggests a loss of $2.5 to $25 billion a year.[7] In his investigation, programs run by the Departments of Labor, Agriculture, Transportation and Housing and Urban Development, the Veterans Administration, the Small Business Administration (SBA), and the General Services Administration (GSA) were shown to have been involved in fraudulent spending to some degree. According to the General Accounting Office (GAO), which is the principal internal auditor, grants, contracts, and loan guarantees have been exploited by false claims for benefits, false statements to win contracts, bribery or corruption or public employees and officials, false payment claims for undelivered goods and services, and collusion involving contractors. Systematic efforts to identify and root out fraud exist but are only indifferently effective. One of the worst areas is the General Services Administration. During the summer of 1978 there were revelations of fraud by managers of GSA buildings and self-service stores. The GSA has 36,000 employees and owns and manages federal government buildings, including the Pentagon. At the time, they spent $5 billion a year on supplies for federal agencies ranging from computers to paper clips. Estimates by federal investigators were that mismanagement in the GSA could be costing taxpayers as much as $100 million a year.

By the end of 1978, thirty-one indictments had been handed down with more expected to come.[8] The investigators reported a pattern of corruption:

1. Payments, often in huge amounts, for work not done or only partially completed

2. Payments for supplies not delivered, involving collusion between managers and employees of the GSA self-service supplies stores and contractors

3. Fraudulent use of government-issued credit cards to charge up hundreds of thousands of dollars' worth of supplies and services for personal use

4. Acceptance of great amounts of poorly constructed office furniture without inspection

An agency of the government that also has widespread fraud and mismanagement is the Small Business Administration. At least $3.5 million in advances to thirty-five concerns in New York alone have never been repaid, while up to $50 million in federal funds is possibly lost. The $3.5 million in New York represents only a fraction of what is expected to be lost. There are possibilities of fraud of more than $2 billion in contracts with firms throughout the country.[9]

These funds are advanced by the SBA to businesses owned by members of minorities that are defined as Black, Hispanic, and Asian only in the New York City area and differently elsewhere. This program allows qualified companies to obtain government contracts without competitive bidding for a wide variety of services from janitorial to computer services in government offices. The SBA advances these companies the money they need to complete the contract with the understanding that it will be paid back when the company is paid by the government agency for which it is doing the work.

One irregularity has predictably been the use of minority members as fronts for majority-owned businesses. Employees of the SBA were involved in this by receiving kickbacks for ignoring such situations, as well as for altering a company's records to show them up to date when they actually were behind in their repayments. It could be argued that the SBA was set up to assist enterprises that are rather riskier than the ordinary run of business. If they were not, conventional bank financing might have been available. However, many of the recipients of its aid were very poor risks, no matter how one stretches the concept and the frauds compounded the problem further.

Red Tape

The idea of red tape, meaning unproductive, time-consuming, and expensive paperwork, is a subjective one. Most people have had grounds to complain about it, but quite often, one person's red tape is someone else's essential constitutional safeguard, protection against fraud, environmental damage, or product dangers, or just simply someone's livelihood. Civil servants, after all, are entitled to defend their jobs, just as everyone is. (And let it not be objected here that private sector jobs invariably have to satisfy stern standards of cost-effectiveness. That is hardly the case in a private sector festooned with protectionism, subsidies, and other material public assistance.)

At any rate, red tape has been extensively studied. In the United States a comprehensive recent study was that of the Commission on Federal Paperwork (CFP); in its final report in 1977, it came up with an estimate of the cost of red tape of $100 billion[10] in the private and public sectors combined. The cost is ultimately imposed on the consumer through higher prices and higher taxes. There are also psychological costs, notably the anxiety, frustration, and anger that people experience when dealing with excessive paperwork and red tape.

The CFP was formed in 1975 for a period of two years to reexamine the policies and procedures of the federal government that have an impact on the paperwork burden, and to recommend any changes to be made. The total costs of federal paperwork were difficult to determine, but best estimates put it at $100 billion a year, or about $500 per capita.[11] Estimates of costs to some of the major segments of society are:[12]

Federal government	$43 billion per year
Private industry	$25 to $32 billion per year
State and local government	$5 to $9 billion per year
Individuals	$8.7 billion per year
Farmers	$350 million per year
Labor organizations	$75 million per year

The Commission decided to study the root causes of paperwork rather than just how to eliminate excessive information requirements. The information requirements studied were considered excessive because they were duplicative, unnecessary to the achievement of program objectives, unnecessarily cumbersome, confusing, and costly.

There are three types of paperwork burdens studied by CFP. First, economic burdens include, but go beyond, the dollar costs of filling out a report: record keeping systems must be set up by the business when the requested information is not available; outside professional, legal, and accounting help may be required to interpret federal requirements; multiple copies may be needed; costs of traveling to government offices and resources spent on paperwork are not available for other, more productive purposes.

Second, psychological burdens may be more important than dollar costs to individuals who experience frustration in completing complex forms, anger when faced with multiple requests for similar data, confusion in reading unclear instructions, and fear that confidential information may be abused.[13] A family spending thirty-five hours filling out a student-aid application or the confusion and anxiety of an individual filling out his own tax return exemplify this burden. But then, the income tax is complicated in large part because of the many special provisions demanded by voting blocs of various kinds and many burdensome and expensive rules on aid payments are designed exactly to reduce fraud—a point we noted earlier.

Finally, cumulative burdens occur when the sum of requests becomes overbearing. For example, one company had to comply with federal requests for 8,800 reports from eighteen different agencies in one year. Some of the more important causes are:[14]

1. Many government agencies fail to analyze the burdens they impose on the public and state and local governments.

2. Often, two or more agencies run similar programs in an uncoordinated way, with a devastating total impact on individuals—for example, the elderly seeking assistance, businessmen reporting financial information, or a state or local government submitting planning information.

3. Timely reforms of laws and regulations that would ease the burden and improve programs are not considered.

4. Federal programs are frequently administered for the convenience of the agency involved rather than the respondents to be served.

The efforts of the commission in part led to the Paper Work Reduction Act of 1980. It turned out to have far-reaching effects, but not, perhaps, as first intended. There is evidence that the laudable effort to cut red tape and the administrative burden of society in general, has likewise backfired in the secretive and restrictive atmosphere generated by the Reagan administration. By increasing the authority of government officials to classify data, cutting back on the collection of statistics, increasing the surveillance of government officials (and the use of lie detectors in this connection), reducing the staff of the national archives, and, above all, by a sustained effort to repeal or gut the Freedom of Information Act and, meanwhile, throwing up administrative barriers to its working, an atmosphere of secrecy has been fostered, such as has not been experienced for many years. Inevitably, the suspicion grows among the public that ever more important information is being hidden and that the public's rights in this regard are being seriously eroded.[15]

No account of fraud and red tape can be complete without reference to the military sector. Although the problem that its enormous size has created for American society will be discussed in detail in chapter 15, the administrative burden within the Pentagon is enormous. The United States has the lowest ratio of combat troops to total employees in its military establishment.[16] From the viewpoint of this chapter, there has been pervasive evidence of duplications of efforts, red tape, cover-ups, conflicts of interest, cost overruns, and diversion of resources to private purposes. GAO reports have been numerous on this subject.

As for reports of major scandals, one need but refer to the extended congressional inquiry into the TFX aircraft which later became the F-111 and was just as poor an investment as its critics had maintained from the beginning.[17] Finally, there is the extraordinary account of A. Ernest Fitzgerald, the "whistle blower" on the C5A transport, which was another star-crossed endeavor. For his pains, Fitzgerald was fired, and his account of the whole series of events that ultimately led to his partial reinstatement makes alarming reading.[18]

Conclusion

This chapter has presented a general discussion of government costs and how they are involved in the computation of social costs. Largely through a discussion of fraud and red tape, it has been shown that important questions of social inefficiency are involved. However, the foregoing admittedly calamitous accounts of government practice cannot be taken in isolation. Similar conditions prevail in some parts of the private sector, and certainly private managements should not feel themselves in any way absolved from the necessity of keeping a sharp eye on their own inefficiencies. Furthermore, the whole problem should not be exaggerated. Conservative politicians, beginning with President Reagan, regularly wax wroth about "fraud, waste and abuse," but it has not gone unremarked that earlier claims of being able to reduce the cost of government materially by eliminating them were no longer being made in 1982, when the problems of public finance clearly transcended such potential remedies.[19]

Notes

1. K. W. Kapp, *Social Costs in Business Enterprise*, rev. ed. (Nottingham, England: Spokesman-B. Russell Foundation, 1978), p. 8.

2. "The Underground Economy's Hidden Force," *Business Week*, April 5, 1982, p. 64.

3. Ibid., p. 70.

4. P. M. Blau and M. W. Meyer, *Bureaucracy in Modern Society*, 2d ed. (New York: Random House, 1971), p. 28.

5. A. Hacker, "Talking Our Way Out of This One," *Newsday*, September 22, 1976.

6. J. E. Ullmann, "White Collar Productivity and the Rise of Administrative Overhead," *National Productivity Review*, Summer 1982, p. 290.

7. Cited in "Few U.S. Agencies Are Equipped to Stop Fraud in Their Programs, Panel Is Told," *Wall Street Journal*, September 19, 1978, p. 6.

8. "G.S.A. Housekeepers Left a Mess," *New York Times*, November 6, 1978, p. A-1.

9. T. Smith, "Millions in U.S. Loans Squandered in Minority Program, Inquiry Finds," *New York Times*, November 9, 1978, p. A-1.

10. Commission on Federal Paperwork, *Final Summary Report* (Washington, D.C.: CFP, October 3, 1977), p. 2.

11. H. Kaufman, *Red Tape, Its Origins, Uses and Abuses* (Washington, D.C.: The Brookings Institution, 1977), p. 32.

12. CFP, *Final Summary Report*, p. 29.

13. U.S. Senate, Committee on Appropriations, *Commission on Federal Paperwork* (Washington, D.C.: U.S. Government Printing Office, 1977), p. 1229.

14. Ibid., p. 1246.

15. D. Burnham, *"Government Restricting Flow of Information to the Public." New York Times*, November 15, 1982.

16. J. E. Reilly, "Armed Forces" in *Problems in the Growth and Efficiency of Administrative and Service Functions*, ed. J. E. Ullmann (Hempstead, N.Y.: Hofstra University Yearbooks of Business, 1978).

17. U.S. Senate, Committee on Government Operations, *TFX Contract Investigation*, 8 vols., 88th Cong. 1963-64.

18. A. E. Fitzgerald, *The High Priests of Waste* (New York: Norton, 1972).

19. T. Wicker, "Targeting the Pentagon," *New York Times*, November 14, 1982.

15
The Military Sector

JOHN E. ULLMANN

> Every gun that is made, every warship
> launched, every rocket fired signifies
> in the final sense a theft from those
> who hunger and are not fed, those who
> are cold and are not clothed. This
> world in arms is not spending money
> alone. It is spending the sweat of its
> laborers, the genius of its scientists,
> the hopes of its children.
>
> President Eisenhower, Speech to the
> North American Society of Newspaper
> Editors, April 16, 1953.

Introduction

As a definition of the social costs of militarism, President Eisenhower's statement, made almost a generation ago, can scarcely be bettered. That military spending takes away from social purposes is explicit in every facet of the Reagan-era budgets, and that more than money is involved is the principal reason why with very few exceptions, economists have consistently misinterpreted and grossly underestimated the effects of military spending.[1]

Some could, however, argue that military spending is part of what a nation decides to do with its money; presumably it buys some sort of service with it. But, such a service transcends the rational when the United States has 9,500 deliverable nuclear warheads which, when applied to the 200 or so significant population centers in the Soviet Union, provides 45 for each one. The 7,000 Soviet warheads produce similar overkill in the United States.[2] This raises not merely questions of opportunity cost but also, to put it mildly, of social efficiency as previously discussed.

Such considerations underlie the rising criticism of proposed spending levels in 1984 ($245 billion) and a growing view that the policies these weapons are expected to enforce have never been properly formulated. It is as if a factory were being crammed full of miscellaneous equipment without having much of an idea of a process or product. A long-term critic, Representative Les Aspin (D.-Wisc.) is quoted: "I don't have any idea what this Administration's defense policy is. I read the [Secretary of Defense's] posture statement, and I still don't know. We are just buying things without any relation to the threat."[3]

Given this poor formulation of objectives and given the realities of modern nuclear and conventional weaponry and the increasing tendency to blur the distinction, the protection offered by military establishments tends to become much like the kind of "protection" offered in the rackets of old: it is protection against dangers created primarily by those offering the protection.

As it became clear in 1982 that the federal deficit would exceed $200 billion, that no relief was in sight for the troubled economy, and that the choice lay between the intended escalation of the arms race and such essential services as social security, the erstwhile consensus behind the Reagan policies disintegrated with a celerity that has few parallels in recent political history. Whether as the result of increasingly vocal criticism from the business community, including such prestigious groups as the Business Roundtable, comments from disillusioned members of the administration like Murray Weidenbaum, former Chairman of the Council of Economic Advisers, the demonstrated strength of the nuclear freeze movement or, perhaps most important, the elections that returned a much less controllable Congress, cuts in planned military outlays appeared inevitable.[4] They were still resisted by Mr. Reagan and some members of his entourage, however, and the amounts of the cuts being mentioned were not nearly enough to provide significant budgetary relief, let alone cope with the damage that decades of military concentration had wrought. A sustained political struggle was clearly in prospect.

Opportunity Costs

When opportunity costs are set against an activity, it is necessary to indicate that what is being proposed has direct urgency compared to what could arguably be presented as a lesser degree of urgency in the area that is being criticized. The criticisms of military spending certainly appear well founded, at least as long as a confusion of aims underlies the whole thing and it remains medically impossible to kill anyone more than once. By contrast, the alternatives to which the funds and efforts could be applied are extraordinary, diverse, and increasingly and desperately urgent. A recent useful compendium of the problems that have arisen is a publication of the Council of State Planning Agencies titled *America in Ruins*. Among other major items it lists the following:

1. The 42,000-mile Interstate Highway System is not yet finished, but it is deteriorating so rapidly that 2,000 miles a year need to be rebuilt. In view of a general loss in industrial capability as well as inflation, the costs of these repairs are likely to be at least as great as the original costs of the roads affected.

2. It will cost $700 billion in the 1980s to maintain the remaining national system of nonurban highways.

3. The nation's 756 largest urban areas will need $75 to $110 billion during the next twenty years to maintain their water system.

4. Bridges, aqueducts, streets, sewers, water lines, transportation facilities, and hospitals in New York City will alone require $40 billion for repair and rebuilding during the 1980s. The water shortage of New York City during 1979-1980 was less the result of reduced rainfall in the watershed than a leaky nineteenth-century supply system that had to be used because a new water line has lain half built for some ten years without the money to finish it.

The total bill for infrastructure renewal is estimated at $3 trillion.[5]

Comparably huge amounts are required for a variety of other projects not merely in the public but also the private sector. Further discussion of these problems will be presented later, but at this point it is appropriate to reproduce a portion of an extensive tabulation which S. Melman prepared, showing some very specific and direct offsets. A selection of eleven items appears in table 15.1. It is particularly noteworthy that several of them are based not on contract costs but on cost overruns, that is, on the mistakes that were made in the original proposals. It is for this reason that the proposed $1.6 trillion which the Reagan program expects to pour into the military is not taken seriously as an estimate. Rather, overruns of $750 billion and more are considered likely, some of these estimates coming from the Pentagon itself.[6]

One of the objections often voiced to this kind of opportunity cost is that money would not be voted for these other and presumably more worthy purposes; it is easier to raise money for war. That may be true; however, there can be a variety of alternate choices if the money is not spent on the military. If items like the ones in the table are not thought suitable or worthy, a whole

Table 15.1
Selected Corresponding Costs in the Military and Nonmilitary Sectors

Seven percent of the military outlays from fiscal 1981 to 1986 = $100 billion = the cost of rehabilitating the U.S. steel industry so that it is again the most efficient in the world

The cost overrun, to 1981, on the Navy's Aegis-cruiser program = $8.4 billion = the comprehensive research and development effort needed to produce 80- to 100-mile-per-gallon cars

Sixty-three percent of the cost overruns, to 1981, on fifty current major weapons systems = $110 billion = the twenty year cost of solar devices and energy-conservation equipment in commercial buildings, saving 3.7 million barrels of oil per day

Two B-1 bombers = $400 million = the cost of rebuilding Cleveland's water supply system

The Navy's F-18 fighter program = $34 billion = the cost of modernizing America's machine-tool stock to bring it to the average level of Japan's

The cost overrun, to 1981, on the Navy's F-18 aircraft program = $26.4 billion = the cost of electrifying 55,000 miles of mainline railroads and the cost of new locomotives

Three Army AH-64 helicopters = $82 million = the cost of 100 top-quality, energy-efficient electric trolleys (made in West Germany)

One F-15A airplane = $29 million = the cost of training 200 engineers to design and produce electric trolleys in the United States

The MX missile system, first cost = $34 billion = the cost of a comprehensive ten-year energy-efficient effort to save 25 percent to 50 percent of U.S. oil imports

The cost overrun, to 1981, of the Army's UH-60A helicopter program = $4.7 billion = the annual capital investment for restoring New York City's roads, bridges, aqueducts, subways, and buses

Ten B-1 bombers = $2 billion = the cost of dredging six Gulf Coast and Atlantic Coast harbors to handle 150,000-ton cargo vessels

Source: S. Melman, "Looting the Means of Production," *New York Times,* July 26, 1981.

variety of others would present themselves, from further tax cuts to reductions in the national debt, to other public or private alternatives. The illusion of the Reagan budgets is that they "cut government spending." They do nothing of the sort: rather, the enormous spending for the military, coupled with tax cuts, is precisely what is producing the expected deficits. And these, which are again widely believed to have been grossly underestimated, inhibit meaningful pump-priming of a sick economy through increasing consumption and the general lowering of interest rates and promise to reignite inflation.

It is thus clear that much wider ramifications are inherent in military spending. These will now be reviewed in some detail.

A Model of Military Spending

The economic, scientific, and technical ramifications of the arms race are shown in figure 15.1. Military spending occupies the center stage and whatever its operational merits it does produce military capability as shown. Arms spending has five input sources. Taxes[7] (2) are the first financial source but they are seldom enough to pay for the military establishment. Thus, increases in the national debt (3) must be used to pay for it as well and this puts further load on the tax base because government debt instruments, bonds, and so forth must be serviced and, at least in theory, repaid. Debt service is budgeted at about $100 billion a year for 1984 but the expected deficits render that figure a fantasy. In practice, of course, debts are "rolled over," for the most part, and looking back over the last generation, at ever higher interest rates. Thus, taxes must shoulder this extra cost (12).

The third domestic input is that of technical and scientific resources (1) which are treated separately in the next section. Their importance to the arms race is central and so are the effects of the wide diversion of these resources to military purposes.

For most countries, the arms race also is fueled by foreign inputs, again of technical and scientific resources (4) whose diversion contributes to the problems of their home countries and, most conspicuously, foreign debt (5). It might be thought that the United States would not be significantly affected by that, but this is not the case. Since World War II, the United States had been pressing West Germany to take on a larger share of the cost of maintaining U.S. forces in Europe. This item was actually the one that first opened the balance of payments gap, of which more later. Eventually, the matter was "settled" by West Germany buying U.S. bonds. Thus, the American taxpayer was not only paying for the troops stationed in Europe but interest on the cost as well. The Landgrave of Hesse-Cassel got a much better deal when he was actually paid for his Hessians two hundred years ago; the United

Figure 15.1
The Arms Interlocks

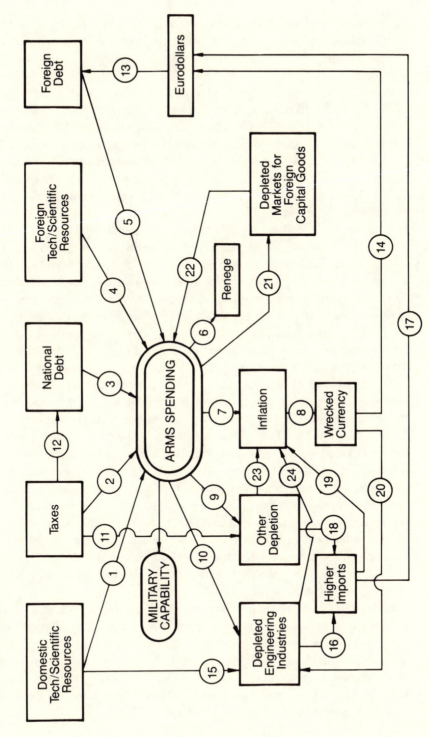

States finances its latter-day Hessians. In the overall indebtedness of the United States, this sort of thing might not bulk large, but it all helps to worsen the overall picture; for other countries, however, foreign debt for arms is an enormous item.

In fact, some countries have begun to renege on that sort of debt (6). The USSR has been affected at least three times, in Egypt, the Sudan, and Somalia. It is also owed huge sums for equipping the armed forces of the Warsaw Pact, whose reliability, except for limited internal repression, is questionable. The United States has likewise been distributing billions of dollars' worth of arms around the world without recompense, beginning with Chiang Kai Shek's aid in the 1940s and continuing to Indochina, Somosa's Nicaragua, and the Shah's Iran; "our men" all lost in those parts.

Returning to the domestic effects of arms spending, the use of debt to finance the arms race immediately and inevitably produces inflation. Large sums are created out of nowhere and no real and operationally definable demand is satisfied by them. In that sense, the effect differs from traditional Keynesian pump priming in which at least an attempt is made to satisfy some verifiable need with the resources invested. Rather, here the ultimate result of the military effort is stored or destroyed in the shape of weapons and the labor component of the military sector likewise does not contribute to the satisfaction of any demand in society.

The point then is that something has to give. In a study for the United Nations Centre for Disarmament, S. Melman[8] analyzed the economies of major nations involved in the arms race, including the United States, the United Kingdom, the Federal Republic of Germany, the USSR, Egypt, and Israel. His findings were that the response in free market economies is inflation. In a planned economy like the USSR, it is rationing and physical shortages, and developing countries that overspend on arms have elements of both rationing and inflation, that is, some of the worst of both worlds. Since Melman's study was completed in 1980, it is becoming clear that shortages may develop even in market economies. Serious questions are being raised whether the American industrial establishment could sustain a military buildup of the size expected without bottlenecks that would impinge drastically on civilian consumption.[9]

Conversely, the communist nations, including the USSR, have had to contend with generally rising price levels. There was a limit beyond which even their planned societies could no longer sustain upward levels of prices. The resulting increases were instrumental in touching off substantial unrest and riots, most conspicuously in Poland but also within the Soviet Union itself, leading to governmental demands for more "discipline" all around and, indirectly, to the internal travail of Poland.

When inflation goes on long enough and proceeds at a greater rate than that of stronger and less troubled economies, the currency is wrecked in the international markets (8). The origins of that problem go back to about 1960, but its later extent was due to the financing of the Vietnam war and the further responses to its ruinous aftermath. The Vietnam war was financed in large measure by increasing the domestic debt; as Wilbur Mills, then the Chairman of the tax-writing House Ways and Means Committee, admitted, an attempt to pay for the war out of extra taxes would have helped end popular support for it even sooner than actually happened. It was, however, also financed by the simple device of letting dollars flood abroad to anyone willing to accept them; U.S. inflation was thereby literally exported.

Originally, these were still full-weight dollars, but actually the rot had already set in. In the early 1960s, as the balance of payments worsened, the Euro-dollar scheme was hatched which, shorn of its euphemisms, simply means that some dollar checks given to foreigners will never be presented for payment and may be used for further credit. Such an arrangement is called "check-kiting" when practiced by individuals and is quite illegal.

The value of the dollar could not be sustained in the face of such policies. Devaluation came slowly at first in the form of minor revaluations of the Deutsche mark and the Swiss franc and then drastically in the float of 1971. The decline has generally continued since. As of early 1982, there were about $1 trillion in the Euro-dollar market, which operates beyond almost all regulation. That is not much less than the acknowledged national debt. For reasons to be explored later, there has been no physical improvement in the U.S. ability to pay. Certainly there has been no return to the days when the United States was able to finance a payments gap created largely by foreign military expenditures (and, to a much smaller extent, by a tourism deficit) by a healthy surplus in the trading account, that is, an excess of exports over imports. Much of the U.S. indebtedness abroad is thus in the form of Euro-dollars, and they are an acknowledged reason for the weakness of the dollar, relative to its historic standing.

A wrecked currency feeds inflation further, of course, mainly by making imported goods more expensive. While countries other than the United States are more vulnerable here, it too has had to cope with very much higher prices for imported energy as a result of the weak dollar. The U.S. government has been of two minds about this problem, however. On the one hand, it professes to be against inflation, but higher energy prices, at least in theory, should reduce demand. The problem is that the price elasticity of energy demand is very much less than people expected before 1973. Furthermore, much domestic conservation requires individual capital investment—new insulation or a new small car—and that sort of thing suffers first whenever the economy is in trouble as it has been in recent years. This is quite apart from the ideologically motivated deemphasis of energy conservation by the Reagan administration.

Depletion and Related Effects

We have so far focused on the financial effects of the arms race. Another and at least equally damaging set of effects is due to the depletion that arms spending works on the rest of the economy. It is convenient to discuss the effects separately for the engineering industries (10) and the rest of society (9). In general, they are the consequences of the preemption of technical and scientific resources (1) which leaves but little for the rest of the engineering industries (15). Not only is a large proportion of U.S. technical manpower so engaged, but the very nature of engineering training has been revised, the better to supply military industry. The ability to develop products commercially and to prepare them for economical quantity production that had been the principal glory of American engineering for decades, gave way to "applied science" orientations in the engineering schools in which manufacturing was looked down upon.[10]

Participation in military research and manufacturing produces a highly deleterious effect. It has been observed that the military industrial firm is not conventionally profit maximizing. Rather, its earnings, by dint of various cost-plus contracts, depend upon the amount of the contract. This leads to a subsidy-maximizing orientation,[11] without much incentive for economy and efficiency. As a result, overhead soars, paperwork threatens to engulf even the smallest product development, and "support services" and second guessing of all sorts must be laid on for engineers no longer trained in product design and manufacturing. One manifestation is that managements even in nonmilitary fields like automobiles demand risk reduction such as separate government contracts for product development. In this manner, research costs of industry, which had traditionally been borne by industry itself as part of the risks and rewards of doing business, were turned from a business cost to a social cost.

These changes in engineering have had very much broader implications in at least three areas: innovation, the decline in manufacturing, and the decline in productivity. By all kinds of measures, innovation has sharply declined.[12] From about 1960 onward there has been a hiatus in technical innovation which contrasts painfully with the enormously productive period between 1945 and 1960. In that time, the antibiotics, steroids, television (black and white and color), new plastics and fabrics, insecticides, computers, and so on all made their debut, as did more star-crossed developments like nuclear power. After 1960, this stream of innovation dried up and then promising leads such as those in solar and other energy, transportation, and sea water desalination were no longer followed up. When some of them were taken up again following the energy problems of the early 1970s it was almost as if everyone had gone to sleep for a good decade.

The beginning of this fallow period coincided with the sharp expansion of American military research and the concentration of effort in those areas, following Mr. Kennedy's alleged missile gap, the escalation of the Vietnam war, and the moon shot. This explanation of what happened has at times been criticized on two grounds. First, there is supposed to have been a spin-off from military and space technology. However, the cost structure of military products was and is such that anything that could be applied, at least in part, to a commercial purpose has to be practically reinvented to avoid Pentagon-size price tags. The record shows, moreover, that most of that "reinventing" was done by Japan where commercial electronic products speedily became concentrated; the period was one in which first radios and then, for practical purposes, television sets ceased to be manufactured in the United States. In products such as video games and television recorders, American entries were for practical purposes non-existent or sharply limited.

The second objection is that the highly active period from 1945 to 1960 was something of a historical freak. However, consider 1920-1935: it brought radio broadcasting, the plastics, synthetic fabrics, diesel traction for the railroads, passenger aircraft, and witnessed the growth of mass merchandising of capital products of all sorts for personal consumption. Or, consider 1895-1910: one need only mention a few names—Edison, the Wright brothers, Henry Ford, and Marconi, all but the last having been Americans.

The decline in the consumer electronics industry has been mentioned. It is only one among many such industries and is part of a general decline of manufacturing. It is rather remarkable to note the equanimity with which this development was long regarded and is still being downplayed in some circles. As manufacturing declined, it was reasoned, people would take up clerical work and services that would offset job losses and would be more fitting for a "postindustrial society" than manufacturing. Such a society, it was reasoned, should not produce "things" but rather "information," forgetting in the process that information, just like things, costs money and that it must be subjected to the same kinds of price determinants of markets as physical products. Other products, it was reasoned, would be imported mainly from factories in foreign countries run by Americans.

That delusion had a long run. It began to run into a number of international realities, not the least of which was that countries, particularly those in the process of industrializing themselves out of Third World poverty, were not about to let foreigners run so vital a sector of their economies. Then, in 1978 machinery and finished products first moved ahead even of oil in the American import bill and hence to the forefront of an increasingly disastrous balance of payments (16, 18). All of this adds further to foreign indebtness (17, 13). It also feeds inflation (19) because a dollar at low value increases the prices of imports and, therefore, provides a higher protective screen for high prices of domestic products. It is of interest in this connection that when it became clear in 1981 that Japan would take a strong role in the development of the next generation (64K) of computer memories and a dominant one in the generation to follow (256K) the matter was regarded even in normally complacent journals with some alarm.[13]

Finally, there is the matter of declining productivity. Figure 15.2 presents the relationship between military expenditures in percent of gross national product and corresponding annual rate of growth in manufacturing productivity, averaged over 1960-1980. The inverse relationship between the two is very clearly evident; one partial exception appears to be Canada, but the Canadian economy is tied very closely to that of the United States and therefore shares a good many of its troubles regardless of its own military expenditures.

Declining productivity is a very troublesome condition for an industrial country. Inflation and unemployment are its direct consequences. As to infla-

Figure 15.2
Military Burden and Productivity, 1960–1978

tion, when American industry was at its peak of innovative capabilities (up to 1960, as noted) it was traditionally able to keep improvements in labor productivity sufficiently high to compensate for consistently rising real U.S. wage levels. Once the decline set in, this was no longer possible, and it became necessary to pass along the ever-rising costs in the form of higher prices. Higher prices in turn depressed markets, and this, coupled with the decline of manufacturing described above, led to unemployment as well. Thus was born "stagflation" which speedily became the pervasive economic pestilence of the 1970s and 1980s.[14] It's role in such other problems as the financing of social security was discussed in chapter 8.

What productivity improvement still took place appeared to be primarily due to production units being made ever larger rather than better. In effect industry worked economy of scale to its limits but as this could not continue indefinitely in finite markets, eventually no further improvements could be gained.[15] There were attempts to blame environmental and other regulations for the decline, but upon closer examination these do not hold water.[16] Some reference to the controversy was made in chapter 5.

Finally, the depletion of engineering industries and other activities is crucially determined by the preemption of capital by military spending. If domestic spending and capital formation are taken over and controlled to the extent expected, none of the capital investments in areas such as energy or transportation or just better maintenance can possibly come to pass. It is distressing that this point is being presented once again as a choice of "guns v. butter." When this phrase first surfaced in Nazi Germany in about 1936, the world generally thought it more than somewhat obscene that a large and economically important nation should decide to face itself with such a choice —obscene, and not a little alarming.

Perhaps the last word on the issue of depletion and its consequences should belong to William Brock, Mr. Reagan's special trade representative. He is charged with negotiating international trade relations, especially at this point the ones with Japan. He is quoted as saying that, "if the United States spent as little as Japan does on defense, we could balance the budget, cut taxes, and have 8 percent interest rates."[17]

The Myth of Military Prosperity

The way out of the present deepening economic crisis must start with an end to the arms race as the central motivator. The arms race continues not merely because of political problems that defy solution or accommodation. It could rather be argued that some of these problems exist in their virulent form because the capacity for organized violence has grown so much. In *Walden*,

Henry David Thoreau said that "men have become the tools of their tools"—
equipment determines behavior. But political support for a cutback in the
arms race requires attention to the problem of conversion, that is, of finding
those involved in it something else to do.

The matter is unfortunately handicapped not only by immediate operational difficulties. Certainly, no society has done a good job so far with finding
people something else to do when their accustomed jobs are no longer
necessary or desirable. In the United States, that includes not only people in
the military industries and the Department of Defense itself but redwood
loggers, tobacco farmers, and others.

Another problem, rather, is the belief that war and its preparations bring
prosperity that is, a social benefit rather than cost. It rests not only on igno-
rance of the kinds of problems discussed here but on an extraordinary mis-
reading of history. Since modern industry began, military contracts have
seemed the way to prosperity. Early literature focused on the profitable "merchants of death"—firms like Krupp, Vickers, Skoda, or Schneider-Creuzot.
Ironically, Krupp, having abandoned arms manufacture after 1945, is today a
prominent victim of the eroded world markets for capital goods. The "merchants of death" model survived into the 1930s but then war preparations
were considered instrumental in getting the world out of the Great Depression; it is that perception that most colors American attitudes. Yet, Americans
should know better because, for over a century, wars have been becoming less
and less profitable.

Circa 1870, a victor could still make the loser pay for the war, as happened
with Prussia and France and in somewhat different form, after the American
Civil War. By World War I, winners and losers lost equally; indeed, repara-
tions had to be abandoned because they could only have been collected in the
shape of goods and that would have ruined the economies of the victors. After
World War II, the winners put the losers back together again and the latter,
profitably demilitarized, then became the strongest industrial economies in the
world. Vietnam showed the enormous adverse leverage of only a "limited"
war; the financial damage to the United States will take generations to erase.[18]
Nevertheless, the alleged military prosperity is being touted by the Reagan
administration as a way out of the deepening economic troubles. These sentiments have been expressed, *inter alia*, by Secretary of Defense Caspar Wein-
berger; he thereby took a different stand from his predecessor, Robert S.
McNamara, who had said to the House Armed Services Committee in
January 1964:

> The Department of Defense cannot and should not assume the respon-
> sibility for creating a level of demand adequate to keep the economy
> health and growing. Nor should it, in developing its programs, depart

from the strictest standards of military need and operating efficiency in order to aid an economically distressed company or community.[19]

These words ring hollow after one war and several Lockheeds but, if they were acted upon, would make excellent sense; as noted at the outset, it is precisely in justifying its needs that the current program is so defective.

There are, however, other indications of the myth of prosperity through military spending. First, while it is true that, as noted above, preparations for World War II helped extinguish the Depression, it is also true that if the government had spent $80 billion in 1941 on *anything*, it would have ended the Depression. As M. Anderson[20] says in a far-reaching study of jobs lost as a result of military spending, the federal government could just as well have replaced worn-out housing, run-down railroads, and decrepit hospitals.

Anderson's study draws upon a previous one by Russett. Using a thirty-year data base, he shows the expenditures foregone by sectors of the economy for each billion dollars spent on the military (table 15.2).[21] Expenditures foregone may be translated into jobs not generated because the money was spent less effectively, it being true that most other activities generate many more jobs than military spending does. (For some examples, see table 15.3.) From this, Anderson derived an estimate of the net gain or loss for each state, depending, on the one hand, on that state's tax contribution to military spending and, on the other, on jobs foregone.

Table 15.2
Expenditures Foregone by Sector of the Economy for Each Billion Dollars Spent on the Military

	$ Million
Services	187
Durable goods	163
State and local government consumption	128
Residential structures	114
Producers' durable equipment	110
Exports	97
Nondurable goods	71
Nonresidential structures	68
Federal civil purchases	48
Imports	25

Source: M. Anderson, *The Empty Pork Barrel* (Lansing, Mich.: Employment Research Associates, 1982), p. 2.

Table 15.3
Estimates of Employment Generated by $1 Billion Federal Spending in
Various Activities

Program	Jobs
B-1 bomber	58,000
Army Corps of Engineers*	69,000
Law enforcement	75,000
Sanitation	78,000
Mass transit construction	83,000
Public housing	84,000
Highway construction	84,000
Conservation and recreation	88,000
Welfare payments	99,000
Social security	108,000
Education	118,000

* Mostly construction work related to rivers and harbors.

Source: G. Adams, The B-1 Bomber: An Analysis of Its Strategic Utility, Cost, Constituency, and Economic Impact, Report of the Council on Economic Priorities, 1976, p. 21.

An analysis of all fifty states shows that 70 percent of the U.S. population lives in states that suffer a net job loss every time the military budget goes up (table 15.4). Every large industrial state in the country, except Texas, loses; it is especially noteworthy that such a well-known aerospace and military electronics state as California is now in the loser column. The Middle Atlantic States except Maryland, the Great Lakes States, and the Midwest (except Kansas) likewise lose jobs. The South is split with Florida, Louisiana, Arkansas, and Tennessee losing heavily while the rest of the South and the Southwest, excluding Arizona and Nevada, are net gainers. The total cost comes to over 1 million jobs. It is therefore not surprising that, as military spending is planned to increase rapidly, expectations of a better economy become more and more problematic.

A Way Out

The foregoing problems suggest that a mechanism for conversion should be put in hand. At present, there is none. The dimensions of the problem were first stated in the early 1960s. One formulation of the problem and suggested solutions by the present writer dates back to 1963.[22] Since that time, Senator George McGovern (D.-S.D.) introduced several bills to facilitate this process

Table 15.4
States in Order of Negative Employment Impact of Military Spending: Annual Average, 1977–1978

State	Number of Jobs Foregone	State	Number of Jobs Gained
1. New York	−288,200	1. Kansas	+600
2. Illinois	−160,750	2. New Hampshire	+650
3. Michigan	−139,100	3. Maine	+2,350
4. Ohio	−131,900	4. Alabama	+3,550
5. Pennsylvania	−112,900	5. Connecticut	+3,950
6. New Jersey	−71,950	6. North Dakota	+4,450
7. Wisconsin	−71,700	7. New Mexico	+7,450
8. Indiana	−64,550	8. Utah	+9,350
9. Minnesota	−54,600	9. Kentucky	+11,100
10. Tennessee	−47,200	10. Colorado	+11,200
11. Florida	−40,150	11. Texas	+15,450
12. Massachusetts	−39,800	12. Alaska	+15,750
13. Iowa	−38,500	13. Oklahoma	+16,000
14. Oregon	−37,850	14. Maryland	+17,050
15. Nevada	−24,100	15. Washington	+20,200
16. Louisiana	−23,350	16. Georgia	+20,950

Table 15.4 *(continued)*
States in Order of Negative Employment Impact of Military Spending: Annual Average, 1977–1978

State	Number of Jobs Foregone	State	Number of Jobs Gained
17. West Virginia	−18,950	17. Mississippi	+23,450
18. California	−13,800	18. N. Carolina	+23,800
19. Arkansas	−12,300	19. S. Carolina	+29,200
20. Nebraska	−6,200	20. Hawaii	+45,200
21. Missouri	−4,500	21. Virginia	+125,950
22. Vermont	−4,250		
23. Rhode Island	−3,650		
24. Wyoming	−3,050		
25. Idaho	−2,850		
26. Arizona	−2,850	Net Jobs Lost	−1,015,450
27. Montana	−2,300		
28. Delaware	−1,200		
29. South Dakota	−600		

Source: M. Anderson, *The Empty Pork Barrel* (Lansing, Mich.: Employment Research Associates, 1982), p. 3.

in one way or another, joined in later years by Senator Charles McC. Mathias (R.-Md). Their efforts were consistently unsuccessful and Senator McGovern was defeated in November 1980. On October 12, 1982, the House Subcommittee on Employment Opportunities held hearings on the latest version of the legislation, H.R. 6618, the Defense Production Adjustment Act, which had been introduced by Rep. Ted Weiss (D.-N.Y.).[23] The details of these solutions go beyond the subject of this chapter; it is, however, important to point out that the matter has received a good deal of consideration and that the human, technological, educational, and economic aspects of it are all capable of a reasonable solution.

Nor is this purely an American problem. Rather, it bedevils the Soviet Union no less than the United States; in a remarkable article, Boris Rabbot, formerly secretary of the social science section of the presidium of the USSR Academy of Sciences and adviser to the Central Committee of the Communist of the Soviet Union, says:

> As you [Brezhnev] know from secret Soviet economic data, the acute and persistent inadequacy of living standards in the Soviet Union springs largely from the fact that about two-thirds of the total number of Soviet industrial enterprises are engaged in military production. You and most others in the Soviet leadership are afraid to risk any fundamental industrial reorganization because that might cause severe dislocations in the militarized segment, resulting in large numbers of people being thrown out of work. . . . What would all these jobless do? Where would they go?. . . . Rumyantsev [Rabbot's former superior at the Academy] . . . tried to put all this into more rational terms with his proposal for a Ministry for Professional Retraining and Distribution of Labor, but your fear of unemployed crowds, ripe for revolt, stopped your ears."[24]

It requires no sophisticated analysis beyond the reading of the day's newspapers to conclude that at the beginning of 1982 both the United States and the Soviet Union were in their own ways making exceedingly heavy weather economically. The Soviet Union appeared to have an increasingly grave cash flow problem. This was aggravated by Western cutbacks in credit to Poland. Rumania likewise had cash flow problems, and these could only be solved by the international banking community after Rumania had secured some support from the Soviet Union. This has in fact led to demands that economic pressure on the Soviet Union would be a proper method of assuring political concessions in other areas. A proper assessment of whether this would, in fact, come about is beyond our scope, but certainly it indicates the economic consequences of the kind of concentration on military work referred to above.

As for the United States, the hope of the business community and others concerned with the nation's economic management appears to be that the enormous cutbacks, deficits, and increases in military spending will somehow be compromised so that worse consequences can be avoided. However, without a truly meaningful cut in military spending, this will not happen. The full consequences, including further upward pressure on interest rates would then continue and far-reaching economic destruction would surely come about. The kind of reformulation of defense needs that is required would entail a zero-base review of military needs and obligations. Such analyses have been carried out in the past, for example, by the Boston Study Group.[25] Only a searching reexamination of this sort can lead to the diversion of resources to national economic and technical reconstruction on a scale sufficient to make a difference. The social costs of the arms race exceed in cash and in kind those of every other activity, encompassing as they potentially do, the destruction of humanity.

The time is at hand for a redefinition of national security, not in the sense of the meaningless arithmetic of overkill but rather in terms of what is needed for the resuscitation of a society badly neglected in some of its most vital parts. Survival of the United States as a successful, prosperous nation, with a substantial private sector and a wide range of personal freedoms for its citizens, calls first of all for a well-functioning economy. It calls for enough raw materials, a sound infrastructure, and a healthy manufacturing establishment to give meaning to the concept of economic health, and they in turn require an intensive technical and scientific effort to give meaning and flexibility to them. If these conditions are present, and if there is a sense of progress and of solving these ever more persistent problems in a compassionate and socially responsible fashion, then social solidarity replaces the current conflict and alienation, and the country's morale rises along with its achievements and its prosperity. Merely to put it this way indicates how far we fall short these days and also how urgent the effort now is—for utilitarian no less than humanist reasons.

Notes

1. S. Melman, "The Peaceful World of Economics I," *Journal of Economic Issues*, March 1972, p. 35; see also M. L. Weidenbaum, *The Economics of Peacetime Defense* (New York: Praeger Publishers, 1974) and a review of it by J. E. Ullmann in *The Wall Street Review of Books*, Spring 1979, p. 149.

2. U.S. Department of Defense and Center for Defense Information, cited in F. Lewis, "Brezhnev's Missile Freeze Is Still Far from Thaw," *New York Times*, March 21, 1982.

3. Quoted in R. Halloran, "Criticism Rises on Reagan's Plan for 5-Year Growth of the Military," *New York Times*, March 22, 1982.

4. "Backers of Defense Spending Start to Break Ranks," *Business Week*, November 15, 1982, p. 14; see also "Guns Vs. Butter," *Business Week*, November 29, 1982, p. 68; and P. H. Stone, "At War Over the Pentagon," *New York Times*, November 14, 1982.

5. S. Walter and P. Choate, *America in Ruins* (Washington, D.C.: Council of State Planning Agencies, 1981). See also "The Decaying of America," *Newsweek*, August 2, 1982, p. 12.

6. S. Melman, "Looting the Means of Production," *New York Times*, July 26, 1981; see also Halloran, "Criticism Rises."

7. Numbers in parentheses refer to figure 15.1.

8. S. Melman, *Barriers to Conversion from Military to Civilian Industry*, Report to U.N. Centre for Disarmament, April 1980.

9. "Is Industry Ready for the Defense Buildup?" *Business Week*, February 8, 1982, p. 94; E. Cowan, "Are Big Defense Dollars Healthy for the Economy?" *New York Times*, January 24, 1982.

10. J. E. Ullmann, "The Responsibility of Engineers to Their Employers," *Annals of the New York Academy of Sciences*, vol. 196, art. 10, February 28, 1973, p. 417; J. E. Ullmann, "Conversion and the Import Problem," *IEEE Spectrum*, April 1970, p. 25.

11. J. F. Gorgol and I. Kleinfield, *The Military Industrial Firm* (New York: Praeger Publishers, 1972).

12. J. E. Ullmann, "Tides and Shallows" in *Management for the Future*, ed. L. Benton (New York: McGraw-Hill, 1978).

13. G. Bylinsky, "Japan's Ominous Chip Victory," *Fortune*, December 14, 1981, p. 52; for an earlier discussion, see Ullmann, "Conversion and the Import Problem."

14. B. Y. Hong, *Inflation under Cost Pass-Along Management* (New York: Praeger Publishers, 1979); see also L. J. Dumas, "Productivity and the Roots of Stagflation," *Proceedings of American Institute of Industrial Engineers*, May 1979, p. 38.

15. J. E. Ullmann, *The Improvement of Productivity* (New York: Praeger Publishers, 1980).

16. J. E. Ullmann, "See What You Made Me Do," in *Private Management and Public Policy*, ed. L. Benton (Lexington, Mass.: Lexington Books, 1980).

17. Quoted in D. Shribman, "Trade Official's Message: Start Competing," *New York Times*, March 22, 1982.

18. T. McCarthy, "What the Vietnam War Has Cost," and J. L. Clayton, "Vietnam: The 200-Year Mortgage," both in *The War Economy of the United States*, ed. S. Melman (New York: St. Martin's Press, 1971).

19. Department of Defense, *Defense Posture Statement*, January 1964.

20. M. Anderson, *The Empty Pork Barrel* (Lansing, Mich.: Employment Research Associates, 1982).

21. B. Russett, *What Price Vigilance?* (New Haven: Yale University Press, 1970).

22. J. E. Ullmann, "Occupational Problems in Conversion," in U.S. Senate, Subcommittee on Employment and Manpower, *Convertibility of Space and Defense*

Resources to Civilian Needs: A Search for New Employment Opportunities, 88th Cong., 1963.

23. U.S. House of Representatives, Subcommittee on Employment Opportunities, *Hearings on H.R. 6618, The Defense Production Adjustment Act,* 92d Congress, 2d. Session, October 12, 1982.

24. B. Rabbot, "A Letter to Brezhnev," *New York Times Magazine,* November 6, 1977. By 1982, there was strong evidence that the problem of conversion was receiving increasing attention by Soviet planners at various levels.

25. The Boston Study Group, *The Price of Defense* (New York: Times Books, 1979); see also a review by the present writer in *America,* September 15, 1979, p. 118.

16
Summary

JOHN E. ULLMANN

If I say 'Give to this people what they
ask because it is just,' do you think I
should get ten people to listen to me?
The only way to make the mass of mankind
see the beauty of justice is by showing
them in pretty plain terms the consequences
of injustice.

Rev. Sydney Smith, *Collected Work*, (1839)

The General Results

It was noted at the outset that social costs are essentially of three types. The first is uncompensated damage in which a social cost exists that is partially compensated by abatement action. The second is that of an outright subsidy, and the third is one of opportunity costs and social inefficiencies, It is therefore helpful to summarize the results of the foregoing investigations in the same terms. This is done in table 16.1. The table shows a rather wide distribution of these characteristics and also indicates that they vary quite substantially in type.

Throughout the volume, quantitative estimates were made for certain of these costs, and in others it was indicated that so far it is not really possible to make that kind of detailed judgment. What is clear, however, is that the presentation of table 16.1 shows a substantial degree of double counting. Unemployment, for example, is not only considered as an independent phenomenon in chapter 7, but is involved in every discussion throughout the book in which the problems of specific industries are set forth, as in energy generation and industrial pollution, occupational disability, transportation,

Table 16.1
Summary of Social Costs

Chapter Item	Characteristics		
	Uncompensated Damage	Subsidy	Opportunity Cost
4 Mining of coal and uranium, environmental and employ- ment costs	X		
Coal combustion	X		
Radiation from nuclear gener- tion and waste	X	X	
Energy policies in general		X	X
5 Industrial pollution in general	X		
Governmental aid in disposal and so on		X	
6 Occupational disability	X	X	
7 Unemployment		X	X
8 Old age (limited, as noted in ch. 8)		X	
9 Slums and poverty		X	X
10 Duplication of capital facilities			X
11 Drugs			X
12 Automobiles	X		X
Railroads		X	X
13 Food subsidy		X	
Farms	X	X	
14 General government		X	
15 Military sector		X	X

farming, and the military sector. No attempt has been made here, nor would one be readily feasible, to share responsibility for this general problem among these areas. It is also not possible for this reason to say that there is a grand total of social costs somewhere in the economy. Apart from the conceptual difficulty, such a measure in any case would have to combine all three kinds, and from the viewpoint of definitions of costs, this is not permissible. Subsidies are indeed cash outlays, but uncompensated damage includes both cash outlays in such matters, for example, as having to pay for houses that have to be painted more often because they are in a heavily polluted area or, on the other hand, the costs of pain and suffering of various sorts that are inadequately compensated or not compensated at all. To the extent that medical costs are not paid for by the culprit, whoever or whatever it might be, it represents a cash outlay not picked up elsewhere. Finally, opportunity cost is defined by what might be instead of what is. It has been emphasized throughout that these losses are real, but they are of a different character from actual payments.

International Implications

To keep the analysis within reasonable bounds, this volume has focused almost entirely on conditions in the United States. The problems it covers are, of course, worldwide, and the methods of inquiry used here could be applied to other countries. However, even a discussion of social costs in a predominantly American context has important international implications that derive both from the example the United States often sets in international matters and from the policies governing its export trade and the activities of multinational business.

First, much environmental protection the world over has taken its legislative and operational cues from the United States. This is not merely a matter of technology, as in pollution abatement; in that area, in fact, the United States is only one among several countries to have come up with major technological solutions. Furthermore, several of them are further ahead or use available equipment more extensively. Rather, American laws for consumer protection, product information, and quality, and such essentially American ideas as the modern national parks have served as models the world over. The profound retrogression that has taken place in all these areas under the Reagan administration cannot fail to have a dampening effect elsewhere.

Second, the conflict between development and environmental protection appears in even crasser forms in much of the developing world than it does in the United States and industrialized countries generally. To be sure, as noted in several areas, this conflict is often the result of political semantics rather than scientific reality. Still, the problem is one that has engaged the attention of scientists in the field for many years.[1] Here too, the use by the Reagan administration and its supporters of allegations of "stopping development" in trying to secure a drastic weakening of environmental laws may well have similar effects elsewhere. Some countries had linked their development plans to an open invitation to foreign developers to come and pollute. Brazil stands out as an example; a strong public outcry there forced a partial reversal of that policy. Environmental protection and other consumer-related legislation still is sufficiently fragile in all too many places to warrant concern.

Finally, there are plans afoot by the Reagan administration for eased policies regarding the export of products that have been banned in the United States for their toxicity, ineffectiveness, or, for other reasons.[2] This applies particularly to agricultural pesticides and to pharmaceutical products. In defending its action, the administration has raised the issue of "regulatory imperialism," that is, if it stopped such products, it would impose its standards on others. Yet, foreign countries and, indeed, the International Standards Organization (ISO) often use the product standards of major industrial nations, such as the British (BSI) Standards, and the German DIN Standards and those of ANSI, the American National Standards Institute. They do that, in part, because, national pride here or there, there is little point in reinventing the wheel. Even today's great industrial power, Japan, based its original standards work on European models. In any event, the issue is quite clearly the potential loss of multibillion dollar businesses that are highly profitable for a rather obvious reason: the U.S. plants turning out these products were built long ago when the products could still be sold in the United States and so are largely amortized. Fixed costs are minimal.

There is, however, a direct consequence to Americans of dumping dangerous products abroad: if banned pesticides are used on the tropical crops that are then imported into the United States, American consumers are again exposed to them, long after they had eliminated such dangers from home-produced items.

The activities of multinational business as such also have important implications for social costs. If an American firm establishes itself abroad, with the intent of then bringing the manufactured product back home, then, in effect, it imports unemployment. If it searches the world for areas where not only low wages prevail, but where workers' rights are more or less ignored and where safety rules for workplaces and products are not enforced, the problems discussed throughout this book become worse in the aggregate and prevent stable and viable industrialization. Lastly, the economy of the United States itself is sufficiently interdependent that its own poor state directly affects others; it may not be true that when the United States sneezes, others get pneumonia but, it has become clear that a deepening global economic crisis will not abate significantly without a *real* American recovery and that that is unlikely for quite some time.

Some Open Issues

The detailed discussions in this book are in their essence an account of conflict. It is conflict between the private and public sectors, and between either or both, and the public at large as individuals and as organized groups. The problems discussed have engaged the courts, the regulatory process, and legislative activities for decades, and have become enormously more important in the most recent times.

The volume, moreover, recounts a sustained effort to come to grips with many of these issues and to try and resolve them equitably and sensibly. Such a human endeavor is seldom successful, and what has been told above is no exception. Matters have been, moreover, greatly affected by the political changes that took place in the United States following the November 1980 elec-elections. There is little point in once more recounting the details; suffice it to say that there has been a general backward movement, thereby making it virtually certain that social costs in the form of uncompensated damage and of opportunity cost will increase still further.

As to subsidies, they will no doubt survive for the benefit of the most politically powerful. The most important such institution is the military sector, although other programs likewise have shown themselves to be powerfully entrenched and likely to withstand really substantial cuts.

It should be finally noted that social costs are not in themselves necessarily a "good" or "bad" thing; rather, they have to be assessed individually, and such an assessment cannot be done without bringing one's own social values into play. This point was noted at the outset in rather more detail, but it deserves to be repeated here. It is simply that economic activities are hard to compartmentalize to the extent that costs can be determined in their totality and allocated purely to those concerned with the activity itself. What is essential, however, for the effective functioning of a modern society is to understand the wide ramifications of social costs and the enormous potential for truly disastrous actions and interventions that modern technology and large organizations have made possible. Coping with social costs in one form or another thus becomes the central challenge of our time. The areas examined in this book, therefore, give an important indication of a yet unfinished agenda, with implications extending far beyond geographic boundaries and far into the future. It would be cold comfort, indeed (or opportunity cost viewed in reverse), to take heart from the avoidance, so far, of the worst.

Notes

1. There is an extensive literature on this subject; the many publications of UNEP, the United Nations Environmental Programme, are especially noteworthy. K. W. Kapp also treated this subject at length, in works dating from his book *Hindu Culture, Economic Planning and Development* (Bombay: Asia House, 1963) to an address delivered the day before his death in April 1976, "Development and Environment: Towards a New Approach to Socioeconomic and Environmental Development," in *Economics in Institutional Perspective*, ed. R. Steppacher et al. (Lexington, Mass.: Lexington Books, 1977), p. 205ff. In the same volume, see also T. Shibata, "Japanese Economic Expansion and the Disruption of the Environment," p. 141ff. For other writings by Kapp, see *Social Costs, Economic Development and Environmental Disruption* (Washington, D.C.: University Press of America, 1983), chapters 1, 5 and 7. For two other comprehensive conferences that treat international conditions, see B. Pregel et al., eds., "Environment and Society in Transition: World Priorities," *Annals of the New York Academy of Sciences*, vol. 261, 1975 and P. Albertson and M. Barnett, eds., "Environment and Society in Transition," *Annals of the New York Academy of Sciences*, vol. 184, 1971.

2. B. Wyrick, "Panel to Submit Eased Policy for Unsafe Exports," *Newsday*, February 17, 1982; Wyrick is the author of a major investigative series in *Newsday* in November 1981 on the worldwide use of U.S. products banned at home.

Appendix
List of Cases for Chapter Three

Case No.	Citation	Nature of Injury	Award Dollars
1	John v. Marshall Field & Co. (Wash., 1970)	Fall in elevator; head injury	20,000
2	Wilson v. Jefferson Transit (Iowa, 1968)	Hit by bus; fractured jaw with complications	1,373
3	Goldstein v. Linden's Restaurant Corp. (N.Y., 1962)	Glass in frankfurter; cut in mouth, broken tooth	2,300
4	Herron v. Yellow Cab Co. (Ill., 1969)	Short stop; multiple minor injuries	1,500
5	Bertucci v. Anheuser-Busch (La., 1973)	Explosion of beer bottle; lacerations and scarring	2,000
6	Jones v. Cranman's Sporting Goods (Ga., 1978)	Rifle backfired; severe hand injury	81,000
7	Younkin v. Pick-Bay Motel (Ala., 1971)	Paint fumes leading to permanent hearing loss	15,000
8	Homka v. Chicago Transit Authority (Ill., 1971)	Painful accident	9,433
9	Premack v. Chicago Transit Authority (Ill., 1971)	Transit vehicle collision; multiple injuries	7,500
10	Royal Indemnity Co. v. Muscato (Fla., 1974)	Defective parade float; extensive leg injuries	52,000
11	Kwarta v. U.S. Lines, (Md., 1970)	Injuries in operation of new tractor	10,255
12	DeSantis v. Parker Feeders (Wisc., 1976)	Child's loss of leg and part of other foot in auger of cattle feeder; posttraumatic personality disorder	840,000
13	Karabatos v. Spivey Co. (Ill., 1977)	Conveyor belt accident; injuries including loss of arm	200,000
14	Western R.R. of Alabama v. Brown (Ala., 1967)	Badly sprained ankle and knee	14,200
15	Costello v. Chicago Transit Authority (Ill., 1976)	Bus accident to 71-year-old woman; injuries and subsequent blindness	75,000

Case No.	Citation	Nature of Injury	Award Dollars
16	Commercial Insurance Co. v. Street (Fla., 1976)	Elevator accident; permanent injuries	27,000
17	McAvin v. Morrison Cafeteria (La., 1956)	Food poisoning	400
18	Pierson v. Borden Co. (La., 1963)	Cockroach in milk	100
19	Dusek v. Campbell Soup (Miss., 1961)	Metal fragment in soup; injury to tongue	600
20	Pensacola Race Assoc. v. Williams (Fla., 1965)	Fall at race track; back injury	30,000
21	Haynes v. Coca Cola (Ill., 1976)	Contaminated beverage	1,000
22	Blevins v. Cushman Motors (Mo., 1976)	Defective golf cart; loss of consortium	91,000
23	Hoffman v. Sterling Drug et al. (Pa., 1973)	Blindness from choloquine	437,000
24	Harrelson v. Norton Co. (Ala., 1975)	Grinding wheel disintegrated; injury to groin	40,000
25	Turner v. Culpepper & Stone (Ala., 1964)	Furnace explosion, improper repairs; loss of consortium	5,000
26	Bradbury v. F. W. Woolworth (Ala., 1962)	Injury; loss of consortium	5,000
27	Bennett v. A & P (Ala., 1958)	Award to husband; wife slipped in store	5,000
28	Deemer v. Reichart (Kans., 1965)	Auto accident; disabling injuries	50,910
29	Cooper v. Christiansen (Mich., 1970)	Attack on plaintiff; lost wages	2,100
30	Ryan v. Twin City Milk Producers (Minn., 1971)	Milk truck collision; damaged vision, loss of hearing, other injuries	85,000
31	Soberaiski v. CMP R.R. (Ill., 1975)	Railroad accident; impaired earning potential	30,000
32	Frisch v. International Harvester Co. (Ill., 1975)	Injury from farm machine; loss of livelihood	125,000
33	Freeman v. DC Transit System (Md., 1970)	Accident; strained muscles, unable to work at usual job	20,000
34	Pitten v. Denison (Mich., 1976)	Loss of arm in hydraulic press at age 67	1,250,000
35	Huston v. Chicago Transit Authority (Ill., 1976)	Death of working woman	150,000
36	Morejon v. Washwell Inc. (Fla., 1974)	Laundromat accident; loss of arm to 87-year-old woman	150,000
37	Means v. Sears Roebuck & Co. (Mo., 1976)	Badly assembled bicycle; extensive injuries	65,000
38	Heiman v. Boatel Co. (Alaska, 1978)	Carbon monoxide poisoning from defective air conditioner	506,000
39	Spurlin v. General Motors Co. (Ala., 1976)	Bus accident; death	70,000
40	Foster et al. v. Marshall et al. (La., 1977)	Car-truck accident	82,500
41	Metropolitan Dade County v. Dillon (Fla., 1974)	Six-year-old child killed by garbage truck	90,000
42	West et al. v. Caterpillar Co. (Fla., 1976)	Grader without backup signal caused fatal accident	125,000
43	Basel v. Fibre Board Paper Products Co. (Tex., 1973)	Asbestosis and mesothelioma; death before trial	79,000

Case No.	Citation	Nature of Injury	Award Dollars
44	d'Hedowville v. Pioneer Hotel Co. (Ariz., 1977)	Hotel carpet fire; killed 31-year-old attorney	500,000
45	Hanson v. Florida East Coast Ry. Co. (Fla., 1976)	Claim of widow of accident victim	600,000
46	Ploof v. B.I.M. Truck Service Inc. et al. (N.Y., 1976)	Cable broke; truck driver killed	375,000
47	Leonard v. Albany Machine Co. (La., 1976)	Fatal sawmill accident	173,000
48	Rudiasaile v. Hawk Aviation Inc. (N. Mex., 1977)	No oil in aircraft engine; fatal accident	235,000
49	McGale v. LI R.R. (N.Y., 1978)	Police altercation resulting in death on railroad property	3,300,000
50	Bjerk v. Universal Engineering Corp. (Minn., 1977)	Incorrect lubrication of rock crusher; head injuries, contributory negligence	106,000
51	West v. Food Fair Stores Inc. (Fla., 1978)	Partially disabled customer falls; 50 percent contributory	12,500
52	Mitchell v. Ford Motor Co. (N.H., 1976)	Badly designed handbrake*	—0—
53	Jones et al. v. Hittle Services, Inc. et al. (Kans., 1976)	Propane gas explosion due to failure to smell escaping gas*	—0—
54	McDaniel v. McNeil Laboratories Inc. (Neb., 1976)	Brain damage from anesthetic*	—0—
55	Schell v. AMF, Inc. (Pa., 1976)	Baking machine cleaned incorrectly*	—0—
56	Schoeffer v. Remington Arms et al. (La., 1976)	Defective ammunition*	—0—
57	Grant v. Parke, Davis & Co. (Wisc., 1976)	Brain damage from vaccine injections*	—0—
58	Dixon v. Gutrecht (La., 1976)	Injury from falling cartons*	—0—
59	Kay v. Cessna Aircraft Co. (Calif., 1977)	Engine failure; pilot did not follow instructions*	—0—
60	Price v. Niagara Machine Works (Calif., 1977)	Punch press injury*	—0—
61	Rogers v. Uninac Co., Inc. (Ariz., 1977)	Laundry injury to arm; improper maintenance rather than defective design*	—0—
62	Rogers v. Ford Motor Co. (Ala., 1976)	Improper lubrication of corn header	1,500
63	Hopkins v. General Motors Corp. (Tex., 1976)	Truck overturns; driver is paralyzed	1,760,000
64	Madison v. Rueben (Ill., 1970)	Child falls through open window	5,000
65	Mielke v. Singara Grotto, Inc. (Ohio, 1975)	Slipping on wax; injuries	210,000
66	Schouline v. Citizen's Hospital Association (Ala., 1972)	Hospital malpractice	5,000
67	Johnson v. Opelika Coca Cola Bottling Co. (Ala., 1970)	Contaminated drink	2,500
68	Savely v. Gray Company, Inc. (Tenn., 1977)	Malfunctioning grease gun	25,000
69	Gonzales v. Bristol Myers (Tex., 1977)	Drug side effects; FDA approvals and warnings cited*	—0—

Case No.	Citation	Nature of Injury	Award Dollars
70	Straley v. Cologne Drayage & Storage, Inc. (La., 1977)	Injuries to warehouse worker; warnings defective	25,000
71	Ayr-Way Stores, Inc., et al. v. Chitwood et al. (Ind., 1973)	Child injured by lawn mower	80,000
72	Frische v. International Harvester (Ill., 1975)	Gas cap emitted flames	125,000
73	Brooks v. Dietz et al. (Kans., 1976)	Accident during furnace repair	262,000
74	Klayer v. General Ordinance Corp. (Pa., 1975)	Mace spray failed, user was shot	42,000
75	Hoods & Sons, Inc., et al. v. Ford Motor Co. (Mass., 1976)	Defective truck assembly; injuries	21,500
76	Banks v. Koehring Co. (Iowa, 1976)	Loss of arm in machine accident	150,000
77	Nowakowski v. Hoppe Tire Co. (Ill., 1976)	Head injuries from exploding tire	105,000
78	Sadowski v. Bombardier, Ltd. (Wisc., 1976)	Snowmobile accident; 25 percent disability	100,000
79	Ball Corp. v. George (Ariz., 1976)	Loss of left eye from exploding soft drink bottle	125,000
80	Raney v. Honeywell, Inc. (Iowa, 1976)	Gas explosion in furnace repair	540,000
81	Meking v. Bishman Mfg. Co. (Tex., 1973)	Defective tire-changing machine	25,000
82	McKass v. Zimmer Mfg. Co. (Ill., 1973)	Broken pin used in fracture	175,000
83	Tibbetts v. Ford Motor Co. (Mass., 1976)	Injuries during tire changing	20,000
84	Levea v. G. A. Gray Corp. et al. (Wash., 1977)	Steel drum fell on machinist	175,000
85	Chamberlain v. Carborundum Co. et al. (Pa., 1973)	Grinding wheel exploded; death of user	103,000
86	Neal v. Whirl Air Flow Corp. (Ill., 1976)	Loss of left hand in machine	120,000
87	Ferry v. Luther Mfg. Co. Inc. (N.Y., 1977)	Hand injured in punch press	64,000
88	Nester v. Consolidated Edison (N.Y., 1965)	Accident due to equipment fault	350,000
89	Troszynski v. Commonwealth Edison Co. (Ill., 1975)	Burns from defective meter	75,000
90	McDowell v. South Western Bell Telephone Co. (Mo., 1976)	Ear damage due to defective telephone	10,000

* Verdict in favor of defendant.

Sources: Corpus Juris Secundum, 2d ed., vol. 25; American Jurisprudence, 2d ed., vol. 22; Commerce Clearing House, Products Liability Reporter: August 1973–November 1975, December 1975–December 1977; Pacific Reporter, 2d ed., vol. 478; Northwest Reporter, 2d ed., vol. 163; New York State Reporter, 2d ed., vol. 235; Southern Reporter, 2d ed., vol. 135; Southwestern Reporter, 2d ed., vol. 106; Southeastern Reporter, 2d ed., vol. 166; Newsday, June 8, 1978, p. 29; Business Week, February 12, 1979, p. 73.

Bibliography

Social Costs

Kapp, K. William. *Social Costs of Business Enterprise.* 1963. Reprint. Nottingham, England: Spokesman-The Bertrand Russell Foundation, 1978.

_____. *Social Costs, Economic Development and Environmental Disruption.* J. E. Ullmann, ed. Washington, D.C.: University Press of America, 1983. Collected papers.

Klein, Thomas A. *Social Costs and Benefits of Business.* Englewood Cliffs, N.J.: Prentice Hall, 1977.

Business and Society

Books in this field usually treat several social costs issues.

Greenwood, William T., ed. *Issues in Business and Society,* 3d ed. Boston: Houghton-Mifflin, 1977.

Kangun, Norman, ed. *Society and Marketing.* New York: Harper & Row, 1972.

Luthans, Fred, and Richard M. Hodgetts. *Social Issues in Business.* 2d ed. New York: Macmillan, 1976.

Perrow, Charles. *The Radical Attack on Business.* New York: Harcourt Brace Jovanovich, 1972.

Steiner, George A. *Business and Society.* 2d ed. New York: Random House, 1972.

_____, and John F. Steiner, eds. *Issues in Business and Society.* 2d ed. New York: Random House, 1977.

The Environment

Among many books on environmental issues, the following concentrates on social costs issues.

Van Tassel, Alfred J., ed. *Environmental Side Effects of Rising Industrial Output.* Lexington, Mass.: Heath-Lexington, 1970.

Employment

Work in America. Report of a Special Task Force to the Secretary of Health, Education, and Welfare. Cambridge, Mass.: MIT Press, 1973. See especially parts I and III.

R. Kazis and R. Grossman, *Fear at Work: Job Blackmail, Labor and the Environment*. New York: Pilgrim Press, 1982.

Governmental Regulations and Related Costs

U.S. House of Representatives, Committee on Interstate and Foreign Commerce, *Use of Cost Benefit Analysis by Regulatory Agencies*. 96th Cong., 1st Sess., 1979, Serial no. 96-157. A wide-ranging compendium of opposing views.

Ullmann, John E. "See What You Made Me Do," in *Private Management and Public Policy*. Ed. L. Benton. Lexington, Mass.: Heath-Lexington, 1980.

The Military Sector

Melman, Seymour. *The Permanent War Economy*. New York: Simon and Schuster, 1974.

_____, ed. *The War Economy of the United States*. New York: St. Martin's Press, 1971.

Index

About the Editor

JOHN E. ULLMANN, Professor of Management and Marketing at Hofstra University in Hempstead, New York, holds degrees in civil, mechanical, and industrial engineering. He is the author of more than sixty books, monographs, and articles including *The Improvement of Productivity*, *The Suburban Economic Network*, and *Quantitative Methods in Management*.